Dashcode®
FOR
DUMMIES®

Dashcode® FOR DUMMIES®

by Jesse Feiler

WILEY

Wiley Publishing, Inc.

Dashcode® For Dummies®

Published by
Wiley Publishing, Inc.
111 River Street
Hoboken, NJ 07030-5774
www.wiley.com

WILEY

About the Author

Jesse Feiler provides consulting services to small businesses and nonprofits. He is the author of a number of books on FileMaker and Mac OS X as well as on new technologies such as Mashups, Facebook, and Bento. Active in the community, Jesse serves on the boards of HB Studio and HB Playwrights Foundation; he previously served on the board of the Mid-Hudson Library System (including three years as president), founded the Philmont Main Street Committee, and chaired the village's Comprehensive Plan Board. His Web site is http://northcountryconsulting.com.

His books include *Get Rich with Apps!: Your Guide to Reaching More Customers and Making Money Now* (McGraw-Hill), *Sams Teach Yourself Drupal in 24 Hours* (Sams/Pearson), *Database-Driven Web Sites* (Harcourt), *How to Do Everything: Facebook Applications* (McGraw-Hill), *How to Do Everything with Web 2.0 Mashups* (McGraw-Hill), *iWork '09 For Dummies* (Wiley), *Using FileMaker Bento* (Sams/Pearson), and *FileMaker Pro in Depth* (Sams/Pearson). He also wrote the iWork minibook of the book *iPad All-in-One For Dummies* (Wiley).

His iOS apps include MinutesMachine from Champlain Arts (http://champlain arts.com).

Author's Acknowledgments

Carole Jelen at Waterside Productions has, once again, provided great support and advice in the development of this book.

At Wiley, Kyle Looper, Acquisitions Editor, guided this book through the approval process and offered very welcome input in its structuring. Kelly Ewing patiently shepherded the manuscript through production and editing.

Publisher's Acknowledgments

We're proud of this book; please send us your comments at http://dummies.custhelp.com. For other comments, please contact our Customer Care Department within the U.S. at 877-762-2974, outside the U.S. at 317-572-3993, or fax 317-572-4002.

Some of the people who helped bring this book to market include the following:

Acquisitions, Editorial, and Media Development

Project Editor: Kelly Ewing

Acquisitions Editor: Kyle Looper

Technical Editor: Dennis Cohen

Editorial Manager: Jodi Jensen

Media Development Project Manager: Laura Moss-Hollister

Media Development Assistant Project Manager: Jenny Swisher

Editorial Assistant: Amanda Graham

Sr. Editorial Assistant: Cherie Case

Cartoons: Rich Tennant (www.the5thwave.com)

Composition Services

Project Coordinator: Katherine Crocker

Layout and Graphics: Lavonne Roberts, Vida Noffsinger

Proofreaders: Melissa Cossell, Rebecca Denoncour, Evelyn C. Wellborn

Indexer: Christine Karpeles

Publishing and Editorial for Technology Dummies

    Richard Swadley, Vice President and Executive Group Publisher

    Andy Cummings, Vice President and Publisher

    Mary Bednarek, Executive Acquisitions Director

    Mary C. Corder, Editorial Director

Publishing for Consumer Dummies

    Diane Graves Steele, Vice President and Publisher

Composition Services

    Debbie Stailey, Director of Composition Services

Contents at a Glance

Table of Contents

Introduction

$\bullet\ \bullet$

Dashcode was developed initially to make it easier to build Dashboard widgets — lightweight apps that run on your Mac and that can be summoned at the touch of a button (usually F4 or F12) to appear to float in a layer on top of your desktop and your open applications. These widgets were built on open standards such as JavaScript and Cascading Style Sheets (CSS) even though they were designed for use on a Mac and did not necessarily have any interaction with the Internet. With the development of Dashcode, people were able to build these small light-weight widgets quickly and easily.

With the release of iPhone, the Dashcode technology was pressed into service again — this time to develop Web-based apps that, when running in Safari on iPhone, could access iPhone features such as telephony and, in the second release, geolocation (where you are in the world).

In other words, no one set out to write Dashcode to make iPhone (and now iPad) Web applications possible. They just weren't on the horizon. But Dashcode's features are a perfect match, and it provides the fastest way to write Web applications for iPhone and iPad.

This book shows you how to write those applications as well as the widgets that were the first Dashcode products.

About This Book

This book provides an introduction to Dashcode and its variety of features. It shows you how to use the Dashcode features by building on the templates that are provided as part of Dashcode as well as by using code and other elements from the Library. What you see in this book is that the combination of the Dashcode tools and the Library parts means that you really don't have too much code to write.

What you do have to do is to think about what it is you're writing — what you want to help your users do. You find guidelines for developing a consistent and intuitive interface whether you're using Dashcode to build a Dashboard widget, a Safari Web application, or a mobile Safari Web application for iPhone.

You can read this book from beginning to end, or you can jump around to find what particularly interests you (or may be causing some problems). When you come to the step-by-step examples in this book, consider taking a few moments to actually work through them. It's very easy to quickly read the steps and think that you've got it all down pat, but when you actually type in the code and (gulp!) try to run it, the learning process really begins.

Conventions Used in This Book

Throughout the book, you find descriptions of tasks and techniques you can use.

You can download example files from `www.dummies.com/go/dashcodefd`. Files that are posted on the Web are indicated in the text.

You find code snippets and URLs in this book. All appear in a monospaced font such as this:

```
http://northcountryconsulting.com
```

or

```
function load()
{
    dashcode.setupParts();
}
```

Much of this code is available in Dashcode itself. If you compare the Dashcode version with the version in this book, you may see some differences in spacing. This difference is simply due to the layout requirements for the book's pages: anything that matters is noted in the text. When you're typing code, you can ignore spacing with the exception of quoted strings. Text within quotation marks needs to be typed as it is intended to appear or be processed. This means that the following code

```
var example = "some text";
```

is not the same as this code:

```
var example = "some

text";
```

When first released, iPhone and iPod touch were powered by the iPhone OS. iPad changed all that. It was tricky to explain that iPad is powered by the iPhone OS. Thus, in 2010, the people at Apple introduced iOS: the operating system for iPhone, iPod touch, iPad and . . . devices to come. Unless otherwise noted, here are the conventions for devices used in this book:

✔ **iPhone** always means iPhone and iPod touch

✔ **iOS devices** include iPhone, iPod touch, and iPad (and possibly new devices)

The book shows you how to develop your own Dashcode projects. Several of them are available for download at www.dummies.com/go/dashcodefd.

The full names for the projects that you build with Dashcode can be quite a mouthful. You can build

✔ **Dashboard widgets:** These widgets run in the Dashboard environment on Mac OS X. The word *widget* is used in many contexts today, but in this book, it always refers to Dashboard widgets.

✔ **Safari Web applications:** In this book, you build these applications with Dashcode. They run in Safari on Mac OS X and Windows.

✔ **Mobile Safari Web applications** run in Safari on iOS devices.

You can also use other development tools than Dashcode (in particular, Xcode) to build iOS apps, iPhone apps, and iPad apps. Those apps run directly in the iOS operating system whereas the widgets and Safari Web applications run in Safari. From the user's point of view, these apps often look very much the same. In fact, making your Safari Web applications and mobile Safari Web applications look like native iOS apps is frequently an important goal. In this book, unless otherwise noted, the word *apps* refers to all three types of Dashcode projects as well as iOS apps.

What You're Not to Read

You don't have to read everything in this book in order to understand the subject at hand. For example, the gray boxes, or *sidebars,* you see throughout this book include information that you don't have to know — if you're interested in them, read away! In addition, you can skip information marked by the Technical Stuff icons (unless you're the techie type that loves those extra details!).

Foolish Assumptions

As I wrote this book, I assumed a few things about you, the reader. I don't assume that you have any in-depth programming experience. In fact, I wrote this book to help novice programmers create iPhone, iPad, and Mac OS X programs in the fastest and easiest way possible. But if you're an experienced programmer; don't worry. I tell you what you need to know to master the syntax of Dashcode.

How this Book Is Organized

This book is divided into six parts.

Part I: Introducing Dashcode and How You Can Use It

This part introduces you to the Dashcode world. If you're used to desktop applications, you have to start thinking a bit differently about software in the world of Web applications and widgets. You have to stop to think about what you're doing with that device. You tend not to think too much about exactly how you use the software because everything "just works," but if you develop software, you have to make an effort to think about it — and make it happen in the ways that users expect.

Part II: Constructing Your Projects' Pieces and Parts

This part introduces you to the components that are built into Dashcode ready for you to use as well as the Dashcode tools that help you work with them. The most important tools are the inspectors that let you inspect and modify aspects of your interface elements and the Library of code and interface elements (not to mention your iPhoto library, which is automatically integrated into it). You also discover how to use behaviors to enhance the user interface.

Part III: Integrating Data

Interestingly enough, the relatively small size of apps and widgets makes sophisticated data management more necessary than ever, and Dashcode provides tools for that purpose. When you have an almost limitless expanse of space in which to display your data (think of a spreadsheet the size of a house), you don't need to worry about its organization and presentation. But when you're using data on the very limited space of an iPhone screen, you need to make the most of it and organize it cleverly. This part goes into all those issues.

Part IV: Trying Out Each Environment

This part provides full-fledged projects from start to finish. They go into the issues related to iPad and iPhone Web apps as well as for Dashboard widget and for Safari Web apps designed to function in a traditional desktop or laptop browser.

Part V: Refining Your Project

This part covers advanced techniques, such as the use of localization to translate your interface, along with the extensive Dashcode debugging tools.

Part VI: The Part of Tens

This part provides lists and tips to help you in a variety of ways. I cover techniques for improving your interface and making your users like you and share a trick that helps you save time and effort in building your Dashcode projects. And the best part is, these chapters are all short and sweet.

Icons Used in this Book

Throughout this book are icons that mark various items of interest:

This icon identifies things to remember. If you want to highlight the text with a colored marker, feel free to do so. If you're reading a book as an e-book, tap and hold the word or words you want to highlight and then tap Note. To see your notes in iBooks, tap the list next to Library in the upper left of each page. You see all your notes in your Bookmarks (tap the list next to Library in the upper left of each page). With Kindle for iPad, tap the center of the page and then tap the open book in the center of the bottom of the screen to see all your notes.

This technical information is highlighted so that you can decide for yourself whether you want to read it at this time. You can skip it, if you want.

This icon provides shortcuts and hints for improving your Dashcode project as well as shortcuts to save time.

Almost nothing is totally catastrophic when you're using Dashcode, with one exception. In your mind, place this warning next to everything you do with Dashcode: Save a copy of your project at every step of the process. If you do make a mistake, just go back to the last saved copy. It's often easier to revert to your project as it was 15 minutes ago than to recreate your steps and undo them.

Where to Go from Here

If you haven't used Dashcode yet, Part I is a good place to start because it helps you jump into the Dashcode tools and terminology. Part III is a great place to begin if you want to use Dashcode to help you organize and present data. (Teachers like this section.)

Scan through the book to look at the screen shots of projects to see what the possibilities are. When you find one that interests you, just jump in there.

Feel free to come back to specific details by using the index or detailed table of contents. (Of course, with e-books, just search.)

You can find more information (including a Cheat Sheet of shortcuts) at the publisher's Web site at www.dummies.com. This book also has sample files available at www.dummies.com/go/dashcodefd.

Part I
Introducing Dashcode and How You Can Use It

The 5th Wave   By Rich Tennant

"We're concerned – Kyle doesn't seem to be able to hot key between apps like all the other children."

In this part . . .

Dashcode can be your entry into the world of iPhone and iPad apps as well as Dashboard widgets. Apps and widgets are all variations of the very modern idea of light-weight and targeted software that's relatively easy to develop and use. Apps and widgets have turned the world of software development upside down — not least from the standpoint of cost and complexity. Writing apps that run on iPad and iPhone requires using Apple's programming tools that are based on Objective-C. Dashcode lets you build Web applications for Safari that have many of the features of full-fledged apps. For example, on iPhone these Web applications can make calls and find your location.

The iPad and iPhone Web apps are built on the same technology as Dashboard widgets: JavaScript, Cascading Style Sheets (CSS), and the graphical development interface of Dashcode. Dashcode is a great way to start producing projects quickly.

Chapter 1

Exploring the World of
Apps and Widgets

In This Chapter

▶ Discovering Dashcode terminology

▶ Getting to know apps and widgets

▶ Working with Safari Web apps

▶ Using iPhone Web apps

From the very beginning, the Mac has demonstrated that it doesn't have to hurt to use a computer. You don't have to type some obscure command; instead, you can move a mouse to click an icon. You don't have to create a program with thousands of lines of obscure computer code in order to generate a program. The folks at Apple have raised the bar higher and higher so that building programs and using them is easier and easier.

And from the beginning, some people have snorted at this concept of making computers easy to use. Talk to old-timers or read some newspaper and magazine articles from the 1980s, and you'll understand how suspicious people were of the mouse . . . not to mention all those pictures on the screen.

Apple and the Mac started to change all those viewpoints. Dashcode is just the latest example of Apple's approach to computers "for the rest of us." Dashcode makes it easy to build software that's easy to use and that does amazing things.

This chapter shows you what you can do with Dashcode and how to do it.

Developing Software for Apple Computers

Apple builds hardware — products such as the Mac itself, iPod, iPhone, and iPad. It also builds software to make those devices work — operating systems such as Mac OS X and iOS. (Formerly called iPhone OS, *iOS* is the operating system for iPhone, iPad, and more wonders to come.) Apple also builds application programs for people to use — products such as Safari, iTunes, the iWork suite (Numbers, Keynote, and Pages), the iLife suite (iPhoto, iMovie, iDVD, GarageBand, and iWeb), along with applications that ship as part of Mac OS X, such as Mail, iCal, Address Book, Preview, and utilities such as Disk Utility, System Preferences, Terminal, and Console.

Apple encourages third-party developers to develop and distribute their own application programs. Some are developed by large corporations such as Adobe (Creative Suite 5, including such products as Photoshop, Illustrator, and inDesign), Microsoft (Word, PowerPoint, and Excel), and FileMaker (which actually is a wholly-owned but independent subsidiary of Apple). Others are developed for in-house use by a wide variety of organizations; these applications you rarely hear about, in part because they often are part of a company's competitive edge. Still others are developed by individual developers for their own use or for specific markets in which they have expertise.

All these software products — the operating systems, the Apple-built programs, and the third-party programs — are created using Apple's robust and powerful development environment that is built around Xcode and Interface Builder along with powerful compilers to generate the runtime code. If you have a Mac OS X installation disc, you find a folder of these developer tools on it. When Mac OS X was introduced, Steve Jobs made a point of noting that the developer tools would always be available as part of the installation disc. The tools are an optional install, but the idea was to make it possible for people to bring their own ideas and innovations to the Mac OS X platform.

For as long as there have been computers, the skills and knowledge needed to develop programs have been in short supply. Various tools and strategies have been developed to provide an alternate way of developing software that had less of a learning curve. On the Mac, tools such as HyperCard, AppleScript, and Automator have eased the way for people to build their own software without needing to go through the complications of tools such as Xcode and Interface Builder (and, before them, Macintosh Programmers Workshop —MPW).

The Web has provided a new set of tools to create sophisticated Web pages that can function very much the way application programs do. The design skills for the developer are much the same whether you're writing for a Web-based application or for one based on a personal computer or other device, but the languages are different, and learning how to use them is often easier in the Web environment.

As with so many things, a tradeoff is involved. Traditional applications may be harder to build, but they can be more powerful than their Web-based counterparts. One important consideration is that traditional applications can access specific hardware features of a computer. Web-based applications run within a Web browser, and it's the browser (not the Web-based application) that accesses the computer's hardware.

Apple has found a way to provide access to specific hardware features through its Safari Web browser and to make that access available to people who develop Web pages. On Safari, a Web page can initiate a phone call on an iPhone; the same page when run in a browser on a Mac properly skips over the phone call code because a Mac can't make a phone call. The same Web page, when run in a browser such as Firefox, can also work properly: Apple's extensions to industry-standard Web pages are designed not to break in other browsers.

The variety of tools and development opportunities has led Apple to focus on three development platforms:

- ✓ **Mac OS X for Macintosh computers:** This environment is centered on Objective-C and the Cocoa development framework.

- ✓ **iOS for mobile devices, such as iPod touch, iPhone, and iPad:** This environment also uses Objective-C along with a customized development environment that handles mobile issues as well as interfaces that may not have traditional menus or resizable windows.

- ✓ **HTML 5 for Safari on Macs, iPads, and iPhone as well as Dashboard on Mac OS X:** This environment also includes JavaScript and Cascading Style Sheets (CSS). Unlike Mac OS X and iOS, these technologies are not proprietary, although some Mac-specific code in Safari is proprietary. The Dashboard environment on Mac OS X also fits into this category because of its use of HTML 5, JavaScript, and CSS as well as the absence of a compiler.

Introducing Dashcode

The goal of the developer group at Apple was to make as much as possible of the functionality of all the Apple devices available on each of these platforms. Xcode and Interface Builder are the pair of development tools for the first two platforms; Dashcode is the tool for the Third Platform.

"HTML for Safari on Macs, iPads and iPhone as well as Dashboard on Mac OS X" is a bit of a mouthful. As described at Apple's Worldwide Developers Conference in June 2010, Mac OS X, iOS, and HTML 5 constitute Apple's software strategy. To avoid that long description, I refer to the *Third Platform* when talking about "HTML for Safari on Macs, iPads and iPhone as well as Dashboard on Mac OS X."

Sure, you can write HTML, CSS, and JavaScript code with any text editor or with a variety of graphical user interface-based editors, but Dashcode is specifically designed to develop Web applications for Safari on mobile devices such as iPhone as well as the Mac itself and iPad. (iPad is definitely a mobile device, but in part because of its size, it fits into the category of Safari for a Mac laptop or desktop.)

Maybe it's because learning how to use the development tools for Mac OS X and iOS is a major project or maybe it's because developing on those platforms takes more time and effort, Dashcode and the Third Platform sometimes get skipped over. No more. This book is your guide to developing for the Third Platform.

By relying on open standards (such as CSS and JavaScript), Dashcode makes the development process for the Third Platform as fast and easy as possible. JavaScript code appears deep inside your Dashcode project templates, but you may never see it. And when you do see this code, you're likely to look at it only to make modifications.

Inspectors make it easy to inspect and change interface elements — their color and size, their behavior, and their interaction with data. A library of reusable interface parts and code snippets further insulates you from the process of starting from a blank piece of paper or an empty file and having to write code from scratch.

Because Dashcode makes it possible to develop very powerful user interfaces, you have the time to think about how you'll interact with the users of your apps and widgets.

The rest of this chapter introduces you to the types of software you can develop with Dashcode for the Third Platform. The examples here are built on Dashcode templates, which means you can build them yourself. In the rest of the book, you find more details on the process and additional features you can add for yourself. In this chapter, the emphasis is on out-of-the-box functionality with minimal customization.

Talking the Dashcode Talk

Here's a brief summary of the terms that you need to know to talk about Dashcode:

- ✔ **You use Dashcode to build *projects*.** These projects can be Dashboard widgets or Web applications for Safari on a Mac or a mobile device. You see examples of widgets and apps throughout this chapter.

- ✔ **Dashcode includes *templates* for projects.** You choose a template and the specific type of project you want to build and Dashcode builds the code. Sometimes you need to customize that template, but other times, the code is complete just by using the template.

- ✔ **Dashcode has a *Library* of reusable interface parts and code snippets.** You can use this Library to build and customize your projects.

- ✔ **Dashcode includes simulators.** The simulators let you run your projects as if they were running in Safari (on a personal computer or on a mobile device) or in Dashboard.

✔ **The end result of a project is a *product*, which can be a widget or an app.** You can deploy a completed project with Dashcode to Dashboard or to a Web site (including a MobileMe site); you can also save a Dashcode project to disk so that you can send it to people or post it on a Web site for further deployment and distribution.

Visiting a Small World: Apps and Widgets

Compared to traditional software programs, apps and widgets are smaller. They're often physically smaller, and their scope is smaller because they tend to focus on one thing. This section shows you some Dashcode projects built from the included templates that demonstrate the point. I also show you some features that Dashcode lets you build into your apps and widgets.

Figure 1-1 shows the Dashcode Utility template built for Safari on a Mac.

Figure 1-1: The Utility template lets you build a small word processor in Safari.

You can change fonts and apply styles, such as underlining or bold. Figure 1-1 also helps demonstrate the difference between Dashcode projects and traditional applications. The Utility template does one thing (word processing) with a number of features, but it's not a substitute for Word or Pages. You can't easily add an image, for example, and you won't find commands to place headers and footers. And search though you might, you won't find a Save button or Save command. What you type is automatically saved.

You can target the same Utility template for mobile Safari on iPhone (see Figure 1-2). In this figure, the Dashcode project is running in the iPhone simulator.

The code is different for the two versions of the app, but it uses similar features. In each case, the template uses appropriate interface elements. For example, the options in Figure 1-3 let you select fonts and sizes.

Figure 1-2:
Build the
template
for mobile
Safari.

If you click one of the pop-up menus in the simulator or tap one of them on your iPhone, the typical iPhone interface element, shown in Figure 1-4, appears. You don't have to do anything special.

Figure 1-5 shows a Dashboard widget built from the Countdown template. It provides a countdown (or countup) clock.

This example shows a project template that may need some customization to work. You can see how far Dashcode is from the complicated programming techniques of old.

The template can count down from a specific date and time to zero; alternatively, it can count up from that given date and time. In version 3.0 of Dashcode, the specific date is 4/1/2010, and the time is 4 a.m. The default is to count down to zero, and so the clock won't run because that date is in the past. To make it work, you can either change the date to a date and time in the future, or you can use the option to count up from the specific date and time.

Figure 1-3:
Select fonts
and font
sizes.

Figure 1-6 shows how you make such a change. This layout has a lot of set-tings, but all you need to do is either change the date and time or choose to count up.

The Countdown template is yet another example of how you can focus Dashcode projects; it isn't a stopwatch. Instead, this example is a count-down/countup clock for a specific date and time. Simple and focused.

Utility and Countdown are just two of the built-in templates. What you might want to take away from them are the following aspects of Dashcode projects:

✔ Projects focus on a goal.

✔ Traditional menu bars are nowhere to be found.

✔ The windows aren't resizable, and there are no scroll bars.

✔ It's easy to build these projects.

Figure 1-4:
The appropriate interface elements are automatically used.

Figure 1-5:
Count down or up from a time.

When I say it's easy to build these projects, I mean that you can make a change to a template to see whether it might work in only a few minutes. Even if you have to do some customization, such as entering a start date for the countdown timer your changes to the templates can often be fast. And if the changes don't work out, just move on to the next idea.

Not all Dashcode project modifications are as simple as changing the start or end time for a countdown/countup clock. Some of the examples in this book can take quite some time to complete, but once you've got the basic structure of an app or widget set up, the tweaks can be accomplished quite simply. In fact, as soon as you can think of a modification, you may be able to put it into place if you already have set up one of the templates.

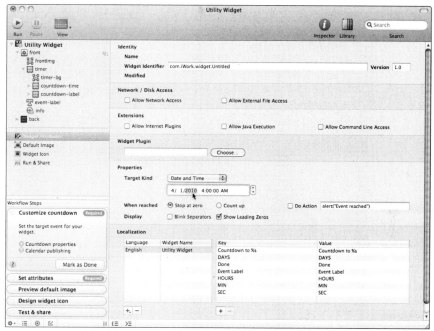

Figure 1-6:
Modify the
settings.

Categorizing Widgets and Apps Apple's Way

As you explore the templates and think about developing your own projects, it can help to categorize your ideas. One of the challenges in designing Dashcode projects is keeping them focused. Identifying the kind of project you're building helps with the focus.

Here are the three categories that Apple uses for apps on iPhone and iPad: they apply very well to Dashcode projects, too:

✔ **Immersive:** These projects are often games. They're immersive in the sense that you can "lose yourself" in them. The whole point is to take you out of your office, the line for the bus, or whatever situation you're in that you'd rather not be in.

✔ **Utility:** These projects provide some kind of service. They often work with the Internet. A utility app can be a currency converter; another example is the Maps Dashboard widget template (see Figure 1-7).

Like the Countdown widget, this widget requires customization. You need to register with Google to get a key to use the mapping system, and you need to supply the initial address. It's just a matter of typing in those two values, as you see in Figure 1-8. (You can see how to get the key in "Chapter 8.)

✔ **Productivity:** Finally, projects such as the Utility template let you create a small word processor. Often, a productivity project is characterized by the fact that the user puts data into it; a utility app often is characterized by the fact that the user gets data out of it (a map, the translation of a word or phrase, and so on).

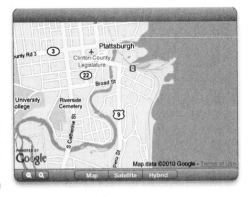

Figure 1-7: The Maps widget is an example of a utility widget.

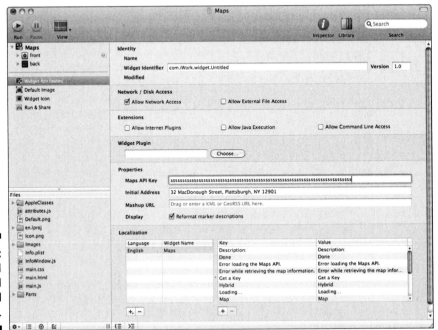

Figure 1-8: Set the API key and the initial address.

Navigating the Data

Dashcode templates provide tools for users to navigate through data easily. One of the handiest constructs is the browser interface tool that is available on iPhone in many apps built on iOS as well as Dashcode. Figure 1-9 shows the Browser Dashcode template in action. This example uses the data that is built into the template: It is information about a number of national parks in the United States.

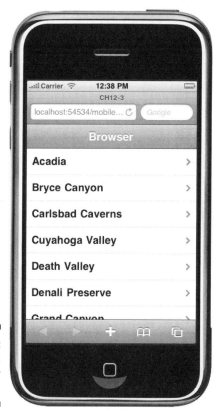

Figure 1-9:
Use the
Browser
template.

Precisely because this interface is used so frequently on iPhone, users recognize it, know how to use it, and know what to expect from it. Figure 1-9 shows a list of parks; the arrows at the right of the park's name take you to details about that park, as shown in Figure 1-10.

The data is provided in this template; you can modify it for your own project. In fact, to modify this project for your own purpose, the only thing you may need to do is to change the data. The project itself doesn't contain any text except for the data.

Figure 1-10:
Details are
provided for
each item.

Dashcode can use data that is included in the project as the National Park data is, but it can also use data that it accesses at runtime from a location on the Internet. In either case, the data needs to be in a standard format — JSON (JavaScript Object Notation) or XML (eXtensible Markup Language). You can find examples of the data files in Chapter 12.

Understanding the Structure of Apps and Widgets

You can work with Dashcode without knowing the details of how it does what it does. (In fact, that's true of most hardware and software.) How deeply you get into the structure of Dashcode is up to you. This section provides a high-level structural view; you find details throughout the book. And if you just want to focus on what you can do with Dashcode, feel free to do so.

Dashcode projects consist of code that is contained within the templates. You create a new Dashcode project by selecting a template. You can add your own code to the project to augment the template's code, but, most often, you customize with specific information on forms (refer to Figures 1-6 and 1-8).

Sometimes, you need to enter information into the code that Dashcode has generated; in those cases, clear comments tell you what to do. For example, Figure 1-11 shows you code that you can drag from the Library into your project. It lets you enable a specific button.

A comment directs you to change elementID to the name of the button you want to enable. Although Figure 1-11 may not be shown in color, Dashcode helps you further by placing elementID in purple. It's hard to make a mistake.

Your Dashcode project consists of a number of separate files; most are written in JavaScript. (See Appendix A for more information on JavaScript.") Other files are CSS files and PNG files that contain graphics for the projects. These file types are used extensively across the Web, so if you want to learn more about them, you can find many resources online and in libraries and bookstores. Remember, though, that you will probably not find the need to go into these files much of the time. And if you do, you can find help in the form of comments in the sections you may need to customize.

You may see a number of other file types in your project, such as property lists (plist), and localization folders (lproj). The only thing you must know about the files and folders inside your project is that you shouldn't move or rename them. Dashcode relies on their having certain names and locations.

Some people think that because the files are visible and editable as well as because they use standard Web formats, you can go into them and modify them at will (see Part II). Look but don't touch.

Figure 1-11:
Customize
the code for
your own
project.

Dashing through Dashboard Widgets

Dashboard widgets can be immersive, utility, or productivity. They can be particularly effective at displaying data from live data sources. Navigating through data is useful, but widgets shine at presenting changing data to you in a way in which you don't have to navigate to find what you want. Podcasts, video podcasts, and RSS feeds all fit the bill: They're changing data, and the widget or app just needs to go out to an address that you specify once to find the latest and greatest information.

Figure 1-12 shows the Daily Feed Dashboard widget template in action. It shows the latest posting from the feed.

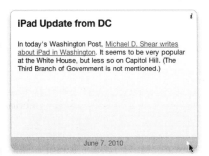

Figure 1-12: Daily Feed shows the latest item from an RSS feed.

You can use the Daily Feed template almost with no changes in the template. All you have to do is to supply the address of the RSS feed, as shown in Figure 1-13.

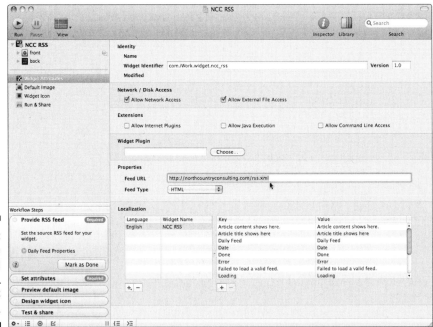

Figure 1-13: Customize Daily Feed with the URL of an RSS feed.

At the bottom of Figure 1-13, you can see a section called Localization. This section supports the ability to customize the interface automatically for various languages. Note that the languages supported are more than just languages: They include dialects and variants, such as UK and U.S. versions of English. The actual languages that are supported for your widget or app are up to you (some topics rely on specific languages), and you must provide the translations. The localization section at the bottom of Figure 1-13 illustrates the basic idea: You specify words and phrases used in your interface, and you then provide translations of them for specific languages. You can find more on localization in Chapter 16, where you see how to implement localization.

Apps or widgets that present RSS feeds are a great way to provide language-specific information to your users. If you subscribe to a feed that is in French, then — voilà — you have a French app or widget. The only thing that isn't in French is any text that is in the widget itself, and that's where localization comes in. Many apps and widgets have no text in their interface other than content: Plenty of icons and buttons in the Library provide functionality without the use of text. But if you do need text, consider localizing it.

Dashboard widgets have a front and a back. The front presents the main information, and the back presents credits, options, and other related information. You flip the widget from front to back by clicking the *i* button. In Figure 1-12, this button is in the upper right corner of the widget. This button normally appears when you hover the mouse over the widget, and it's typically in one of the four corners of the widget. The behavior to flip the widget (complete with an animation of the flip) is built into your Dashcode project.

When you want to flip back to the front, a Done button does the trick, as you can see in Figure 1-14.

RSS feeds are so useful because after you set them up, the feed you're presenting does all the work. That's one of the reasons why Dashcode has several RSS feed templates. Daily Feed shows the latest item from a given Feed. The RSS template takes another approach: For a given feed, it shows you the latest stories rather than just the most recent one. Figure 1-15 shows the RSS template in action.

Figure 1-14: Flip back to the front with Done.

Figure 1-15:
RSS shows
several
stories.

Dashcode lets you specify the feed as with Daily Feed, but you also can specify how many stories to show and the date range to use, as you see in Figure 1-16.

In addition to the options you specify in the widget, the back of the RSS widget has an option that the user can set (see Figure 1-17).

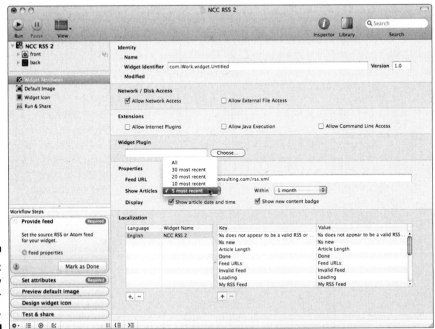

Figure 1-16:
Specify
options for
RSS.

Figure 1-17:
Users set
options on
the back of
Dashboard
widgets.

Trekking with Safari Web Apps

Safari is available on Mac OS X, Windows, and the iOS devices. Safari is compli-
ant with the standards for the Web, including HTML 5, which is the latest version
of the basic Web programming language. HTML has a number of major additions
that Safari supports, along with many other browsers. Safari also has some additional features that come into play when it is running on iPhone or iPad.

The two most important aspects of HTML 5 that matter to you are its ability to
handle embedded media well and the ability to store data on the user's computer. The ability to handle embedded media well can be a complicated and
contentious issue, but its basic consequence is that Flash isn't needed in many
cases and, in fact, isn't supported on devices, such as iPhone and iPad. If you
get too deeply into the issue, you may find yourself dealing with a lot of personal
theories. Steve Jobs has posted a note about Flash (www.apple.com/hot-
news/thoughts-on-flash) that provides some information. In a nutshell, his
point is that there are some security issues, on mobile devices Flash uses a lot of
battery power, and there are some performance issues. Agree or not, HTML 5 is
where Apple and much of the industry are heading. It's fully supported in Safari.

The fact that HTML 5 allows users to store data through their browser means
that your Dashcode apps for Safari (on mobile or other devices) have a way
to store data through HTML 5 and without going through some database or
file structure. In fact, it's Safari's implementation of HTML 5 that interacts
with the file system or a database. It doesn't matter from your point of view:
All you care about is that you don't have to do it in your Safari Web app.

The Utility template (refer to Figure 1-1) runs in Safari and uses the HTML 5
data storage features. Figure 1-18 provides a look at another Safari Web app:
It's the RSS Web app that re-implements the RSS Dashboard widget in Safari.
Figure 1-18 shows the RSS Safari template running in the simulator.

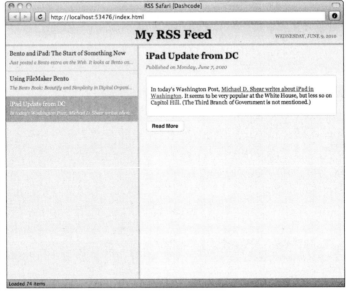

Figure 1-18: RSS Safari Web app behaves like the RSS Dashboard widget.

The interface looks different, but it has the same information. As you can see in Figure 1-19, the settings are the same as for the Dashboard widget. You provide the URL for the feed, and the settings for the display.

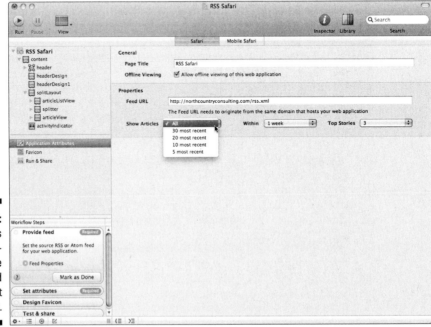

Figure 1-19: Settings are similar to the Dashboard widget setup.

Calling iPhone Web Apps

The Safari RSS template allows you to build a mobile Safari version for iPhone at the same time. So, without further ado, Figure 1-20 shows the same RSS feed on the iPhone simulator.

Figure 1-20: The same RSS settings let you produce an iPhone product with Dashcode.

The difference in the interface reflects the size and features of iPhone: Dashcode has done all the work for you.

Figure 1-21 shows how you can drill down to articles on iPhone. One reason for drilling down is that you have a much smaller screen to deal with than on a laptop or desktop computer.

If you want to read more, Safari on iPhone can display the original article, as you see in Figure 1-21.

The settings for the mobile Safari version are shown in Figure 1-22. The feed and the options (number of stories, for example) are the same settings as they were for a regular Safari Web app. You don't have to enter them again; they're the same values.

In Figure 1-23, you do see some additional settings that apply only to mobile devices, such as iPhone. For example, you see the viewport settings, which handle rotation of the device between horizontal and vertical orientations. The issue of rotation applies only to mobile devices because rotating a desktop computer and its display from horizontal to vertical isn't a supported or recommended behavior.

In the Dashcode templates, you typically provide only the bare essentials, such as the URL of an RSS feed. The templates provide the code to implement the functionality appropriate for whatever your product will run on: Dashboard, Safari, or mobile Safari. (Not all versions are supported for all templates.)

Figure 1-21:
Drill down to
an article on
iPhone.

Figure 1-22:
You can see
the original
article in
Safari on
iPhone.

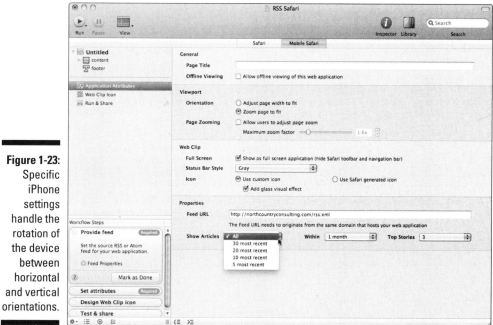

Figure 1-23:
Specific
iPhone
settings
handle the
rotation of
the device
between
horizontal
and vertical
orientations.

Chapter 2

Getting to Know Your Development Tools

Dashcode packs a great amount of functionality into one window. Almost everything that you'll want to do in order to construct a widget for Dashboard or a Web app for iPhone or iPad is available in the Dashcode window.

This chapter helps you explore the Dashcode window. As you do so, you'll discover how Dashcode works. (You'll also appreciate many of the user interface techniques used in Apple products — and that you can use in your own widgets and apps.)

Don't think that you have to memorize everything you find in this chapter. It's a guide to Dashcode, and you'll come back to specific parts of the Dashcode window throughout this book. In fact, as you go through tasks such as working with data or Internet connections, you'll come back to the Dashcode window in step-by-step guides.

In this chapter, just take a look at the window and what's inside it. (The next chapter puts the window to use.)

Getting Dashcode Installed

The first step is to get Dashcode and install it on your Mac. (Yes, you need a Mac. Dashcode runs only on Mac OS X, and although apps in general can run on many devices, in this book, we focus on Web apps built with Dashcode.)

Log on to `developer.apple.com` and follow the links to download developer tools. This path changes from time to time as Apple rearranges the developer site, but rest assured that you have opportunities on almost any page to register to become a developer if you haven't done so yet. You can choose from a variety of types of membership, some of which are free. All require you to provide a valid e-mail address and to agree to Apple's terms and conditions for developers.

After you register, download the Developer Tools package, which is automatically installed on your Mac in the root directory of your hard disk; the folder is called Developer. Inside that folder is a folder called Applications, which contains Dashcode. (You may want to drag that icon to the dock so that you can launch Dashcode whenever you need it.)

The download of Developer Tools can be fairly large; after all, it contains all of the tools needed to develop any Mac OS X application as well as those for iPhone and iPad. (This same software is used to build Mac OS X itself.) During the installation process, you can choose which components you want to install. The best choice is to use the default installation. If you're short on disk space, you can pick and choose, but if you're short on disk space at this stage of the game, you may soon get into trouble.

Introducing the Dashcode Window

The Dashcode window is compact and powerful. Unlike some other development environments, you won't find yourself opening and closing a variety of windows: Everything is available in the Dashcode window. Figure 2-1 shows the window in action as you work on a project. The window will probably look different depending on what project you're working on and what preferences you set for Dashcode. In addition to preferences, you can show or hide different parts of the window as well as expand or contract them.

What you see in Figure 2-1 is a project using the RSS template for Safari with the mobile Safari (iPhone) interface displayed.

Choosing a template is the first step in Chapter 3, which walks through the process of developing a mobile Safari Web application using the RSS template.

The Dashcode window is divided into three basic parts:

 ✔ The *toolbar* at the top
 ✔ The *navigator* at the left
 ✔ The *canvas* at the right

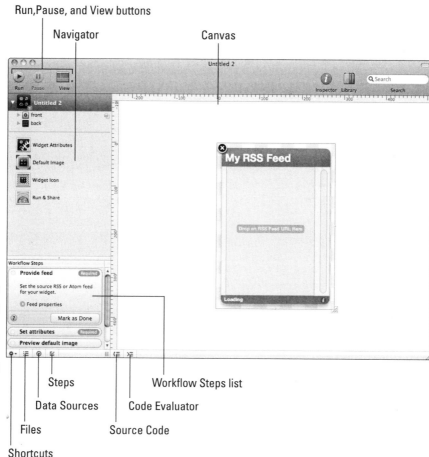

Figure 2-1:
Work on a
project in
Dashcode.

If your project is destined for both Safari and mobile Safari, a tab bar appears
just below the toolbar so that you can switch between the two versions, as
shown in Figure 2-2.

Tooling through the Dashcode toolbar

The Dashcode toolbar is a standard Mac OS X toolbar, so you can show or hide
it as you want. The small lozenge-shaped button in the top right of the window
frame does the showing and hiding. You can also choose View➪Show/Hide
Toolbar or the keyboard shortcut ⌘T to show or hide it.

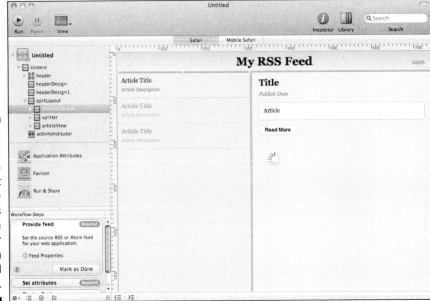

Figure 2-2:
You can
develop
a project
for mobile
Safari as
well as a
version for
Safari on
Mac and
Windows.

As for the contents of the toolbar, as with any Mac OS X toolbar, you can choose View➪Customize Toolbar to open the customization sheet, shown in Figure 2-3. Just drag the items you want to add into the toolbar, drag the ones you want to remove out of the toolbar, and move the remaining items from side to side.

In this book, the default toolbar is used without customization, but as you become more advanced at using Dashcode, you can explore the additional items.

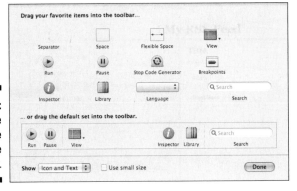

Figure 2-3:
Customize
the
Dashcode
toolbar.

Using the toolbar or menu to decide what to view

The View item is relevant to all three panes within the Dashcode window. (*Pane* is the term for parts of a window that you can show or hide individually in response to buttons, menu commands, or the running of an application.) Figure 2-4 shows the choices for View.

If you look carefully at Figure 2-4, you see gray lines that divide the choices into three sections. In the first section are panes that can appear in the Canvas pane at the right of the window (yes, panes can contain panes, something you'll appreciate as you need to use them to present information in your apps and widgets):

- ✔ Canvas
- ✔ Run log
- ✔ Stack frame
- ✔ Breakpoints

Because canvas is the initial and most frequent view shown in the large area at the right of the Dashcode, it has given its name to the entire area. I describe the Canvas pane in the section "Starting Out with the Canvas," later in this chapter. I discuss run log, stack frame, and breakpoints, which are used in debugging, in Chapter 19.

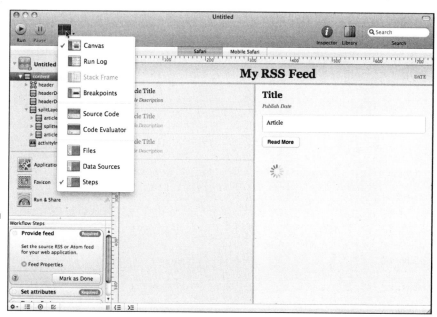

Figure 2-4: Choose what to view from the toolbar.

These panes appear at the top of the Canvas pane. You can see only one (or none) of these four panes at a time.

The next set of panes, which Chapter 19 discusses in detail, appears at the bottom of the Canvas pane: Source Code and Code Evaluator. As with the first set, only one of these two panes can appear at a time. In Figure 2-4, you see the Canvas pane. If you add a Source Code pane, it appears at the bottom (see Figure 2-5).

You can drag the dividing line to increase or decrease the size of the top and bottom panes.

If you click View in the toolbar or choose View⇨Source Code to stop showing the Canvas pane, the Source Code pane automatically fills the Canvas pane at the right of the window, as shown in Figure 2-6.

The next set of panes, shown in the navigator, is Files, Data Sources, and Steps. (For more on the navigator, see the following section.) The panes are grouped together in the View item. Those groupings have the same meaning as the other groups: Only one Navigator pane can appear at a time. Furthermore, the pane's location is predetermined: It always appears at the bottom of the navigator.

I discuss the Files and Steps panes in the next section "Using the icons in the window frame to decide what to view." I cover the Data Sources pane in Chapters 9 and 10.

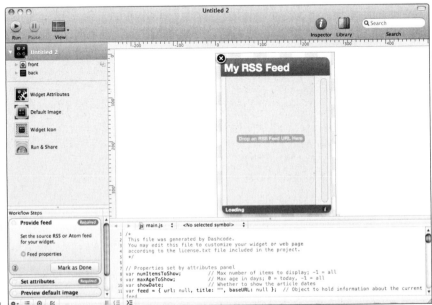

Figure 2-5:
Add a
Source
Code pane.

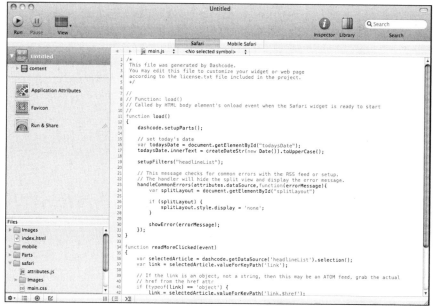

Figure 2-6:
Dashcode
expands
panes when
it can.

Using the icons in the window frame to decide what to view

You may think that the people at Apple have crammed as many options as possible into the View menu and View in the toolbar, but wait — there's more! Look at the bottom edge of the window frame shown in Figure 2-6. At the left are four small icons, described from left to right:

- ✓ **Shortcuts:** This gear icon appears throughout Apple's interfaces. It always means that a drop-down or pop-up menu of commands and actions will be revealed when you click it. You'll find the gear icon in Finder windows, in many applications on Mac OS X, and in widgets and apps. In most cases, its menu of commands consists of commands that are also located in other places, such as the menu bar.

- ✓ **Files:** This icon consists of three horizontal lines that are somewhat reminiscent of a file list in a Finder window. It shows and hides the Files pane in the navigator.

- ✓ **Data sources:** The bull's-eye-like icon represents data sources.

- ✓ **Steps:** The check mark is for the Workflow Steps list.

The View menu, View in the toolbar, and the icons in the lower left frame of the window give you at least three different ways to show and hide files, data sources, and the Workflow Steps list.

- ✓ **Divider:** Moving along to the right, the three vertical lines are the divider for letting you drag the divider between the two window panes (that is, the navigator and the canvas).

✔ **Source code:** The three horizontal lines with a curly bracket to their left let you view the source code in the canvas.

✔ **Evaluator:** The next icon with three horizontal lines and an arrow is for the Code Evaluator. The arrow represents the pointer that indicates the current line of code when you're debugging your project.

The icons in the navigator show or hide their respective tools. Because the Canvas pane consists of two panes that you can resize, this second set of icons shows or hides tools in the lower pane, which may be sized out of view at the moment. Although the icon may appear to have no immediate effect, if you drag the bar at the bottom of the canvas up to reveal the lower pane, you'll see that your choice appears.

Navigating the navigator

At the left of the Dashcode window is the *navigator*. The navigator contains various pieces of information in panes that you can choose to display.

In Figures 2-1 and 2-2, two appear in the navigator:

✔ **Stack Layout pane:** At the top is the project's Stack Layout. The Stack Layout represents your project. The small *disclosure triangles* next to various items let you expand and contract them so that you can see more or less detail. When you click the disclosure triangle next to a folder, everything folds up into the icon that's named after your project. In the first figures of this chapter the project is new and has not yet been saved, so it has the default name of *Untitled* (or *Untitled 2* or *Untitled 3*). After you've saved a project, the name is changed to the name of the file in which you save it.

You can find out more about the Stack Layout later in this chapter in the "Providing Information and Interaction with Views and View Hierarchies" section.

The Attributes, Favicon, and Run & Share links appear at the bottom of the Stack Layout and let you navigate to major Dashcode tools. (See Chapter 3 for more information.)

✔ **Steps pane:** At the bottom of the navigator in Figure 2-1 is a pane containing a list of workflow steps. You can find out more on the Workflow Steps list later in this chapter in "Working Through the Workflow Steps List."

You can add, remove, and resize panes in the navigator, which is why your navigator may look different from the one shown in Figure 2-1.

The lessons of the Dashcode interface

In order to create your own Dashboard widgets and iPhone or iPad apps, you'll need to use Dashcode and know your way around the window. But Dashcode's window can play another very important role for you because it's a good example of how you can squeeze data and functionality into your own apps and widgets. Every software developer knows that the screen never has enough room for everything that developers and users want to have visible. (Developers refer to the screen as *real estate* for obvious reasons.) When it comes to apps and widgets, they have even less space than traditional applications because they run in smaller windows (Dashboard widgets) or on devices with smaller screens (such as iPhone), so the problem of how to fit everything in is made even worse. Don't just explore Dashcode so that you can know how to use it: Explore Dashcode to see what concepts and ideas you can borrow.

Dashcode uses a wide variety of interface elements and techniques to fit all the information into its window. It packs a great deal of information into its window — and that window is fairly large. You can resize and reshape it, but you can't make it so small that you can't see all three parts. Here is the smallest you can make it:

Your apps and widgets are going to be even smaller than this resized Dashcode window, so you are going to have to consider many of the Dashcode techniques yourself to present your data. For that reason, don't just learn how to use the Dashcode window; get in the habit of looking at it critically and asking yourself why the people at Apple made the various design choices that they have made. You're going to encounter the same issues of presenting data and functionality in your apps and widgets that the Dashcode designers have encountered.

You can construct very complex sets of rules; if they're clear to the user at some level, they can make for a successful and powerful interface. As an example, consider the View menu and the View item in the toolbar: They bring up the same menu of views. Most Dashcode users probably think that they just control what the user wants to view, but that is just the beginning of their functionality.

The little dividing lines in the menu shown in the View command and by View in the toolbar group some of the items together, and for many users, that logical grouping isn't worth a second thought. However, those groups determine sets of panes — at most one of which can be displayed at a time. Most Dashcode users probably don't think about this behavior; it's one of the aspects of the interface that "just works."

Remember that not only do you have much less space on the interfaces of your apps and widgets, but you're unlikely to have an instruction manual. In that environment, you and your users need every bit of available help to make using your projects easier. One thing to learn from the Dashcode interface (and, indeed, from almost all the Apple interfaces) is the benefit of consistency. If certain interface items always behave in the same way, users can learn that without having to think through the steps that are involved.

Despite your ability to remove panes from the navigator, you can never remove the stack layout; it always appears at the top of the navigator. Furthermore, the top-to-bottom sequence of panes always remains the same. For example, the Steps pane is always below the Attributes pane when both appear.

You can choose which panes to view by using the View menu or by using View in the toolbar, as shown in Figure 2-4.

Exploring the canvas

The large area at the right of Figures 2-1 and 2-2 is called the *canvas*. The canvas is where you design the appearance of your project.

In fact, the canvas section can contain a variety of panes, as described in the section "Tooling through the Dashcode toolbar," earlier in this chapter. Because the canvas is the most commonly used pane, I devote an entire section to it later in this chapter.

Working Through the Workflow Steps List

By default, the Workflow Steps list is shown in the navigator for a new project. When you show or hide the Workflow Steps list, the menu command is Show or Hide Steps. The Workflow Steps list consists of steps that you should do as you work on your project. You can mark each step finished or unfinished, and you can come back or jump ahead as you work on the project's steps.

Users can show or hide the Workflow Steps list just as they can show or hide any other of the interface elements by using the View menu or the View item in the toolbar.

Each project template can have its own steps, but the overall format of the Workflow Steps list is the same. Figure 2-7 shows you the Workflow Steps list for the mobile Safari template that is developed in Chapter 3. It also demonstrates the effect of the View⇔Use Small Navigator Icons command.

You can expand and collapse each step by just clicking in its background. In Figure 2-7, the first step (Provide Feed) and the last step (Test & Share) are collapsed. The small circle at the left of the title of each step indicates whether or not the step has been completed. If you click in that circle, you reverse the completion status; you do the same thing by clicking the Mark as Done/Mark as Not Done button in each step.

Each step has a brief description. If you want more information, you can click the question mark to open the documentation for you in its own window. You may see links shown as arrows within small gray circles. These links take you to the part of Dashcode where you can perform the step.

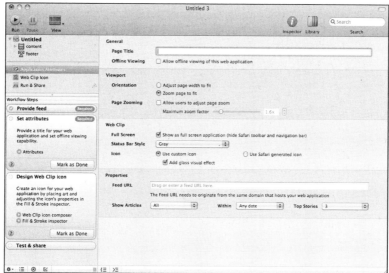

Figure 2-7:
Using the
Workflow
Steps list.

Note once again how much functionality is presented in a small space (a space you can make even smaller by collapsing it).

The steps are presented in an order that makes sense to the project template designer, but you can perform them in any order that you choose. For example, some steps, such as icon development for your widget or app, may depend on other people. You don't have to wait for them to accomplish some of your other steps. You can go through the steps in a different order, and you can even switch steps that have been marked as done to not done. (Alas, marking a done step as not done often happens in the testing step at the end of the workflow.)

Managing project files

Most of the time, you don't need to manage your Dashcode files; Dashcode does it for you. On the few occasions when you need to manipulate the internal Dashcode files, use Dashcode and not the Finder to do so. You can manage your Dashcode files by choosing View⇨Files, clicking View in the toolbar, or clicking the Files icon in the lower left frame of the Dashcode window.

Looking Inside an App or Widget

One of the simplest projects is the RSS project: It's available for Safari (mobile or desktop) and for Dashboard. An RSS project lets you specify an RSS feed. When you run the app or widget, the latest postings appear. (Chapter 3 describes a basic example.)

If you look inside the finished app or widget, you'll see that more than 30 separate files are involved. Figure 2-8 shows the files in the RSS Dashboard widget; Figure 2-9 shows the files in the RSS Safari app.

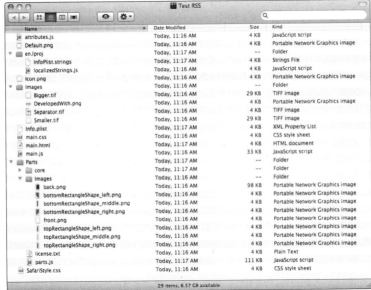

Figure 2-8:
Looking at the RSS widget files.

The files are organized into folders, which give you a good idea of what is going on. Basically, you have a set of files that are in the Core folder, which is inside the Parts folder. The files in the Core folder are the main files that provide the support (mostly in JavaScript) for your project. These files are automatically included in your project; you don't have to do anything, and, in almost all cases, you do nothing with them.

In many ways, these files provide some of the basic functionality that is provided by Objective-C code in Xcode and Interface Builder for OS-based apps.

For Safari Web applications, you see a Safari folder and a Mobile folder (if you have both versions). Your project is implemented inside these folders and outside of the Core folder (which has general support for all projects). And, as you see throughout this book, all you do is point-and-click in Dashcode.

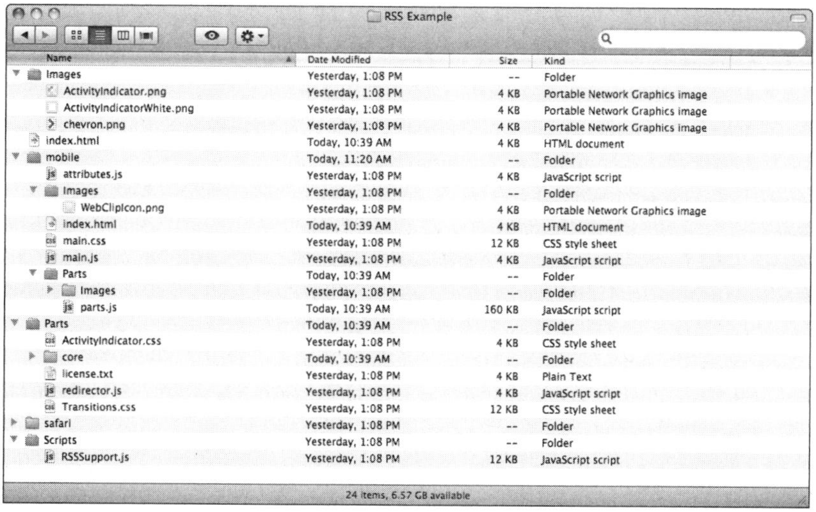

Name	Date Modified	Size	Kind
▼ 📁 Images	Yesterday, 1:08 PM	--	Folder
ActivityIndicator.png	Yesterday, 1:08 PM	4 KB	Portable Network Graphics image
ActivityIndicatorWhite.png	Yesterday, 1:08 PM	4 KB	Portable Network Graphics image
chevron.png	Yesterday, 1:08 PM	4 KB	Portable Network Graphics image
index.html	Today, 10:39 AM	4 KB	HTML document
▼ 📁 mobile	Today, 11:20 AM	--	Folder
attributes.js	Yesterday, 1:08 PM	4 KB	JavaScript script
▼ 📁 Images	Yesterday, 1:08 PM	--	Folder
WebClipIcon.png	Yesterday, 1:08 PM	4 KB	Portable Network Graphics image
index.html	Today, 10:39 AM	4 KB	HTML document
main.css	Yesterday, 1:08 PM	12 KB	CSS style sheet
main.js	Yesterday, 1:08 PM	4 KB	JavaScript script
▼ 📁 Parts	Today, 10:39 AM	--	Folder
▶ 📁 Images	Yesterday, 1:08 PM	--	Folder
parts.js	Today, 10:39 AM	160 KB	JavaScript script
▼ 📁 Parts	Today, 10:39 AM	--	Folder
ActivityIndicator.css	Yesterday, 1:08 PM	4 KB	CSS style sheet
▶ 📁 core	Today, 10:39 AM	--	Folder
license.txt	Yesterday, 1:08 PM	4 KB	Plain Text
redirector.js	Yesterday, 1:08 PM	4 KB	JavaScript script
Transitions.css	Yesterday, 1:08 PM	12 KB	CSS style sheet
▶ 📁 safari	Yesterday, 1:08 PM	--	Folder
▼ 📁 Scripts	Yesterday, 1:08 PM	--	Folder
RSSSupport.js	Yesterday, 1:08 PM	12 KB	JavaScript script

24 items, 6.57 GB available

Figure 2-9:
Looking at
the RSS
Safari files.

Deep inside Dashcode, those actions often cause sections of code to be added to your project. In fact, sometimes a single click of the mouse can add an entire file to your project.

You create none of these files for a Dashcode project. In later projects — particularly those involving data sources — you may worry about one or two files, but that's about all.

Packaging Your Apps and Widgets

All these files are what make your app or widget run. You typically don't see these files. Apps and Dashboard widgets have different packaging methods.

Packaging a Safari Web application

For a Safari Web application, the files are packaged exactly as you see in Figure 2-8 — they're in folders, such as Parts and Images. This structure is exactly what any Web site might use. Figure 2-10 shows the RSS template folder with all the subfolders collapsed. Collapsing the subfolders makes the structure of the basic folder clearer.

If you name your deployable project something like RSSExample (the space is removed for simplicity), you can upload it to a Web site. If someone types `www.yourURL.com/RSSexample`, basic Web rules provide that if an `index.html` or `index.php` file is found, that file is displayed in the user's browser.

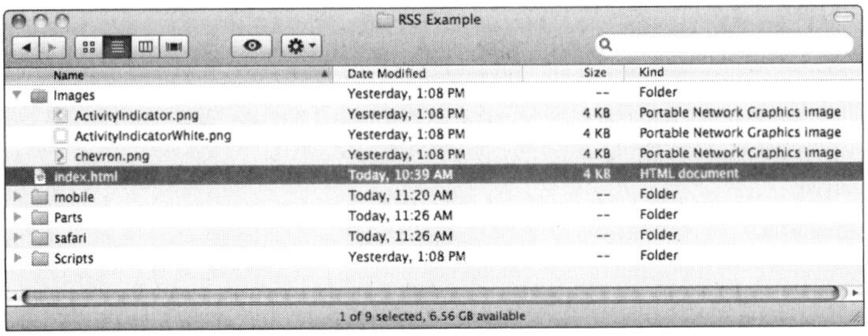

Figure 2-10:
Looking at
the top
level of a
Safari Web
application.

In Figure 2-10, the folder contains the `index.html` file. When this whole folder is uploaded to a Web server, someone can type `www.yourURL.com/RSSExample` to be launched into your Safari Web application.

From `index.html`, user mouse clicks and other interactions launch JavaScript code, and your app appears in Safari as you would expect. For these steps to work, all you have to do is upload the entire folder to your Web site. (And just to make things easier, Dashcode can do that task for you.)

The process described here relies on Web standards; they aren't special Dashcode implementations. As a result, here are some characteristics of Dashcode Web apps to remember:

✔ **Dashcode Web apps work on any Web server.** The Web server needs to know nothing about apps, Dashcode, iPhone, or iPad or anything except standard run-of-the-mill Web processes and files. You don't need permission from a webmaster or IT manager to deploy a Dashcode Web app. If you need permission to deploy any JavaScript-based files on the Web server, that's a separate matter. What's important for many people is that they don't have to get Dashcode-, iPhone-, or iPad-specific permissions.

✔ **Dashcode Web apps are self-contained, and you can move them from one Web server to another.** You can also move them from one domain to another even if those domains are on the same server.

✔ **Dashcode Web apps work only on Safari and browsers derived from WebKit (which is at the heart of Safari).** Extensions to the Safari Web browser provide additional functionality to some of the JavaScript code included in your app. This additional functionality does tasks such as interact with the telephony features in iPhone or the mapping software on any of the supported products. If you access the URL from another browser, the code inserted in your Dashcode app simply bypasses these features.

✔ **Files inside a Dashcode Web app shouldn't be moved or renamed outside Dashcode.** You can do any moving or renaming inside Dashcode, which then takes care of adjusting the internal links. After the `index.html` file is running, it (and other files in your project) may have *relative links* to other files. Relative links are files that are addressed not by full URLs, such as `www.yourURL.com/RSSExample/anotherfile.html`, but through links that take `index.html` or another file as a starting point. For example, from `index.html`, you can access a file in an adjacent folder called Parts as `../Parts/anotherfile.html`. Moving or renaming a file breaks these internal links. (Using Dashcode for the renaming preserves them.)

Packaging a Dashboard widget

The structure of a Dashboard widget is basically the same as for a Safari Web application (see preceding section) except for two differences:

- ✔ **Dashboard widgets have no alternate environments.** For Safari, you can have mobile or desktop environments. You have only one environment for Dashboard widgets. (A word to the wise: This structure handles widgets and apps equally well. If the people at Apple wanted to dream up a second or third environment for Dashboard widgets, it would be no problem.)

- ✔ **Mac OS X can hide the files using a *package*.** Mac OS X has a concept called *packages*. Most applications are packages. Packages appear to be files just like any other file on your disk. However, if you hold down the Control key while you click an application program's icon, you see a shortcut menu (sometimes called a *contextual menu*) that includes Show Package Contents. If you select that command, a new window opens with a single folder called Contents. You can navigate through that window as through any Finder window view files and folders within it.

When you finish putting together a Dashboard widget with Dashcode, Dashcode packages up the project into a widget file; Dashcode can install the widget for you in your own Dashboard. You can also share that widget file with other people. If you use the Show Package Contents command to look inside the widget, you see the file structure shown previously in Figure 2-8.

Because widgets are only used on Mac OS X, you can safely package them up in this way. Your Safari Web applications need to be deployed on Web servers that may not be running Mac OS X, so they don't necessarily support the concept of packages. That is why you have to generate Web apps as a set of files rather than as a package.

Packaging a Dashcode project

The concept of packages on Mac OS X is used in Dashcode itself as well as for widgets. When you create a project, you can save it to disk just as you would any other file. The Dashcode file itself is a package. Figure 2-11 shows you the contents of a typical Dashcode project.

Figure 2-11:
Dashcode
projects
rely on
packages.

Dashcode automatically provides two files with information about your project. The rest of the files in the project are the actual code to make it run.

- ✔ **wdgtuser:** This file, which is prefixed with the Mac OS X user name, contains information about the user.

- ✔ **projectinfo.plist:** This *property list* file contains information about the project.

In addition to the project files, the Dashcode project package contains these two files so that it's a self-contained entity for Dashcode to use. When you're running your app or widget, you need only the files inside the project folder; you need these two other files only when you're using Dashcode to create or modify a project. In order to deploy an app or widget, the safest method is to use Dashcode: It creates the appropriate run-time files. Do not attempt to install a Dashcode project file as a Web app or a widget: It won't work.

Apple uses property lists extensively throughout Mac OS X. Property lists are all XML files, so they're readable in any text editor. You can use the Property List Editor, which is part of Apple's Developer Tools, to display and edit them. (You must be a registered developer and have installed the tools unless you have a Mac OS X installation disc handy.) Figure 2-12 shows a Dashcode `projectinfo` property list file. This information is inside every Dashcode project no matter where you move it. Your preferences and settings for Dashcode and this project are part of the project. The location of preferences and settings inside the project is a difference from other applications where the application settings are preferences for your account and are stored in your user account folder.

As you can see in Figure 2-12, this property list stores your settings for the Workflow Steps list including which steps have been completed.

To finish up the files in the Dashcode project package, look at the `wdgtuser` file, shown in Figure 2-13. It, too, is an XML file, shown in BBEdit so that you can see the raw XML.

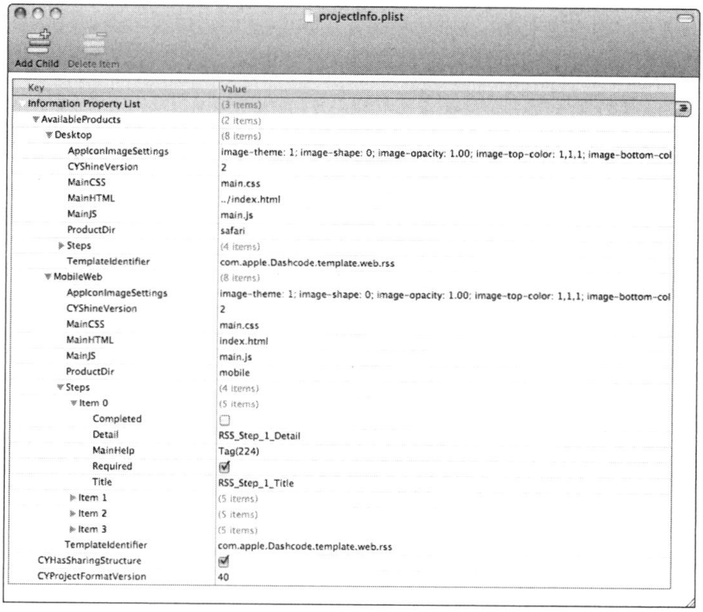

Figure 2-12:
Look inside
a Dashcode
project
property list.

In Figure 2-13, you can see the settings for this project and this Dashcode user.

Figure 2-13:
Look inside
a wdg-
tuser file.

Introducing Views

Everything you see on an app or widget is a *view.* Views come in many different types, ranging from buttons to text fields to containers that display a photo or a video clip, but they all have a number of common characteristics. Each view, for example, has a specific location and a specific size. Views can contain other views, so when you speak of a view's *location,* you're actually talking about its location within the view that contains it.

On the canvas in Figure 2-14, you see a representation of the RSS template. You can click a view to highlight it; the date view is highlighted in Figure 2-14. You can then change settings and attributes of the view.

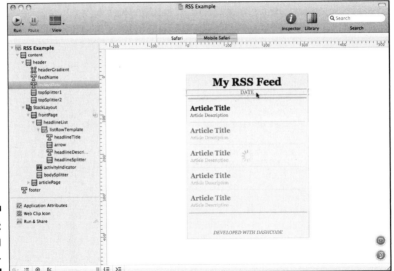

Figure 2-14:
Exploring
views.

At the top of the navigator, you see a view hierarchy. The todaysDate view, which is selected in the canvas, is highlighted in the navigator.

Like all views, the todaysDate view has two locations:

✔ **Visual location:** On the canvas, this view is highlighted with an outline and small handles to resize it. It has a specific location on the canvas (and, later on, on an iPhone). With Dashcode, you can move the view around and place it exactly where you want it.

✔ **Structural location:** A view also has a structural or hierarchical location. Look at the navigator at the left of Figure 2-14, and you see that the view is also highlighted there. Disclosure triangles let you expand and contract any of the views in the navigator; when they're expanded, you see the *subviews* within them.

As you build your interfaces, you need to be aware of both types of location. In this case, `todaysDate` is inside a view called `header`. The `header` view is inside another view called `content`. Proceeding up the hierarchy, (you see that `content` is directly inside the entire project. The project has only two *subviews*:

- ✔ `content` contains a number of subviews.
- ✔ `footer` has no views.

In a view hierarchy, the final view at the bottom is `footer`; it contains the phrase "Developed with Dashcode."

In Dashcode's navigator, the icons next to view names provide indications of what type of view you're looking at. A *T* for example, indicates a text view — a view that contains text such as "Developed with Dashcode."

Most of what you do in Dashcode consists of manipulating views. You may decide to add or remove views from the templates; you may move them around and resize them. You can change their colors, and, perhaps most important, you can change their behaviors.

Yes, views can behave. Their three main characteristics are

- ✔ They can display data.
- ✔ They can contain other views.
- ✔ They can respond to events.

Buttons, which are views, respond to mouse clicks or taps, and other types of views respond to other types of events.

Views and the windows in which they appear are much the same as they are in desktop applications, but apps and widgets have two critical differences:

- ✔ **Scrolling:** You can scroll many windows on the desktop, allowing the window to display much more data than fits in its frame. Resizing is one solution to this issue, but scrolling is another classic approach. In almost all cases, you can't scroll widgets and apps.

- ✔ **Multiple windows:** Part of the graphical user interface structure is the ability to work with multiple windows — even inside the same program. For example you can have several spreadsheets open at the same time in a spreadsheet program. That is not the case for apps and widgets: For a given app or widget, only one window at a time belongs to it. On Dashboard, you can have 15 widgets open in 15 windows. Some of those widgets may even be open several times in what are called several *instances* of the widget. Each instance is independent. Likewise, with Web apps, you may have the same Web app open several times and displayed in several Browser windows, but each one is independent.

Sorting out views, panes, and menus

You see views in the navigator and displayed in the canvas as you use Dashcode. You also work with views in Dashcode itself. If you want a quick introduction to the difference between windows and views, check out the View and Window menus in Dashcode.

The View menu (and View in the toolbar) lets you show and hide panes in the Dashcode window. If you want to be precise, you can view or not view the panes (hence the menu name). Inside the Dashcode app, the panes are displayed as views. *View* is the programming term, and *pane* is the term that most users use.

Next to the View menu, the Window menu lets you minimize or hide the Dashcode window. You can also show or hide two other windows

in Dashcode: the Library and the inspector. You can also show or hide these windows from the toolbar.

Closing a window is done from the File menu because in most cases that involves saving changes to a document that is portrayed in a view — a File menu operation. The Window menu lets you show or hide a menu; even a hidden window is still open.

Developers use these very specific terms to describe the behavior of apps and widgets as well as all Mac OS X applications. Using specific terms helps you navigate through developer documentation by knowing the correct terms to search for and look up in an index.

Unless someone points out the fact that your app or widget has only a single nonscrolling window, you may not even notice that fact.

You can also resize windows — and even dialogs — on desktop applications. You can't resize a window on an app because you don't see a frame, which is what you use to resize it. However, an app's interface frequently does change size as you zoom it as well as when you rotate the device between horizontal and vertical orientations.

Checking Out the Library

The *Library* is just that — a repository of information and, more important, practical elements that you can add to your projects. The Library is always present in Dashcode, but you can show or hide the Library window from the Window menu or by clicking Library in the toolbar. (Clicking Library in the toolbar when the Library window is open hides it.)

As you start to explore the Library, you see how the pieces of Dashcode come together in the files that make up your project. Open the Library window if it isn't open. It doesn't matter what project you have open because at this point you're just exploring the Library window. (Without a project window open in Dashcode, you have no toolbar and no Library menu.)

Figure 2-15 shows the Library window.

At the top of the Library window are tabs to control three panes: Parts, Code, and Photos. In each pane, you find a list of the items available as parts, code snippets, or your own photos.

No matter which pane you select, the bottom of the Library window contains a field that lets you search that particular pane. For example, if you search for *checkbox* in the Parts pane, you find the checkbox part. In the Code pane, you find some code snippets.

In the lower left corner of the Library is a shortcut menu (as always with the gear). This menu helps you organize the items in whatever pane you're viewing, as shown in Figure 2-16.

Some familiar organizational tools appear in the shortcut menu. One of the great features of Mac OS X is its use and reuse of the same powerful interface techniques. Smart collections appear in Bento, smart groups in Address Book, and smart folders in the Finder. As in all these applications, you can have groups that you configure and update just by dragging items from the pane into them in addition to smart groups that are automatically updated. The option to show the banners for groups can further customize and organize your Library window. (Note that the banners are turned on in Figure 2-16.)

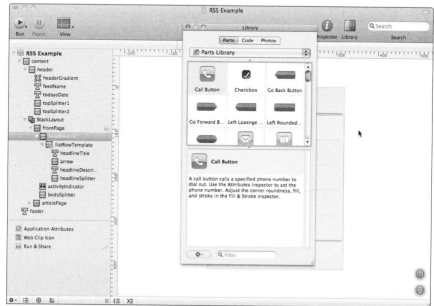

Figure 2-15:
Exploring
the Library.

Figure 2-16:
Use the
shortcut
menu to
organize
your Library.

The idea behind the Library window is that you can drag an item from the window into your Dashcode project. Nothing is exciting about this until you think back on those dozens of files that are hidden inside your Dashcode project. When you drag an item from the Library into your project, you're dragging references to specific files and parts of files into the code that you also don't normally see in your project. Dragging items from the Library is a far cry from writing code!

Looking at parts

In the Parts pane are graphical elements that you can insert into your apps and widgets. These elements are sorted into a number of categories controlled by a pop-up menu (see Figure 2-17). You can also use the search box at the bottom right of the window to find specific items.

Use shortcuts, such as the option to show banners to organize the window. As always, use yourself as a test subject so that not only do you use the interface, but you think about how it works so that you can create your own interfaces effectively. Use the pop-up menu at the top of the Library window, shown in Figure 2-17 to find what you're interested in. At the bottom of the window is a description of what is happening. In this example, you're both user and developer of the same item — a pop-up menu.

Note also from the description at the bottom of the menu exactly what will happen to your project when you drag that pop-up part into it. You'll be automatically adding JavaScript code that you can refine using the Attributes and Behavior inspectors — see Chapters 4 and 7.

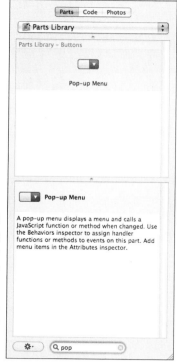

Figure 2-17:
Use the
pop-up
menu and
search field
to narrow
your list of
parts.

Exploring code

The Code pane, shown in Figure 2-18, shows snippets of JavaScript code instead of icons for interface parts.

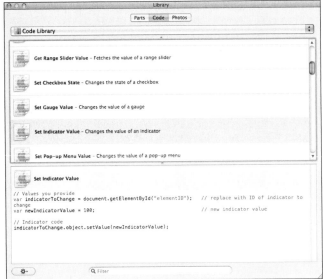

Figure 2-18:
The Library
contains
snippets of
code for you
to use.

Sometimes the code contains comments that let you know that placeholder text needs to be customized for your use.

If you're not interested in writing code, you can create many apps and widgets without ever bothering to use code snippets.

You can use the search field to search the titles of the code snippets; it doesn't search for text within the code snippets.

Using your photos

The Photos pane interacts with your iPhoto library, which lets you add photos to your apps and widgets, as shown in Figure 2-19.

Although the iPhoto library was originally for photos, it has become a cleverly indexed and organized collection of many other images, diagrams, illustrations, and logos.

The iPhoto library is specific to the user account on your Mac. You can create a separate user account that is used for development (and often work in general). The iPhoto library in that account has photos and other images that you can use in apps and widgets without worrying. Personal photos can live in another account — often one that is synchronized with iPad or iPhone.

Figure 2-19:
Your iPhoto
library is
integrated
with
Dashcode.

Starting Out with the Canvas

The *canvas* is where you create your app or widget. On the canvas, you see
the interface that you create by dragging parts or photos from the Library
window.

After you drag these items to the canvas, you can resize them and rearrange
them. (The Align and Distribute menu commands let you organize them as
you do in many other applications.) You can further customize these parts
for your project by using inspectors (see Chapter 4). On rare occasions, you
may also use a code snippet.

Chapter 3 describes this general process in more detail.

Testing and Deploying Your Work

When you finish the first draft of your project, Dashcode helps you test it.
The final item in the Workflow Steps list lets you test. For Dashboard widgets,
clicking Run & Share presents the pane shown in Figure 2-20.

Figure 2-21 shows the corresponding pane for a Safari application.

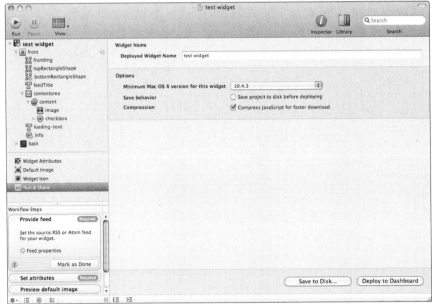

Figure 2-20:
You can run and share a Dashboard widget.

Figure 2-21:
You can run and share a Safari application.

Notice the two buttons in the lower right of the window. The Save to Disk button lets you save all the project files in their folders to a location on disk that you specify. If you save the Dashcode project by choosing File⇨Save (or when you're warned about unsaved changes when you're closing a Dashcode project), you save the project in the package structure described previously. All the files are there, but they're normally not visible in the Finder except through the Show Package Contents command or the Go to Folder command from the Go menu.

The Deploy button takes your project and deploys it to Dashboard on your own computer or to a location you specify on a Web server.

As always with Dashcode, still more options are available. As you're developing your project, you can run it inside Dashcode. You don't have to deploy it to test it. Dashcode includes a simulator for iPhone as well as Dashcode. This simulator provides a quick way to see what your project will look like before it's deployed for final testing.

Chapter 3

Creating Your First Dashcode Project

The Dashcode window is a marvel of user interface (UI) design. The window arranges a wide variety of functions and a great deal of information so that all items are available in a logical and compact environment for developers to create amazing apps and widgets.

Just as the proof of the pudding is in the eating, the proof of the developer tool is in the development. In this chapter, you develop your first Dashcode project.

Stepping Through the Development Process

Dashcode provides you with the Workflow Steps list at the bottom of the navigator to help you move through the development process. Not unreasonably, the Workflow Steps list focuses on those steps that you take with Dashcode.

Developing your app or widget has a few steps to it in addition to those in the Workflow Steps list. Note that each project is somewhat different, and each developer and development environment has their own characteristics. For example, a project that you create for your own use is different from one that you're creating for a corporation or for use by the general public. You can create many special-purpose projects with Dashcode, such as the ones in this book that are designed to demonstrate the Dashcode features.

Not withstanding the many variations, here's a reasonably full list of things to think about on your way to completing your first Dashcode project:

- ✔ **What do you want people to be able to do with the project?** Even if you're just playing around to try to learn more about Dashcode, think of what your project should enable people to do. Often, the most successful projects (like the most successful applications) are quite clear about what they enable people to do. Thinking about what you, the developer, want to do can often make the end result less successful than if you focus on the user.

- ✔ **How should people be able to achieve their goals with your project?** This question is the beginning of your interface design. There is a great deal of information, theory, and opinion about interface design. Here are a few questions that you should answer before you start.

  - **Who are your users?** What terminology do they understand and use? (Think of the difference between the terminology of people who watch television and people who produce the shows.)

  - **What language do your users speak?** Dashcode lets you internationalize your projects.

  - **What is the end result of the project?** Is it entertainment so that the end result is a chuckle or the pleasurable experience of having concentrated on things other than what is going on around them? Are you providing information to your users? Are you helping them organize their own information?

  - **What content will your project need?** Does your project need to access a data file or Web site to find data to present to the user? Will it contain graphics as part of its interface, be they logos, drawings, or photos? For any content that you do not create, do you have it available (or know where to get it), and do you have the rights to use it?

- ✔ **What type of project will it be?** Remember that Dashcode lets you create Safari Web applications as well as Dashboard widgets. For Safari, you can create Web applications designed for the desktop Safari browser where the windows are movable and resizable. You can also create Safari Web applications for mobile devices such as iPhone and iPad. In those cases, the Safari window isn't movable or resizable. Furthermore, you have access to a wide variety of Safari extensions that take advantage of iPhone or iPad features. Remember that Safari and Safari Web applications run on both Mac OS X and Windows.

  You don't have to choose one type of project. Without too much difficulty, you can make a single Dashcode project that runs on mobile Safari or desktop Safari; you can reuse much of the code for a parallel Dashboard widget.

- ✔ **What is the time frame?** How much time you have is a key part of the project. If you're not going to be able to finish everything in the time allotted, you're better off confronting that issue at the start. That way, you can plan for a Phase II and a Phase III before tempers are frayed.

Thinking about What a Mobile Device Is for the Purposes of a Web App

"What is a mobile device?" is a pretty simple question, but the answer is complicated. Your choice in Dashcode 3.0 is Safari or mobile Safari. Mobile Safari is for iPhone. Everything is packaged together in the file and folder structure (see Chapter 2 for details). Inside the folder is a subdirectory called `safari` and a subdirectory called `mobile`. (These names are case-sensitive names, which is why they appear lowercased and some other names are not.) At the root level of your file/folder structure, in addition to these folders, you have folders called `Parts` and `Images`. They contain files used in both the mobile and desktop versions of your app. The only other thing at the root level is `index.html`, which is the default file that starts your app running.

If you follow the code, you'll see that `index.html` wanders through a variety of the files and functions that are included with every Dashcode project. At one point, control gets to `redirector.js`, which is inside the `Parts` folder at its root level. (Note that `Parts` folders are within both the `mobile` and `safari` folders as well.)

Inside `redirector.js` is where the magic happens to use either the `mobile` or the `safari` folder. The logic relies on the fact that every browser identifies itself to every Web site that it visits. This identification consists of a user agent string that looks something like

```
Mozilla/5.0 (Macintosh; U; Intel Mac OS X 10_6_3; en-us)
AppleWebKit/531.22.7 (KHTML, like Gecko)
Version/4.0.5 Safari/531.22.7
```

This code is the user agent string for Safari on the desktop of Mac OS X version 10.6.3.

The user agent string that Safari on iPhone sends back changes the last section to something like

```
Version/4.0.5 Mobile/7B334b Safari/531.22.7
```

Notice that the word *Mobile* has been added. (At the beginning of the user agent string are some other minor changes, such as the substitution of iPhone for Macintosh.) If `redirector.js` finds Mobile in the user agent string, it uses the files in the `mobile` folder instead of those in the `safari` folder.

With the advent of iPad, this logic becomes wrong. Testing for the word Mobile isn't sufficient because it identifies both iPad and iPhone as mobile devices. True, they're both mobile devices, but for Dashcode purposes, a *mobile device* means a Web app that uses the files in the `mobile` folder rather than those in the `safari` folder. And that's wrong for iPad. iPad should use the `safari` folder's files because its screen is big enough to display full pages.

If your version of Dashcode resolves this issue (that is, it lets you choose iPad as a destination for your Web app), you have no problem. You also have no problem if you're building a Dashboard widget. If you're developing a Web app for iPad, you definitely need this fix. If you're building a Web app for iPhone and you have even the remotest possibility that someone will use it (or experiment with it) on iPad, then you should use this fix.

Here's what you do to use the `safari` folder's files on iPad. I explain the reasoning behind these steps in Chapter 19.

1. **Open your Dashcode project.**

   Before going any further, save a copy of the project to a safe location in case something goes wrong. You can choose File⇨Save As from inside Dashcode, or you can do so in the Finder before getting started.

2. **Choose View⇨Stop Code Generator.**

   The code generator works behind the scenes to keep the files in sync with the interface you're drawing. The only evidence that you've actually stopped the code generator is that the command changes to Start Code Generator.

3. **Show the files in the navigator, as shown in Figure 3-1.**

   To show the files, choose View ⇨Files or click the second button from the left in the bottom frame of the Dashcode window.

4. **If necessary, open the Parts folder to show `redirector.js`.**

   You can use the disclosure triangle next to the Parts folder to open this folder.

5. **Click `redirector.js` to view the code.**

   At the top of the function, you see this line of code. Note that the spacing is different in the book than it is in the file, but it's the same line of code:

   ```
   var DCshowiPhone = RegExp(" AppleWebKit/").test(navigator.userAgent)
     && RegExp(" Mobile/").test(navigator.userAgent));
   ```

6. **Add && !RegExp("iPad").test(navigator.userAgent) at the end so that it now reads**

   ```
   var DCshowiPhone = RegExp(" AppleWebKit/").test(navigator.userAgent)
   && RegExp(" Mobile/").test(navigator.userAgent)
   && !RegExp("iPad").test(navigator.userAgent);
   ```

Figure 3-1:
Show the
project's
files in
navigator.

The line you add changes the test to look for `mobile` but not `iPad`. In that case, you use the `mobile` folder, which is correct for iPhone and not for iPad.

7. **Save the file.**

8. **Choose View⇨Start Code Generator.**

9. **Save your Dashcode project.**

Looking at Your First Dashcode Project

I chose the first Dashcode project to introduce you to the process and illustrate what you can easily do with Dashcode and some of the choices you need to make in real life.

Figure 3-2 shows you what that project will look like after you complete it in this chapter. The project appears in the iPhone simulator available through Dashcode.

Code for this and the other projects in this book is available at www. dummies.com/go/dashcodefd. Download links appear. Where appropriate, I provide additional files. For example, in this chapter's files, you find not only the Dashcode project but also the photo that I use in Figure 3-2.

Figure 3-2:
Your first
Dashcode
project:
Chapter 3
version.

Casting an eye to design

As a Dashcode developer, you should develop the habit of looking at new apps and widgets, not just with an eye to using them, but also with an eye to how they're designed.

Dashcode can help you build Dashboard widgets, as well as Web apps for iPhone and iPad. I purposely chose to design this first Dashcode project as an iPhone Web app. In large part because of the small size of the iPhone screen, coming up with an interface design for iPhone is often more difficult to come up with than one for iPad or widgets. All types of interfaces you can create share many common features and design challenges, but many people find it easiest to work with the most restrictive environment — the iPhone — and then modify the interface from that.

Modifying the interface isn't just a matter of making everything bigger when you move from iPhone. Rather, you need to consider many of the issues explored throughout this book. But, by building what is in some ways the most difficult interface first, you may find moving on from the iPhone to another interface easier.

Note that many people disagree with this theory: It's largely a matter of personal preference and experience. After you've developed a few apps and widgets, you'll be able to decide which types are the most difficult for you.

Whatever you find most difficult may be the right place to start in a multiplat-form development process.

What else do you see in this very simple app?

✔ **Photo:** The photo is simply illustrative. As the project evolves, you can make it "hot" so that it responds to mouse clicks in one way or another.

✔ **Dashcode credit line:** At the bottom is the *Developed with Dashcode* line of text that Dashcode inserts. You can modify or remove this line, but I left it alone in this first example.

✔ **Caption:** Another line of text, *HB Studio,* appears as a caption for the photo. Wouldn't it look better if it were centered? You can see how to center text in Chapter 5.

✔ **Web page address and search fields:** At the top of the window are the standard browser fields. Web apps on iPhone are very specially crafted Web pages, so they have addresses. You can hide these browser elements so that your end results look like an iPhone OS app (see Chapter 8).

✔ **Empty space:** Beneath the photo, you see something that should make your interface-designing mouth water: empty space. An ironclad rule of interface design is that you never have enough space, or (*real estate,* as it is commonly called). Here, you've got the UI equivalent of a large vacant lot that's crying out for development. Here are some of the items you could add:

- A link to further information, perhaps even a regular Web page: (This example is for a theater school, so perhaps the link should be to a list of teachers.)

- Next or Previous buttons: If the photo is shown as part of a tour of a neighborhood, a Next button may take you to an important build-ing around the corner.

You can explore the options for using that empty space in Part II.

Navigating around your app

You need to think about another issue when you look at this app. In fact, this issue is something you don't see: How do you navigate around the app? You can easily imagine all sorts of links and buttons relevant to the information that's displayed here. These navigational aids all take you away from this screen and to another one.

But how did you get to this screen? Web apps are all Web pages, so you can get to them by typing their address. But you can get to a page in other ways that are easy to implement in Dashcode. You can find parts in the Library to help you implement browsers and navigators, such as those that you find throughout iPhone OS apps for both iPhone and iPad. You can put such a navigator or browser around pages like the one shown in Figure 3-1 to provide a more fully featured UI.

After you look at this project, you can start building a Dashcode project of your own.

Creating a New Project from a Template

Whether you're writing the next great novel or the next great software product, nothing is more terrifying than a blank piece of paper or an empty programming window. Starting from scratch is hard to do, but Dashcode can help you avoid that challenge.

When you create a new Dashcode project, you choose a template to use. The template includes supporting files that are generalized for the type of project you're creating (a Safari Web application or a Dashcode widget) as well as customized files for the specific template, such as a Podcast or an RSS feed reader. So the first step in creating a new project is choosing a template.

Here's how you choose a template for a new Dashcode project:

1. **Launch Dashcode.**

   The New Project dialog may be visible, as shown in Figure 3-3. If so, skip to Step 3.

2. **Choose File⇨New Project.**

   You select your template in this dialog. If you want, you can click any of the templates to see a brief description of it at the bottom of this dialog.

3. **Choose your project's destination by clicking Safari in the left pane.**

4. **Click the Custom template.**

   For this first project, choose the Custom template. This template is custom in the sense that it's the most basic template, and you can customize it as you want. The other templates all have at least the basics of a specific type of app implemented in them. Thus, the Custom template is the simplest one.

5. **Select the Mobile Safari check box.**

   It doesn't matter whether the Safari check box is selected at this point.

Figure 3-3:
You can
choose a
template.

6. **Click the Choose button.**

   You can also just double-click the template you want to use, but make
   certain that you've selected the appropriate check boxes before double-
   clicking the template if you're using a Safari template.

   Your created project is ready for you to work with. It may look like
   Figure 3-4, but because Dashcode's interface has so many options, it
   may not. (Refer to Chapter 2 to see the ways in which you can configure
   this window.)

What you care about most right now is the canvas, so make certain that it's
visible either from the View menu or View in the toolbar. Also, remember
that you're interested in mobile Safari for your iPhone app. If you left the
other check box turned on in Step 5, you see buttons just below the toolbar
that let you switch between Safari and mobile Safari. Make certain mobile
Safari is selected.

The Developed with Dashcode line at the bottom of the window is created as
part of the template (but you can modify it as described in Chapter 5). If you
refer to Figure 3-1 (the completed app), you can see that you need to add a
photo and some text as a title.

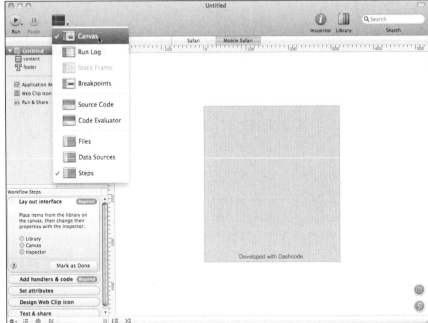

Figure 3-4:
Dashcode
sets up your
project for
you.

Testing your project in the simulator

After you have your own copy of the app, you can test it in the simulator.
Test the app you created from the template to see how (and if) it works
before you've made any changes or customizations. This first step is a good
one to take any time you create a new project.

Many templates do run successfully at this point. Templates that rely on data
often contain sample data in their templates; you can modify that data with
your own data as you see fit. However, templates that have links to Web sites
may not run without customization. Sometimes they have built-in links to
Apple Web sites, but in other cases, you may need to make changes.

The Custom template, though, works right out of the box. Click the Run
button in the upper left corner of the window. The iPhone simulator starts,
as shown in Figure 3-5. This simulator is a separate application that commu-
nicates with Dashcode, so you see a new application icon in your Dock. You
see what appears to be an empty page, but if you look at the bottom, you see
the *Designed For Dashcode* text that is part of the template. That's the beginning of your app.

The simulator takes quite a while to start, so don't worry if you don't immediately see your project.

Figure 3-5:
Test the
project
in the
simulator.

Adding the photo

As you can see in Figure 3-1, a photo appears in the center of the app window, so you need to add it. You can add one of your own photos from iPhoto, or you can use the downloaded photo from www.dummies.com/go/dashcodefd.

You first need to add the photo to iPhoto. (Obviously if you're using an existing photo you can skip this step.) Just drag the photo you want to add to iPhoto or choose File⇨Import to Library to add it.

After you have the photo in iPhoto, add it to your project:

1. **Open the Library window.**

2. **Select the Photos tab.**

   A pop-up menu at the top lets you choose from your iPhoto albums.

3. **From the pop-up menu, select the album you want to browse or leave it set to iPhoto to browse all photos.**

   You can customize the display with the shortcuts icon in the lower left corner of the window.

4. **Drag the photo you want to use into the app on the canvas, as shown in Figure 3-6.**

   Place the photo in the approximate position you want to use. Don't worry what it looks like at this point.

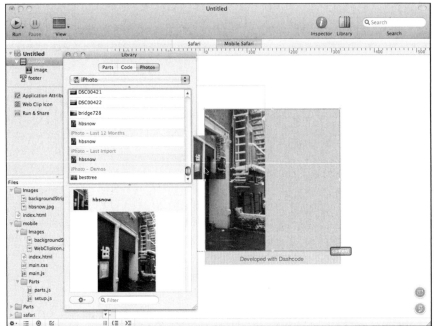

Figure 3-6:
Drag the
photo into
the project.

That's all you have to do to add a photo to your project: Just drag the photo where you want it.

Every specific part that you add to the interface works the same way: Select from the Library, drag it into your app on the canvas, place it where you want it, and then resize it. As the project grows, you'll have a whole hierarchy of views in the navigator — views within views within views. As a result "where you want it" can sometimes be a complex matter of the actual visual location and the hierarchical location. But never fear: If you keep an eye on the canvas as well as the navigator, you'll see the visual location and the hierarchical location at the same time.

Following the photo as you add it to the project

When you drag a photo from the Library window in Step 4, a small thumbnail appears under your pointer. If you do Step 4 very slowly, you'll be able to see what happens at the precise moment the point with the thumbnail underneath it enters your app on the canvas:

✔ **An image part is created within the content part in the navigator at the top left of the Dashcode window.**

The template starts with two parts: content and a text part called *footer*.

✔ **The part into which you're dragging the image is highlighted and identified in the lower right corner of the app image.**

Notice the box that says content in the lower right corner. If you drag the image into the footer that contains the *Developed with Dashcode* text, that part automatically expands.

✔ **The file is added to the file list in the bottom of the navigator.**

Notice that hbsnow.jpg is now placed within the Images folder of your project. Because desktop and mobile versions of your app may need to have different images to accommodate the different sizes of the windows, you find three Images folders in your project: One of them is at the root level, another is in the mobile folder, and a third is in the safari folder. As you drag a photo from the Library window to the project, Dashcode puts the photo in the correct folder.

Experiment with adding other photos to your project and then removing them so that you get the hang of it. Notice that any photo removed from the project isn't removed from the files list automatically. You can select the photo in the Files pane and press the Delete key to remove it.

Adjusting your photo's size

Depending on the size of the image, the photo may be too large or too small. When you drop your photo into your project, it appears selected and has eight small handles, as shown in Figure 3-7. You can use the handles, which are in the four corners and half way along each of the four sides, to resize the photo.

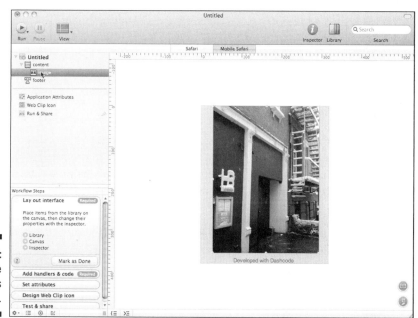

Figure 3-7: Resize the photo as needed.

As you resize the photo, the photo itself retains its shape while you're manipulating the box around it (known as the *bounding box*).

For this example, place the photo at the top of the canvas, as shown in Figure 3-8.

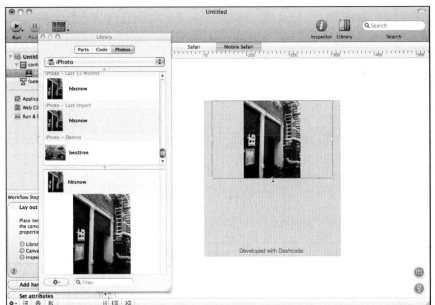

Figure 3-8:
Place the
image at the
top.

You can always come back later and tweak things. In fact, as you develop a UI, you'll frequently make little adjustments until everything is in exactly the right place.

Adding the Text

In the example, a line of text appears just below the photo (refer to Figure 3-2). Everything in your interface is going to be a part. You can't just type in the interface: You have to add a text part and type inside it. The reason is that having a text part makes modifying the interface much easier: You just move the text part around and adjust its handles. You can align and adjust the text inside the text part as you want. If you want to add more text than will fit in the part, the text can still remain inside the part; if you expand the part, the text will be visible.

If you're thinking that having text parts that contain text and that you can move and resize is how page layout programs work (or the layout templates in Pages), you're absolutely right.

Now you're ready to add the text part, position it, and type the text.

1. **Find the text part in the Library and drag it into the app on the canvas, as shown in Figure 3-9.**

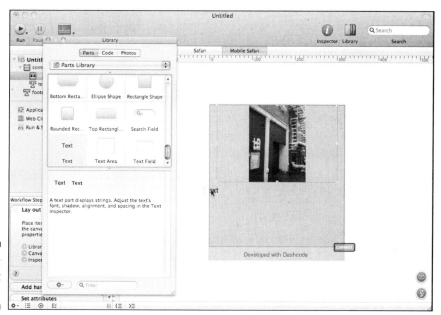

Figure 3-9:
Add a text part.

At the moment the pointer enters the image of the app on the canvas, a box containing the name of the part into which the part will be inserted appears in the lower right corner of the image.

Also note that the Library contains a text field and text area, which are just like the HTML constructs that allow entry of a single line or multiple lines of text. The Text part displays text and allows no user entry, which is what you want.

2. **When you have the part about where you want it, double-click to make it editable and type your text, as shown in Figure 3-10.**

Text parts are only editable when you're accessing them through Dashcode. Users can't modify them.

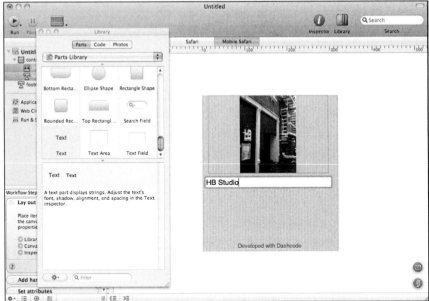

Figure 3-10:
Type the
text.

As you move the parts, around blue guidelines appear to help you align them with either the edges or centers of the other parts.

3. **If you haven't already done so, save your project.**

Testing Your Project

You can test your project with the simulator by clicking the Run button at the upper left corner of the Dashcode window. Testing your project gives you a good approximation of what users will see on the Web, on their iPhone, or on their iPad.

However, in order to fully test your Dashcode project, you need to upload it to a Web site or install it in Dashboard. Dashcode can do either or both of these tasks, depending on the type of project you have built.

Before you can deploy your project, you need to set up at least one *destination* to which you can deploy it. (You can deploy it manually, but the process is more complicated — see the upcoming section "Deploying your App.")

Setting Up Your Destinations

Setting up your destinations is something that you do for all your Dashcode applications. The two most common destinations for your project are your own Web site and a MobileMe account. You can create additional destinations if you want to deploy your apps in other places.

For an individual app, you start with Run & Share at the top of the navigator. Select which destination you want to use by choosing from a pop-up menu, as shown in Figure 3-11. Setting up the two most common destinations (your own Web site and MobileMe) is easy. What you have to do in Dashcode is . . . almost nothing.

Because a web server is built into Mac OS X, and because every account has its own Web site to use as the account owner sees fit all you have to do is turn on that Web site. Deploying Dashcode apps is just one of the uses for your built-in Web site, and you don't need to do anything special for Dashcode. If you have enabled your own web server, Dashcode automatically includes it in the destination pop-up. If you haven't turned your Web site on, you need to turn it on as described in the following section.

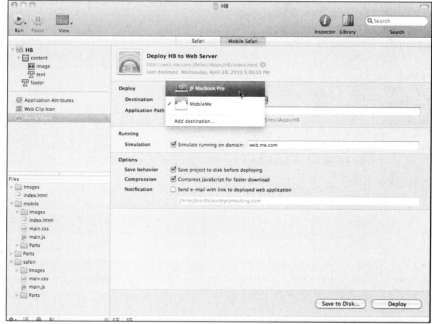

Figure 3-11:
Select a destination when you deploy your project.

MobileMe is often set up when you install Mac OS X. Like your own web server, your MobileMe account is configured in System Preferences. If you haven't configured your account, the section "Turning on Your MobileMe Account," later in this chapter, shows you what to do. As a result, for most people, Dashcode can use either a personal web server on Mac OS X or a MobileMe account with web hosting privileges (or both) for a deployment destination.

Turning on your web server

If you need to turn on your own web server, go to System Preferences (-System Preferences) and click Sharing, as shown in Figure 3-12.

Figure 3-12: Open System Preferences.

The Sharing pane opens, as shown in Figure 3-13.

Select Web Sharing, as shown in Figure 3-13. (Note that the Sharing pane shown in Figure 3-13 is different — and simpler — in Snow Leopard and later than in previous versions of Mac OS X). Settings for the internal firewall are automatically adjusted.

As you can see in Figure 3-13, selecting Web sharing enables two web servers: one for your computer and one for your account (the longer URL that includes your account name).

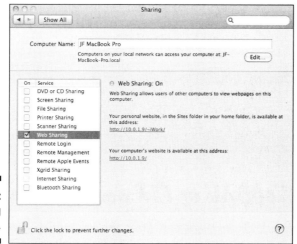

Figure 3-13:
Set sharing
preferences.

The URLs that you see in Figure 3-13 are the ones that anyone can use to get to your Web site. For most people, these addresses start with 10 or 192; these special Internet addresses are reserved for local area networks without too many devices attached to them. They're often the addresses you automatically get if you're connected to an Airport base station or a local router. Although the base station or the router has its own Internet address that is visible to and accessible by the outside world, devices on the local network are normally not visible from outside the network.

If you have a different type of URL, it will be configured (automatically in most cases) in System Preferences. Dashcode picks up the proper URL as long as you have turned on Web sharing.

After your Web site is enabled, putting files on it is simple. Take the HTML files (or any other files) that you want to publish on your Web site and simply drag them to the Sites folder inside your home directory.

When you ask Dashcode to deploy an app to your local Web site, that's all it does.

Turning on your MobileMe account

If you need to turn on MobileMe, go to System Preferences and click the MobileMe settings. Type your member name and password, as shown in Figure 3-14. (Note that your account name is your MobileMe e-mail address but without @me.com at the end.)

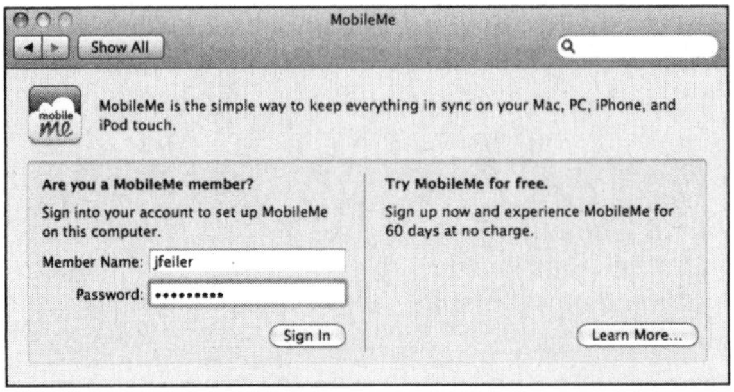

Figure 3-14:
Configure
MobileMe.

Adding WebDAV or FTP destinations

You can add other destinations beyond your own web server and MobileMe (refer to Figure 3-10. If you choose to add a different destination, you see the dialog shown in Figure 3-15.

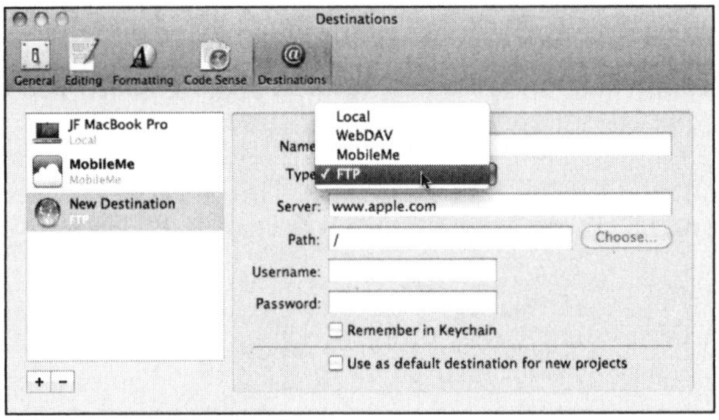

Figure 3-15:
Add other
destinations.

You choose the type of destination you want to add and provide the log-in information. If you want to add another destination, click the + beneath the list of destinations at the left of the dialog. To remove a destination, select it and click the –.

If you've set up a web server or MobileMe in System Preferences, those destinations are automatically added to your destination list, and you can't delete them. (They're grayed out to remind you.) The only way to delete these destinations is to turn off the web server in the Sharing pane of System Preferences or to remove your MobileMe account, which is also in System Preferences. Logging out from MobileMe doesn't remove MobileMe from the list of destinations.

You can also get to the dialog shown in Figure 3-15 by choosing Dashcode⇨Preferences.

There is no limit to the number of destinations that you can create, but in practice, most people have no more than a few — one or more Web sites, a MobileMe account, a WebDAV account, and an FTP site or two.

Deploying Your App

With your destination set up, you're ready to deploy your app. To do so, click Run & Share in the navigator, as shown in Figure 3-16.

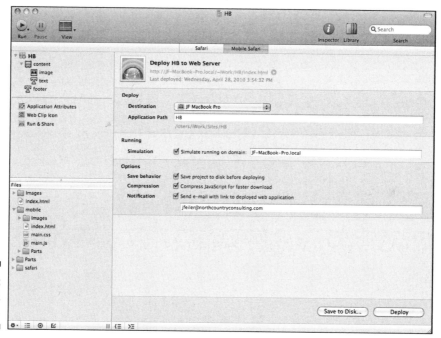

Figure 3-16:
Click Run &
Share.

You have a number of deployment options, but in most cases, the default settings are fine. The only thing that is required is the destination. After you select the destination, click the Deploy button.

When you're deploying your app, you see two URLs for the destination. At the top of the window is the URL that people can use to access your app. An arrow at the right takes you to the destination. You also see a message with the time of the last deployment.

As you see in Figure 3-16, beneath the Application Path field is the address of the location where the files are being placed. This address is usually different from the URL that people use to access your app. For example, for MobileMe, the URL for access is something like `http://web.me.com/jfeiler/iApps/yourapp/index.html`. The location of the files is something like `http://jfeiler@idisk.me.com/jfeiler/Web/Sites/iApps/yourapp`.

The easiest way to keep these addresses straight is to choose the option to send yourself an e-mail with the correct URL. You can then forward that URL on to friends (or copy and paste it onto a Web site).

Sometimes you don't want to deploy the project with Dashcode. You can use the Save to Disk button in the lower right corner to have Dashcode write all the files and folders to a location that you specify. The most common reason for not deploying the project with Dashcode is because you want to deploy your project on a web server to which you don't have access. You can do all your testing in the simulator, and then, when you're done, you can save the files to disk and forward them (perhaps in a compressed ZIP archive) to your webmaster.

Deploying a Widget

Although this chapter has shown you how to build and deploy an iPhone Web app, it is worth taking a moment to look at the Run & Share options for Dashboard widgets. The settings are quite similar, but you don't have to worry about a destination. You either deploy your widget to Dashboard on your own computer, or you save the files to disk.

Cross-site scripting

Cross-site scripting is a situation in which a script running on one Web site calls a script that runs on another Web site. Cross-site scripting has proven to be a very serious security issue in many cases. (Estimates range up to 80 percent of security breaches using this technique.) For that reason, browsers such as Safari for iPhone often prevent scripts on one site from running scripts on another site. You won't encounter problems running any number of scripts from the site you're visiting, but bouncing around behind your back from one site's scripts to another is where the problem can arise. For testing, you can simulate running on a specific site using the deployment dialog.

If you save the files to disk, they're saved as a package with all the files bundled inside it. You can then take that package that appears as a single file and send it to other people or post it on a Web site for downloading. Because Dashboard widgets run only on Mac OS X, you won't have a problem using packages that are only supported on Mac OS X. (In an all-Mac world, the files deployed for a Web app may be in a single package and not in a structure of files and folders.)

Figure 3-17 shows the widget deployment interface.

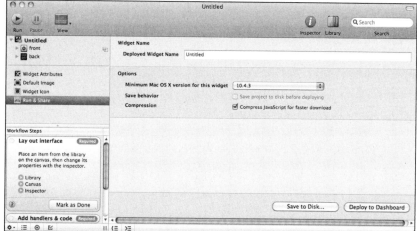

Figure 3-17:
Save or
deploy a
Dashboard
widget.

Part II

Constructing Your Projects' Pieces and Parts

The 5th Wave — By Rich Tennant

"What I'm looking for are dynamic Web applications and content, not Web innuendoes and intent."

In this part . . .

You don't have to write much code with Dashcode: It's more an assembly process, using an array of pre-built interface elements and snippets of code that all fit together. In this part, you see how to work with those construction tools — inspectors, the Library, behaviors, and styles — to assemble, style, and debug your projects. Using these features is a lot easier than writing code!

Chapter 4

Inspecting the Inspector

In This Chapter

▶ Working with inspectors

▶ Managing parts and their attributes

▶ Formatting text

Dashcode isn't just a tool to help you create apps and widgets. It contains a vast amount of content that you can use to build apps and widgets. Some of that content is in the templates, but much more of it is in the Library. Some of the Library content is actually your own (your iPhoto library), but more of it is in the form of code snippets and graphics from the Dashcode team. As you use these components and others that you create, you often need to adjust their settings so that their appearance and performance is exactly what you want. You can do all these things with the inspector, which is next to the Library in the toolbar.

This chapter focuses on a few of the ways you can use the inspector window You also see how the Library and inspector can work together and help you write your own JavaScript code based on Library code snippets.

Using the Inspector Window

The inspector window is an interface feature that you've probably seen. It's used in the iWork applications (Numbers, Pages, and Keynote) as well as in the Finder. Like the Library window and Dashcode itself, the inspector window puts a great deal of information and functionality into a very compact area.

You open the inspector window by clicking Inspector in the toolbar or choosing Window⇨Show Inspector. Figure 4-1 shows the inspector window.

Like the Library window, the inspector window floats in front of other Dashcode windows. In fact, these windows appear in a plane that is above everything else on the desktop. You can move them around, close them, and reopen them as you wish. On this plane, you can click a Library or inspector window to move it in front of the other one.

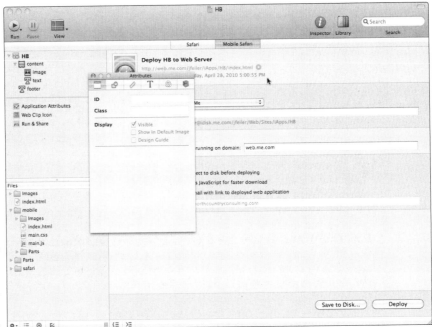

Figure 4-1:
Open the inspector window.

Handling elements in the inspector window

Your Dashcode project's interface consists of *elements,* which can be buttons, fields that contain text or images, and controls, such as browsers that manage other elements. The inspector window displays information about whatever elements are selected.

Parts in the Library become elements on the canvas. Also, Dashcode is an object-oriented environment (as is most software today); just about everything is an object. When you're writing or looking at the JavaScript code, you see that the things on the canvas are *elements;* you can get them programmatically by using the standard JavaScript function GetElementByID.

And just to make life more interesting, in Xcode and Interface Builder (the developer tools that you use to build native iPhone and iPad apps as well as applications and that the people at Apple use to build Mac OS X and their own applications), the Dashcode/JavaScript elements are mostly views. A button on a Dashcode canvas is a JavaScript element, but a button that looks and behaves the same way in an Xcode/Interface Builder app or application is an Objective-C view. What is critically important is that things that look the same must always behave the same so that users know how they work.

If you select more than one element (perhaps you select a button and a text field), the information shown in the inspector window applies to both of the elements. In some cases, information applies only to a single element. In those cases, you don't see information when you have two elements selected.

As you click to select another element in your app, the data in the inspector window changes to reflect the new element. To further enhance its power, the inspector window recognizes selections made in the navigator at the top left corner of the Dashcode window as well as selections that you've made by clicking in the app or widget on the canvas. You can even click a button in your app or widget on the canvas, hold down the Shift key, and click a text field in the navigator. It doesn't matter how you select the elements to be displayed in the inspector window.

Exploring the inspector window tabs

At the top of the inspector window are six tabs. Each tab lets you view and set values for different sets of data in the selected element. From left to right, the tabs are

- ✔ **Attributes:** These values identify the element by its name (which is unique), its class, and whether or not it's visible. For more information on this tab, see the upcoming section "Using Attributes."

- ✔ **Fill & Stroke:** Here are all the settings for style and effects — things such as shadows, the roundness of rounded corners, fill for lines, and the like. Chapter 5 discusses these items in more detail.

- ✔ **Metrics:** This tab is where you set the size of your elements. You can use the handles to resize elements, but you can specify the size in pixels in the Metrics tab. (If you use the handles, the size in pixels is updated here, and vice versa.) You also have autoresizing and layout options. For more information on this tab, see the section "Using the Metrics Inspector," later in this chapter.

- ✔ **Text:** These settings are what you'd expect: font, style, color, alignment, and the like. These settings are also discussed in Chapter 5.

- ✔ **Bindings:** A *binding* lets you set the value of something such as an element's size by setting it to data that is read from a data file or other source. You can find out more about bindings in Chapter 10.

✔ **Behaviors:** Elements can respond to events such as mouse clicks if you configure them to do so. For each type of element (such as a button or text field), you find a list of events to which that type can respond. Each event can have a *handler,* which is the code that executes when the event happens. The name of the event lets you know what it is — for example, `onclick`, `onmouseover`, and `ontouchstart`. For more on this topic, see Chapter 6. The combination of an event and a handler is a *behavior.*

Using the Attributes Inspector

The inspector window shows information about the selected items in your app or widget in the canvas, so in order to start working with the inspector window, you need to create a new project and explore its elements. Create a new Safari app using the Custom template (see Chapter 3). However, create the app only for Safari; don't create a Mobile Safari version. The Custom template for Safari provides you with a jumping-off point for further development. All it creates is a blank Web page.

Using attributes to identify elements

Attributes include class and id — two standard HTML attributes used extensively in the Document Object Model (DOM) and JavaScript. Dashcode uses them in their standard way.

You have to be able to identify every element in your project. That way, you can write code that will let you find an element and do something to it. On Web pages, every element can have an ID; developers and designers provide them when they know they'll need them for JavaScript or other code. In Dashcode (and in many modern Web projects), IDs are treated as required. Dashcode creates an ID automatically for every element you create. You can change the ID, but you can never change it to an ID that already exists. That way, each ID is unique. Most people change the IDs for elements that they'll be using in code so that the IDs are meaningful. The others, you can leave as Dashcode created them.

Adding elements to your project

Your new blank Custom project needs to have some elements added to it so that you can use the inspector window to explore and change settings. To add a part to your Web page and follow its progress in the Attributes inspector:

1. **Make certain that you can see the navigator at the left.**

   If you closed the Dashcode window after creating your new project, reopen it by choosing File➪Open.

2. **Open the inspector window.**

3. **Select the Attributes tab, if it's not already selected.**

   The name of the inspector window changes to reflect which tab you're looking at. The inspector window is now called the Attributes inspector (or whatever tab you have selected).

4. **Open the Library.**

   To do so, choose Window➪Show Library or click Library in the toolbar.

5. **Click the Parts tab at the top of the Library to see the available parts in the Library**

6. **Choose Shapes from the pop-up menu.**

   You see various shapes, as shown in Figure 4-2. A description of a selected shape appears at the bottom of the Library. In addition, a help tag appears when the pointer is over a shape. Both are shown in Figure 4-2.

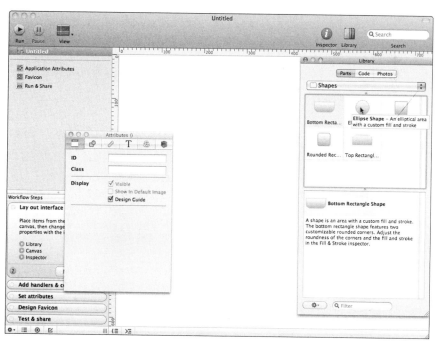

Figure 4-2:
You see
various
shapes.

7. Drag an Ellipse shape onto your canvas, as shown in Figure 4-3.

You can put the first shape anywhere you want on the canvas. If you add a second shape, you may be constrained in where you can place it. (If you're unable to place a second shape exactly where you want it, see the section "Using Metrics," later in this chapter.)

As soon as an element is added, it's automatically selected — standard behavior for dragging any object into a container or document. The selected element in your canvas shows up in the Attributes inspector.

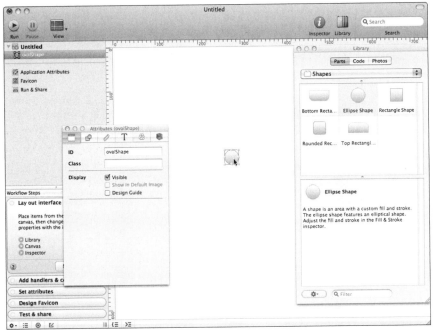

Figure 4-3:
Add a
shape.

Because every element has a unique ID, you can demonstrate this by dragging another Ellipse Shape onto your canvas. It will be selected when you release the mouse button, and its ID will be ovalShape1.

If you don't like the default IDs, you can change them in the Attributes inspector. For example, change the ID of `ovalshape1` to `ovalShape`. Tab out of that ID field to go into the `Class` field. Before you can get there, you get an error message, as shown in Figure 4-4. You can't have duplicate IDs. When you dismiss the dialog, you see that the name is unchanged, but the `Class` field is selected, waiting for you to type in some data.

You may want to try again to make the ID a bit more human-friendly. Try to change it to oval shape. Again, it won't work. IDs can't contain special characters or spaces (see Figure 4-5).

Figure 4-4:
IDs must be
unique.

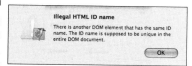

Figure 4-5:
IDs can't
contain
special
characters
or white
space.

When you start to use code snippets from the Library, you see how important it is that every element has a unique ID so that it can use the JavaScript
GetElementByID function. An example of this use is shown in the code that
gets the value for a gauge element. You use this code when you want to take
that value and perhaps display it to the user as text or to pass it into another
function where it will be processed in some way. Moving information from
interface elements, such as sliders and gauges, means that users can take
advantage of the graphical object to enter data that they would otherwise
have to type.

To see an example of GetElementByID in action, select the Code tab in the
Library and choose GetGaugeValue. (It's probably the first item in the list).
You see the snippet shown in Figure 4-6.

Figure 4-6:
Many code
snippets
rely on
Get
Element
ByID.

This code is standard JavaScript code; there's nothing specifically Dashcode-y about it. You may not have paid much attention to this code in the past, or you may not have used it. These two lines of code reappear throughout the code snippets in Dashcode.

The first step in getting the gauge's value is to get the gauge page element. Because page elements have unique IDs, you can call the JavaScript function GetElementByID, store the result that is returned in a variable, and then check its value.

Here is the actual code snippet (the lines are spaced differently on the page than in the Library):

```
// Values you provide
var gaugeValue = document.GetElementById("elementID");
// replace with ID of gauge

// Gauge code
gaugeValue = gaugeValue.object.value;
```

Comments in the code snippets help you understand the code and guide you to what you must customize. (Remember that single line JavaScript comments are introduced by // and continue to the end of the line. One of the most common customizations is to insert an ID.) When you've laid out your interface with parts from the Library, you may not be worrying about IDs. However, because they're there and unique, when you want to add code to your app or widget, you just open the Attributes inspector and check the ID.

Because IDs appear in your app or widget code in this way, remember that changing the ID of an element can break existing code that uses the prior ID. If you're going to change IDs to create a meaningful name, do it right after you create an element. For example, you may want to change a text field from its default name (textField) to something more meaningful like (textField-ForFirstName).

Using other attributes

The attributes in the Attributes inspector other than the ID and class are all optional:

- ✔ **Class:** You use the standard class attribute in HTML most often in a cascading style sheet (CSS).
- ✔ **Visibility:** The check box that controls visibility allows you to place objects in your interface that aren't seen. Note that if you make an object invisible, you'll have a tough time working with it in the future because you won't know where to click to select it.

However, all is not lost. Every element is shown in the navigator at the upper left corner of the Dashcode window. You can click an element, open the Attributes inspector, and then change the check box so that it is visible. And, of course, if you need to refer to an invisible element in JavaScript, you can do so by using its unique ID, which enables you to place some unseen information in a text field, for example. However, that approach is a very round-about way of handling the issue of storing some data away from the user's view. See Chapter 13 for several better ways of handling this issue.

✔ **Default image:** When a widget is loading, Dashboard displays a *default image* until the full widget has loaded. The default image is constructed automatically from the visible interface of the front of the widget. In part because this use of the default image may require a smaller version of your interface, you may choose to eliminate some interface elements from it. Do so by selecting the interface elements that you want to include from the default image and check Show in Default Image.

You can further customize your default image by clicking Show in External Editor in the lower right of a widget Dashcode window so that you can use a graphics application.

✔ **Design guides** can be very useful as you're creating an interface, particularly if it's complex and crowded (which is often the case — there's never enough room). Figures 4-7, 4-8, and 4-9 illustrate the problem and its solution using design guides. The problem begins when you place one object in front of another one either in whole or in part, as you see in Figure 4-7.

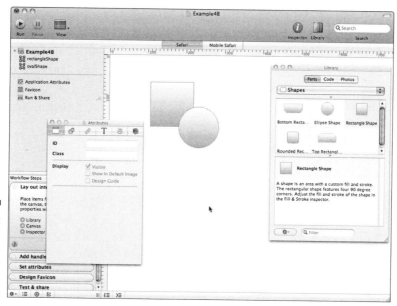

Figure 4-7:
Place a shape partially over another one.

Like many graphics programs, Dashcode treats visual elements as being layered. You can drag elements on the canvas around in two dimensions, but to move them forward and back, you need the Arrange menu. Select the element you want to move forward or back and then choose from the Arrange menu's commands:

- ✔ **Bring Forward**
- ✔ **Bring to Front**
- ✔ **Send Backward**
- ✔ **Send to Back**

In Figure 4-7, the ellipse is in front of the rectangle. By default, each new object you create is in front of the previously created objects, but the Arrange menu is the safest way to control the front-to-back ordering.

When you select an object that is behind another one, it's highlighted with its frame and resizing handles. Thus, in Figure 4-8, the rectangle is highlighted, and therefore it can be seen in its totality even though it's behind the oval. If you click another element so that the rectangle is no longer highlighted, you see that it's partially obscured by the oval just as it was in Figure 4-7.

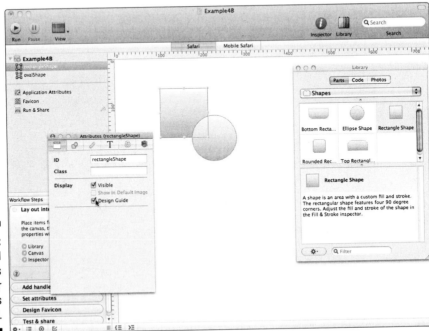

Figure 4-8:
Selected objects have their borders highlighted.

With the rectangle selected, you can enable Design Guide in the Attributes inspector. With Design Guide selected, objects that are behind other objects are partially visible. Thus, in Figure 4-9, you can see a faint image of the rectangle showing through the oval. This is true even if Design Guide isn't selected.

You may want to turn design guides on and off as you work. The advantage to having design guides turned on is that if you accidentally place an object on top of another one, the rear one shows through, and you can rearrange them if that isn't the effect that you wanted. The disadvantage is that you see an interface that users will never see because they see the front-most objects only. (You can modify this in some cases, but by and large, the front-most objects are the ones visible.)

If you've been playing around with shapes and IDs, you may want to get rid of them. If you haven't saved your work, just close the Dashcode window and ignore the warning about unsaved changes. Alternatively, select all the objects you've been experimenting with (in the canvas or the navigator) and delete them.

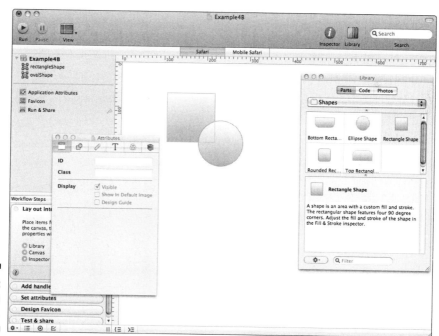

Figure 4-9:
Use design
guides.

Manipulating Text with Element Attributes and Library Code Snippets

Plenty of code in the Library takes advantage of element IDs. Here is a practical, simple example of how to use code snippets together with element IDs. You can use this basic code structure in a variety of your Dashcode projects. This example is an app with two text fields that automatically switch contents as soon as it launches. Later on, you can add a button to initiate the switching and build on this code in many ways.

To build this simple example, you need to create two text fields and then provide the code to switch their contents.

Creating two fields

To create the text fields:

1. **Open the Library, if it isn't open.**
2. **Drag a text field into the canvas.**
3. **If it isn't open, open the Attributes inspector.**
4. **Change the ID of the text field you just added to `sourceText`.**
5. **Type hello into the field.**
6. **Create another text field and rename it `destinationText`.**
7. **Type world into this field.**
8. **Rearrange the text fields so that they're next to one another.**

   Dashcode provides you with guidelines as you move a field near another one, as shown in Figure 4-10.

9. **Save your work.**
10. **Test by clicking Run at the top left of the Dashcode window.**

    The result looks like Figure 4-11.

Get into the habit of testing (and saving) your work as you go along. Undoing the last change you made is easier than going back through a whole set of changes that you entered over an hour or more. I omit testing and saving most of the steps in the book, but you should still be performing them.

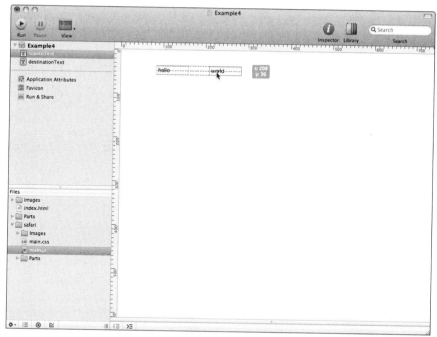

Figure 4-10:
Set up two
text fields.

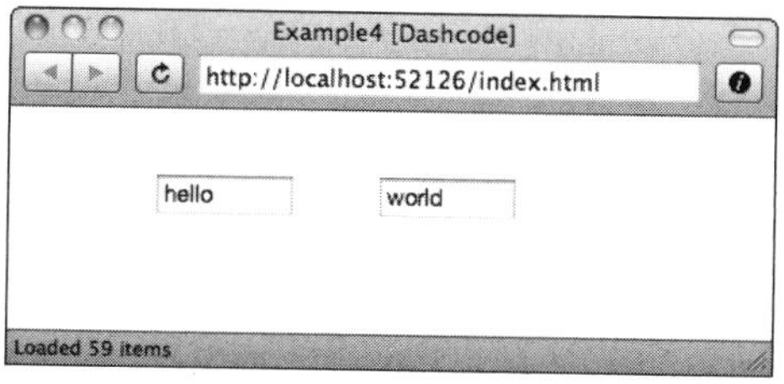

Figure 4-11:
Test your
work.

Writing code to switch field contents

After you create the text fields, you need to write the code that switches field content. The code is in the Library, so here's how to find it and customize it.

To write the code:

1. **Make sure that the list of the project's files appears in the lower left corner of the navigator.**

   If not, choose View➪Files, click View in the toolbar, or click the Files shortcut in the lower left frame of the Dashcode window.

2. **Click main.js in the file list.**

The file opens, and its code appears (see Figure 4-12). If you don't see it, make certain that the source code pane is visible. You may have to drag up the divider between it and the canvas.

Figure 4-12:
Open
`main.js`.

3. **Find Get Text Field Text in the Library, as shown in Figure 4-13.**

   This text is in the section called Text Parts. If you know the name of a snippet or can guess it or part of it, you can use the search field. In most cases, using the pop-up menu to get to the appropriate section gives you a limited number of choices from which you can easily find what you're looking for.

4. **Drag the code into `main.js`.**

   Drag it by using the icon next to the name either in the list of parts at the top of the Library window or in the code snippet in the bottom pane.

5. **Place the code after the only line of code in the function.**

   That code is `dashcode.setupParts ();` (see Figure 4-14).

6. **Check that the code is in the right place.**

   The main thing to watch for is that the start of the code snippet starts on a new line and isn't appended to an existing line of code (see Figure 4-15).

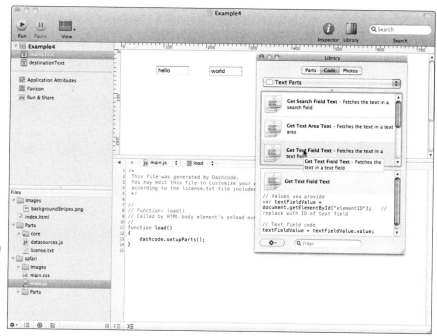

Figure 4-13:
Find Get
Text Field
Text.

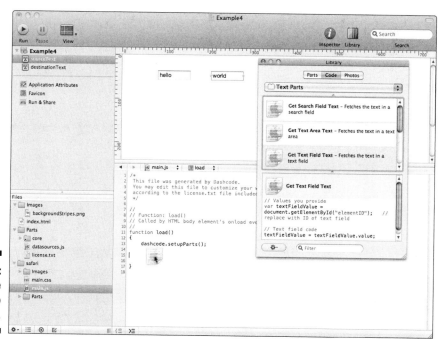

Figure 4-14:
Drag the
code into
`main.js`.

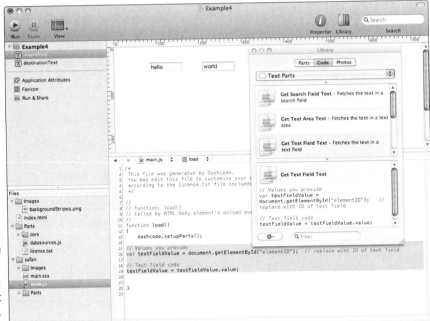

7. **Change** `elementID` **to the ID of the first field —** `sourceText`.

   Always review the code you insert for comments indicating customizations and replacements.

8. **In the same way that you dragged Get Text Field Text into the code in Step 4, drag Set Text Field Text into** `main.js` **and position it right after the Get Text Field Text code you just inserted.**

9. **Change** `elementID` **to the ID of the second field —** `destination-Text`.

10. **Delete** `var newTextFieldText = "String to display";`.

    The snippet changes the text field to this string. You don't need to change it to a specific string: You want to change it to the value of `sourceText`, which the first snippet stored in `textFieldValue`. So you need to delete this line.

11. **Locate** `textFieldToChange.value = newTextFieldText;`.

12. **Change** `newTextFieldText` **to** `textFieldValue`.

    `textFieldValue` is where the value from the first field was stored. The project looks like Figure 4-16.

13. Save, test, and run.

The results look like Figure 4-17.

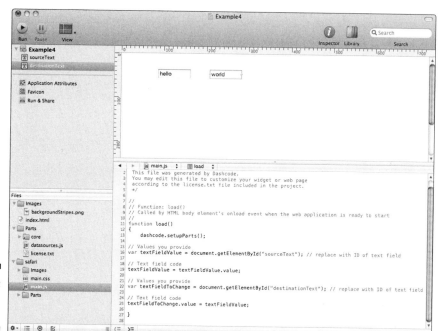

Figure 4-16:
Finish the
code.

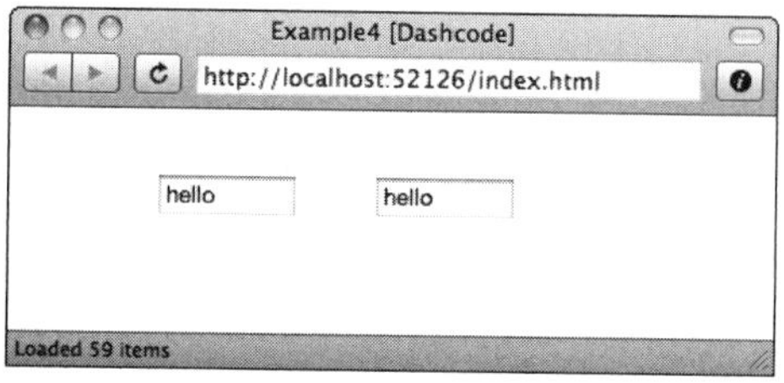

Figure 4-17:
Run the
project.

Looking at Attributes for a Text Field

As you change the IDs of the text fields in the "Creating Two Fields" section, earlier in this chapter, the Attributes inspector changed. Not only does the inspector display information about the currently selected object, such as its name, but the attributes also vary depending on the type of object. The Attributes inspector for a text field looks like Figure 4-18.

Figure 4-18:
Attributes
inspector
for a text
field.

If you want to use a text field for user data entry, it must be enabled (the default setting). You also may want to limit the number of characters that can be entered in the field. As you add other parts to your projects, you can set additional attributes based on the type of object the inspector is looking at.

Working with Fill and Stroke

The Fill & Stroke inspector lets you adjust the way in which elements are drawn. Many of the effects that you can create in the Fill & Stroke inspector can be very impressive, and you don't have to write a single line of code to use them.

The best way to learn about the Fill & Stroke inspector is to create a new project from the Custom template for Safari (you see a blank canvas). Then add a few shapes and experiment with them. In Figure 4-19, for example, you see two rectangles.

The lower right rectangle appears to be in front of the other one, but that isn't really the case because the canvas is two-dimensional, and nothing appears in front or behind anything else. The illusion of depth is created through the use of *opacity* — the degree to which one object can be seen through another one. Opacity is built into the operating system in a section called Core Graphics, which is available on Mac OS X and on iOS.

You can create beautiful effects with opacity, but if you use it too aggressively, you'll make objects appear invisible because things behind them are visible. You should make data entry fields and any elements that require user interaction as visible as possible, which frequently means toning up the opacity toward 100 percent so that nothing is seen through that object.

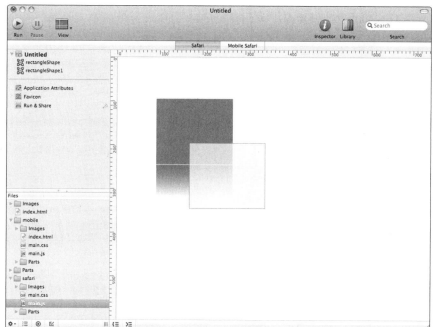

Figure 4-19:
Change
styles of
rectangles.

The other rectangle in Figure 4-19 demonstrates *reflection*. The object is rendered in the normal way, but its image appears as if in a reflection. It's not a complete reflection as a mirror might show; rather, it's more like a reflection in a pond. Here, too, be careful not to overuse this feature. Figure 4-20 shows the Fill & Stroke inspector.

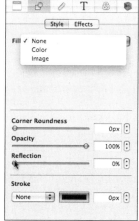

Figure 4-20:
The Fill
& Stroke
inspector
lets you
choose
styles and
effects.

Choosing colors

You can use the Fill & Stroke inspector to set the color for the fill of an object and the stroke of lines. Both the fill and stroke use a classic interface element — the color picker that lets you choose colors (see Figure 4-21.) Once again, you find an enormous amount of functionality in a very small space.

The color picker contains four main areas. The main action takes place in the center of the window. There, you find colors displayed in several different ways, which you control by the tabs at the top of the window. From left to right, the tabs display these color models:

✔ **Color wheel:** Shown in Figure 4-21, the color wheel shows a wide range of colors. At the center of the wheel is white — the color that is the combination of all colors of light. (The combination of all colors of pigment to reflected colors is black.) As you move to the edge of the color wheel, you find major colors, including primary colors.

✔ **Color sliders:** These sliders let you construct a color by moving pointers along them, which creates numeric values for the various models. RGB colors, for example, consist of values for red, green, and blue that range from 0 to 255. An RGB value of 255, 0, 0, is red, while 0, 255, 0 is green. Other sliders adjust gray scale with brightness ranging from 0 (black) to 100 percent (white). CMYK (Cyan-Magenta-Yellow-Black) uses values from 0 to 100% percent for each of these colors; it's used primarily in printing. The point of the sliders is to convert a given color to a specific set of numeric values.

✔ **Palettes:** Palettes are sets of colors used primarily in the operating system. You can choose compatible colors for your apps and widgets.

✔ **Spectrum:** Like the color wheel, spectrum displays a range of many colors.

✔ **Crayons:** A set of colors arranged like crayons in a box, this color model limits the number of colors you have to choose from, which can be a good thing!

When you see a color you want to use, you can drag it to the horizontal rectangle near the top of the window. From there, you drag it into a *color well,* such as the one in the center of stroke settings at the bottom of Figure 4-20.

More important, you can drag the color to your own palette, the row of boxes along the bottom of the color picker. You can create a limited palette for your Dashcode project in this way. You don't have to poke around in the color picker to try to match the green you used for a background; just drag it from its box in your palette to where you want to use it.

Figure 4-21:
Use the color wheel to select your color.

A warning about looking at color

Color is one of the most subjective experiences humans have. Most people can see color, and if any light exists, they experience colors all the time. Any color is experienced in the context of other colors, and it can appear to change drastically depending on these interactions. The classic book on this subject is by Josef Albers's *Interaction of Color* (Yale University Press). Albers demonstrates amazingly how one color can look like two, and two colors can look like one just by varying their neighboring colors.

In addition to color interactions, color is perceived differently when it's viewed as *reflected light* (such as an image on a printed page or a painting) than when it's viewed as *transmitted light* (such as an image on a computer screen).

The only way you can evaluate the colors in your app or widget is to look at it on the devices that they'll be used on in the ambient light that may surround them. That may mean taking your iPod to the beach (purely for the sake of research!) as well as taking it into a fluorescent-lit lecture hall in addition to a living room. Do this evaluation before you finalize your design choices. In particular, look for combinations of colors and lighting that wash out distinctions between two colors, thereby making parts of your interface less noticeable or even invisible.

Setting effects

The Effects tab lets you add complex visual effects. You can choose from two categories of these effects. The first category (Glass) lets you add effects that are somewhat like the appearance of glass objects. The second category, Recess, lets you work with the appearance of depth and shadows.

You can use effects to create a subliminal sense in your users' minds that several objects are somehow or other related. They don't have to connect the dots; all you have to do is to make certain interface elements share some graphical characteristics.

For this type of design to work, you have to avoid scattering visual effects around haphazardly. Create a pattern and then use it consistently so that the user learns what is behind the pattern. Having a consistent pattern really can speed up learning how to use an app or widget.

Using the Metrics Inspector

The Metrics inspector lets you view and set dimensions for a selected element. It also lets you control some automatic sizing and positioning.

Positioning objects with document flow and absolute settings

Figure 4-22 shows three shapes and the Metrics inspector. The selected rectangle is positioned using the document flow setting in the pop-up menu at the top of the Metrics inspector. If an element uses absolute settings, you can place it anywhere on the canvas.

Document flow settings cause objects to flow from top to bottom of the canvas. Dashcode places a gray line beneath the bottom of the lowest document flow element on the page. You can move that element lower, and that line will move down with it. However, if an element above that element also uses document flow settings, you can't move the element up beyond the bottom of the document flow item above it. (Document flow is why you may not have been able to move shapes around exactly as you wanted to.) Absolute positioning gives you total freedom to place objects where no user will be able to see them.

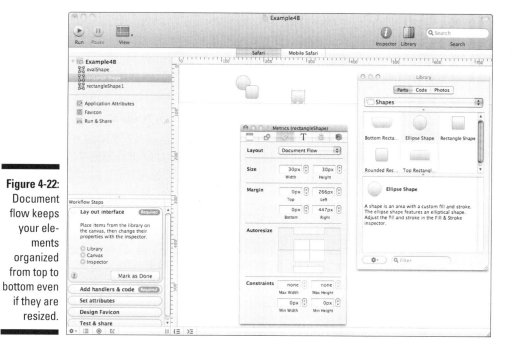

Figure 4-22:
Document
flow keeps
your ele-
ments
organized
from top to
bottom even
if they are
resized.

Widgets usually aren't resized, so Dashcode uses absolute positioning by
default. For Web applications, most elements are automatically set to use
document flow by default. This setting lets them move around as windows
are zoomed and as the device's orientation changes.

Adjusting the autoresize settings

On the desktop, you resize and reshape a window by dragging its frame (usually the lower right corner). On iPhone and iPad, you resize and reshape a
window by rotating the device between landscape and horizontal orientations. Your apps can control what behavior occurs at this time. You choose
the behavior from application attributes, which you can always access from
the navigator, as shown in Figure 4-23.

In general, for iPhone and iPad, the best setting is to adjust the page size
automatically. People may not even notice these adjustments because it's
exactly what they would have expected if they thought about it.

To make the user experience most rewarding, you often want to adjust the
autoresize settings in the Metrics inspector. You can set the autoresize

settings for any object in the interface. This means that the object's location and dimensions can change automatically as the object inside which it is located changes size and shape.

Here's an example of what happens when you use autoresize and how you can control what happens:

1. **Create a mobile Safari app from the Custom template.**

   You do so in the same way described in the earlier "Using the Attributes inspector" section.

2. **Make certain that your application attributes are set to adjust the page size automatically, as shown in Figure 4-23.**

   Use the Orientation setting under Viewport in Application Attributes in the navigator.

3. **Select the content element from the navigator or by clicking in the center of the canvas, as shown in Figure 4-24.**

   Note that the *Developed for Dashcode* text is inside the footer part, which is below the content part.

4. **Open the Metrics inspector and look at the autoresize section.**

   The horizontal and vertical lines control autoresizing (see Figure 4-25). The box in the center represents the selected object. (It's always a box regardless of the shape of the selected object.)

5. **Click a spring inside the box.**

   The spring changes to a straight line. Springs indicate that the dimension is adjustable, as shown in Figure 4-26.

   The autoresize springs and lines function in pairs to control horizontal and vertical size and location. Make certain that you set them back to the way they were in Figure 4-25 before continuing. The lines and springs within the box control the object's size; those outside the box control the object's location.

6. **Place a shape on your canvas, as shown in Figure 4-27.**

   You can place the shape anywhere except the exact center of the canvas. Placing it in the center makes the rotation effect less noticeable.

7. **Use the Metrics inspector to change the shape's layout setting to absolute positioning rather than document flow.**

   You can see how to do so in "Positioning Objects with Document Flow and Absolute Positioning," earlier in this chapter.

8. **Rotate the canvas.**

   The content is resized, but the shape is neither resized nor moved.

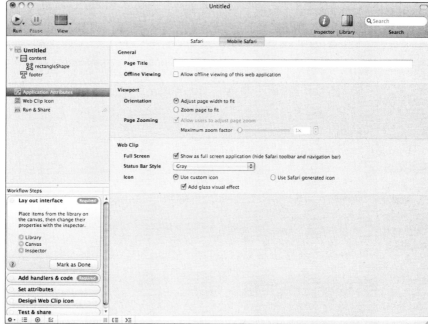

Figure 4-23:
Control how
your app
responds to
a change in
orientation.

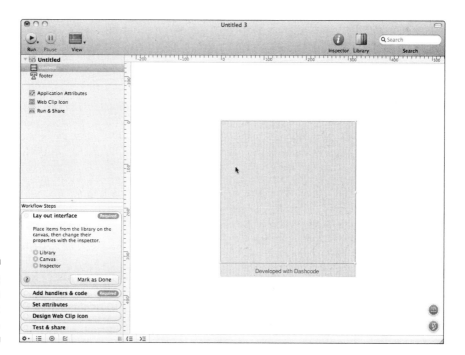

Figure 4-24:
Select the
`content`
part.

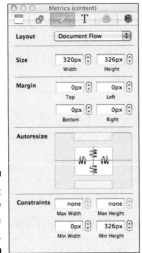

Figure 4-25:
View
autoresize
settings.

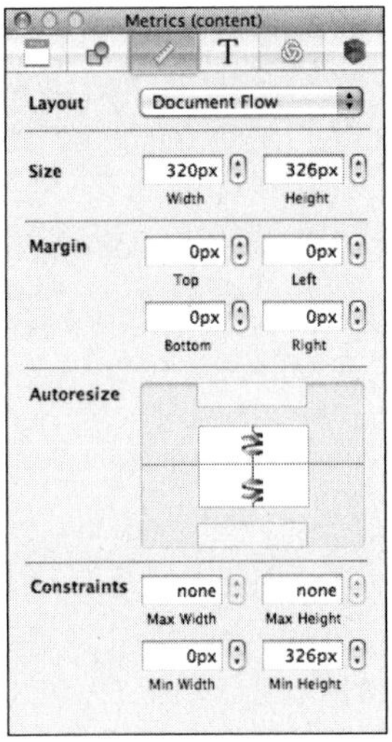

Figure 4-26:
Adjust
autoresize
settings.

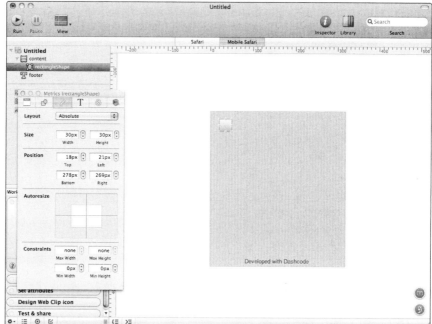

Notice the two buttons in the bottom right of the canvas. The one at the top toggles the canvas display so that it's the exact size of the iPhone. (Somehow, it looks much smaller in Dashcode.) Most people leave the larger setting for the canvas because it's easier to work at that scale.

These buttons' settings are also available in the View menu as Show Size Accurate and Show Pixel Accurate.

The curved arrow below the size settings lets you rotate the canvas. It, too, is available in the View menu as Rotate to Portrait and Rotate to Landscape.

9. **Use autoresize to make the shape move.**

With the shape selected, open the Metrics inspector and look at the autoresize section. What the spring suggests is that this distance is flexible as the device is rotated. Thus, in Figure 4-28, the distance from the left side of the object to the left size of the content object is flexible, and the distance from the right side of the object to the right size of the content object is fixed.

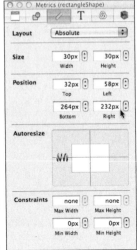

Figure 4-28:
Adjust
autoresize
settings.

10. **Rotate the canvas with the button in the lower right corner in order to move the shape, as shown in Figure 4-29.**

You may have to get out a ruler to prove it, but the distance from the right side of the shape to the right edge of the viewport is exactly the same because you made the opposite side flexible by changing it to a spring.

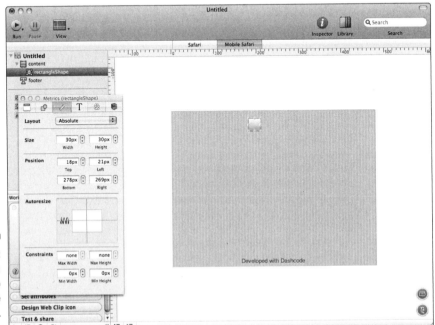

Figure 4-29:
Rotate the
canvas to
move the
shape.

11. Rotate the device a few more times to get the hang of it.

This type of autoresizing lets you position something that appears to many people not to move while it actually does move. Perhaps the most common example is a button that you want people to expect to always find in the "same" place. (A button in the lower right corner of a view is a very common example.) For this button to always be in that "same" place, it has to move so that it's always in relatively the same place when compared to the viewport.

12. Resize and move an object at the same time.

But there is more to autoresizing. You can resize the element itself as well as move it. You don't have to do anything in this case: It's part of the template. Select the footer (with *Developed for Dashcode* in it) and examine the Metrics inspector, as shown in Figure 4-30.

These settings keep the footer the same size and the same relative location in the center of the bottom of the canvas. Try rotating it and changing the settings to see how it functions (see Figure 4-31).

Now if you rotate the canvas, you see that the media part changes its size as the device is rotated, as shown in Figure 4-32.

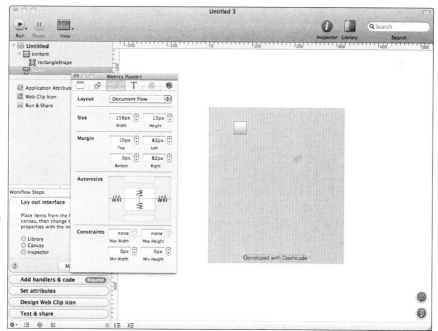

Figure 4-30: The footer stays the same width and stays in the middle.

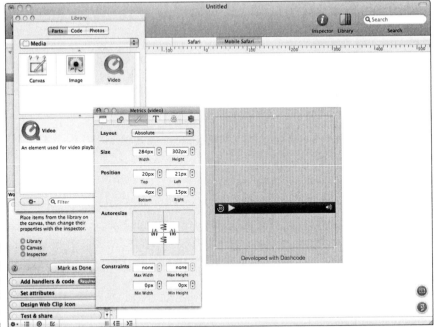

Figure 4-31:
Make a
media part
resizable.

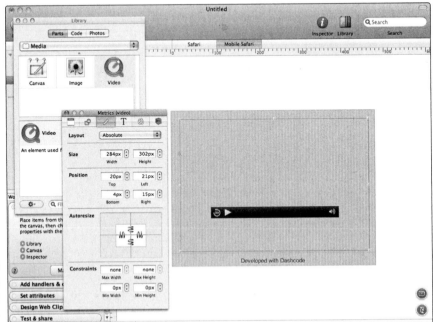

Figure 4-32:
Rotate a
media part.

Chapter 5

Working with Library Parts

*E*veryone has different ways of working on apps and widgets — and sometimes the approach varies from project to project and day to day. However, many people fall into a common routine. After selecting a template, the Library comes into play, and you can quickly assemble your interface. But when you start putting the pieces together, all sorts of issues you never thought of seem to crop up. At this stage of the game, though, you can easily make changes.

As the rough interface takes shape, you can use the inspector to adjust it and tweak it until it's just right. That process often continues throughout the entire development cycle. As you progress, you can add the behaviors that make the objects start to function. At that point, you have something that is ready to test for usability. This early version may always serve up the same hard-coded data as a graphic instead of accessing a database, but you and others can start to get a feel for what works and what doesn't.

The good part of this rapid development process is that your project looks pretty good early in the process. The negative part is that you have to remind yourself (and, perhaps, your boss) that a major part of the development work still lies ahead. Those pixel-by-pixel tweaks to get the exact right position for a button can take a lot of time. Settling on the precise colors for your interface can also be a painstaking process. (If you're developing an app for iPad or iPhone, make certain that you include testing and evaluating the colors outdoors as well as indoors. Colors look very different in varying types of lighting conditions.)

This chapter focuses on the Library and the parts that you use to assemble your interface. Together with Chapters 6 and 7, you can see pretty much the whole interface development process.

Knowing What You Can and Cannot Do with the Library

The Library consists of reusable interface elements (parts), code snippets for you to customize, and your own photos and other images that you've added to iPhoto (see Figure 5-1). In the Library, parts are customizable only in certain ways.

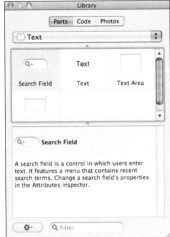

Figure 5-1: The text parts are used to display or enter text.

TIP

In general, you use the inspector to perform these customizations. If you want to get your hands dirty, you can go into the JavaScript code that is generated for you by Dashcode, but doing so runs the risk of creating an interface that doesn't adhere to the standards people expect. Using nonstandard behavior can make your app harder for people to learn.

The code snippets are designed for customization, but comments highlight the areas you should customize. Yes, you can customize others, but the same problem of creating potentially nonstandard behavior can occur. Your photos, of course, are totally your own, and you can do anything you want with them.

By now, scores of thousands of Mac applications, iPhone and iPad apps, and Dashboard widgets have been created. Designers and developers have confronted just about every interface issue that commonly arises (including issues on other platforms and even noncomputer environments). New devices often require you to rethink interfaces, but chances are that in the world of apps and widgets, other people have confronted the interface issues that you face.

Every time you realize that the Library has no standard part for you to use in implementing some functionality your app, think again (and cross-examine yourself) as to whether you need that functionality in that way. Reusing these parts over and over doesn't reflect a lack of imagination on your part. Rather, it reflects a consideration for your users who will approach your app already knowing what those interface elements do and how to use them. As a result, a new user of your app is likely to understand what it does and how it works at a single glance.

That said, do get in the habit of checking out the inspector window for every interface object you use. Many customizations are available so that you can put your own look on your interface.

Chapter 2 explores the basic functionality of the Library window.

Working with Text Parts from the Library

Some apps and widgets are totally text-based, such as eBooks and other references. Others, such as games or utility apps, have no text whatsoever. But most apps and widgets have at least some text. Even the iPhone Camera app, which is almost totally visual, has a Done button and a Camera Roll button to help you navigate.

When it comes to your interface, anything that you can implement graphically is usually better than a textual implementation. But when it comes to your app's data (if it has data), you're often dealing with text.

If your app or widget may be used in another language, all the text in the interface needs to be localized. After you localize the text, your interface itself may need to change. For example, the button may not be big enough for the word it needs to carry in another language. And you may wind up in a situation in which you just can't translate something into a single word.

When you use text in your interface, translation into another language isn't the only problem you may encounter. Winston Churchill (or Oscar Wilde or George Bernard Shaw — the attribution is murky) referred to the United States and England as two countries divided by a common language, and he was right. Parliamentary procedure in England uses the verb "table" to describe the process of laying something on the table for discussion. In the

United States, the exact same word is used to describe the process of laying something down on the table as a way of putting it aside.

Internationalization is a particular issue for apps and widgets because they're distributed almost exclusively by electronic means, which means that they can fly around the world. You may think that only a handful of people in your city are likely to use your app or widget, but you may very well be proven (happily) wrong.

In addition to text parts, other parts, such as buttons, may have text on them, but these parts are designed specifically for manipulating text.

Using the search field when possible

The search field is a good example of how Dashcode packages interface functionality into the Library parts. Experiment with a search field by adding one to your canvas and then opening the Attributes inspector, as shown in Figure 5-2.

Figure 5-2:
Inspect the search field with the Attributes inspector.

Most of the time, part-specific attributes are at the bottom of Inspector panes below common settings, such as ID and Class in the Attributes inspector, shown in Figure 5-2. However, the bottom part of the Attributes inspector provides new attributes for the search field:

✔ **Placeholder:** This gray text can appear in the search field before a user types into it. As soon as the first keystroke is received by the search field, the placeholder text disappears. Placeholder text is a very efficient use of space. Rather than provide instructions, you simply give an example of what you can type or why. For example, at the bottom of the Library window shown in Figure 5-1, the word *Filter* lets you know what that search field can do.

- **Predicate:** You can specify the kind of comparison the searching will be doing, such as searching for *like* or *contains*.

- **Saved results:** If this attribute is set to any number greater than zero, a small downward-pointing arrow appears at the left of the search field to let you choose from recent searches. Saved results is the number of items that will be shown. Remember that lists of more than about seven to ten items are hard to keep track of. You can set the saved results to 1,000, but your users will be mystified. Usually, people want to repeat one of the last few searches. (Not just the single last search.)

- **Search mode:** If you use an incremental search, the search is carried out as you type. The Library window's search field uses incremental search. Letter by letter, type in t-e-x-t-space-f and watch the window as it responds to your key strokes to quickly hone in on *text field*.

Using text areas and text fields

Text areas and text fields are the basic HTML elements for text entry. *Text areas* allow more than one line, but *text fields* are single line, data entry elements. Figure 5-3 shows the Attributes inspector for a text field. The Attributes inspector for a text area is the same except that the value field is larger and you can't set the maximum length.

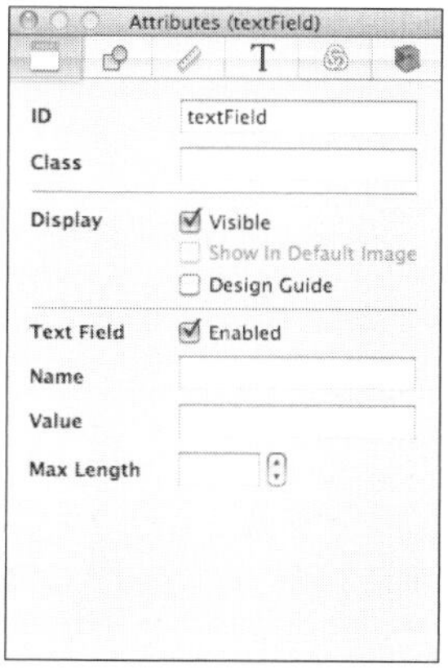

Figure 5-3:
Set attributes for text fields and areas.

As always, the bottom of the Attributes inspector has those attributes for the selected element. When that selected element is a text field, here's what you see:

- **Enabled:** All fields that can allow user input let you enable them.

- **Name:** In HTML, the name of an element identifies it in the same way that ID identifies a JavaScript element. You can use both, but ID is required.

✔ **Value:** Value is the initial text that is placed in the field. You can enter it in the Attributes inspector or just type into the field in Dashcode.

✔ **Maximum length:** You can limit text entry for text fields. Note that if you're collecting text, you can normally limit its length in the input field as well as in a database to which it may be stored. These numbers obviously should be consistent (and usually identical).

Text fields are limited to a single line of text. No resizing handles allow vertical resizing. In addition, the Metrics inspector doesn't allow you to change the height of the field. The only place where you can change the height of a text field is in the Text inspector, as shown in Figure 5-4. You can change the font size, and then Dashcode adjusts the height of the field accordingly.

Figure 5-4: Adjust font size for text fields.

The Text inspector has two panes: Character, shown in Figure 5-4, and Alignment & Spacing, shown in Figure 5-5.

Figure 5-5: Use Alignment & Spacing to control text.

The Dashcode Text inspector is the standard Text inspector that you find in many applications that use Apple's Cocoa development framework. If you use iWork, you'll recognize the Text inspector from Keynote, Numbers, and Pages, which is also is used in many third-party products.

Part of the ease of use of Apple's software comes from this use of consistent interfaces. That's why you don't need to learn the details of common tasks over and over with minor tweaks and adjustments for each application.

You're building apps and widgets with Dashcode. The sophisticated styling that you can use in a multipage word processing document in Pages may not be appropriate on the small canvas of an app or widget.

In the case of Safari Web applications designed for desktop browsers, you need to remember other considerations. These text formatting features depend on support from the browser and its operating system. Fonts have long been an issue on the Web because not everyone has the same set of fonts installed. For many years, there was a concept of *web-safe colors* — colors that all browsers and all platforms could safely use. Today, web-safe colors are less of a concern, but the same color (at least according to numeric values such as RGB and CYMK) can appear quite different on different displays and operating systems even without taking into account interaction with adjacent colors.

For most apps and widgets, though, the issue of space is the primary concern. Note in Figure 5-5 that you can control what happens when the text for a text part overflows the bounds of that part. Particularly when you're displaying data that a user has entered, you may need to gracefully handle cases in which that text overflows the bounds of the field. The overflow setting can be a big help.

Working with Media Parts from the Library

The Library contains four media parts that you can use

- ✔ Video
- ✔ Image
- ✔ Canvas
- ✔ Quartz Composer

Video

The Video part lets you load and run a QuickTime movie at runtime. You can provide settings in the Attributes inspector, as shown in Figure 5-6. (As always, the top part of the Attributes inspector has the ID, class, and display settings.

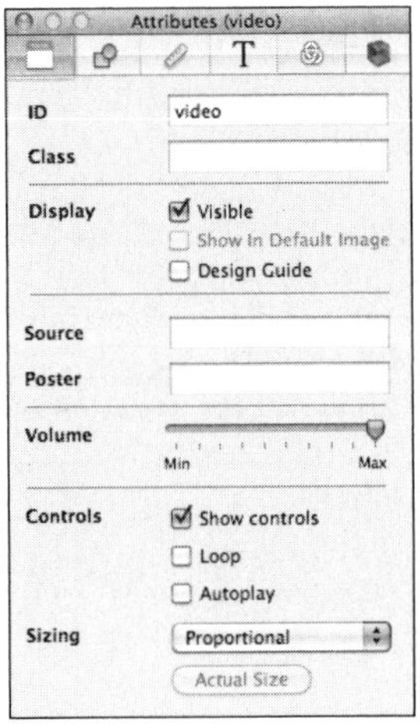

Figure 5-6:
Set attributes for a video part.

The Source is the URL of the video to be loaded. The Poster is the source for the poster image to be shown when the video is loading.

The settings for Sizing and Controls are exactly what they look like.

You can loop a video and set it to autoplay. Autoplay is an interesting setting. Sometimes people think that the moment they select a video, it should play automatically. Other people think that after the video has loaded, they should have the choice to play it when they want to. A lot of this discussion has its root in how long it takes to load the video. If the user experience is that the video plays instantaneously (or nearly so), it should probably start playing immediately. You may need some kind of delay when there are slow connections or very large videos.

Image

An image part displays an image that is loaded at runtime. (If you want to display a known image, you can add it to your app and widget so that it's placed in the relevant Images folder.)

The Attributes inspector lets you set the location and treatment of the image to be displayed in the image element. You type the URL into the Source field, and you choose how the image should be resized. (These parts of the Attributes inspector look the same as they do for video parts that are shown in the Attributes inspector — see preceding section.) Your choices are no resizing, proportional resizing (the image isn't reshaped), and size to fit. In the last case, the image is sized to fit the image part's shape even if that causes distortion of the image. Resize to fit works very well with abstract images and solid colors.

Canvas

The canvas media part provides you with a canvas on which you can draw anything that you want. *Canvas* is a word that is frequently used for such a drawing environment, but it is used in a variety of contexts. When it comes to Dashcode, the canvas that you see in the Dashcode window is the canvas on which you design your app or widget. The canvas media part is a Dashcode part that you can place on the Dashcode canvas.

Code snippets, shown in the Library in Figure 5-7, let you draw whatever you want on the canvas media parts.

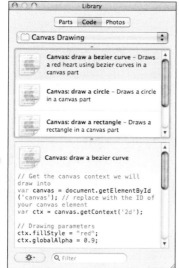

Figure 5-7: Start from code snippets to draw on a canvas media part.

If you have an app or widget that needs to draw shapes perhaps in response to changing data, using the canvas drawing code snippets is one of the ways you can do so. Many people already have their drawing code written for another environment, so the structure of these procedures and calls may let you reuse existing code and analysis.

Quartz Composer

Quartz is the native imaging engine on Mac OS X and iOS. It takes advantage of hardware acceleration wherever it can and is considered one of the fastest-responding graphics engines.

The disadvantage of using Quartz Composer may be that you already have code written in other structures that are easier to port to the Image media part. The advantage is the speed.

As you can see from the Attributes inspector for a Quartz Composer part (shown in Figure 5-8), Quartz Composer was developed in an environment of video and animation rather than simply that of two-dimensional graphics.

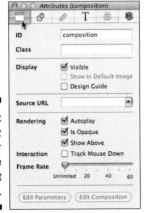

Figure 5-8:
Use Quartz
Composer
for the
fastest
graphics.

Chapter 6

Behaving Well with Buttons

*T*he inspector lets you adjust the visual appearance of interface elements — everything from fonts, colors, size, and location to the way in which objects behave as the container in which they're located is resized either manually or by rotating an iPhone or iPad. In this chapter, the Behaviors inspector receives its moment in the spotlight.

You can attach behaviors to any object, but they're most frequently attached to buttons. In this chapter, you see how to work with the visual aspects of buttons by dragging them from the Library to the canvas and then modifying their visual attributes. Then you see how to attach handlers to their events, and then you implement some buttons for real.

Handling Behaviors

Behaviors are sections of code that run when a specific event occurs; at that time, a handler is executed. Without a handler for an event, an object can't respond to it.

Figure 6-1 shows a Safari app built on the Custom template (the one that starts with a totally blank Web page). In Figure 6-1, an image part has been dragged from the Library onto the canvas. With that image part still selected from the drag, the Behaviors inspector is opened. You see two columns: At the left are the events to which the Image part can respond. At the right, an empty column awaits you to add whatever handlers you want to use.

With names such as `onclick`, `onmousedown`, and `onmouseover`, it doesn't take too much imagination to figure out what these events are. Remember, events apply to this object only.

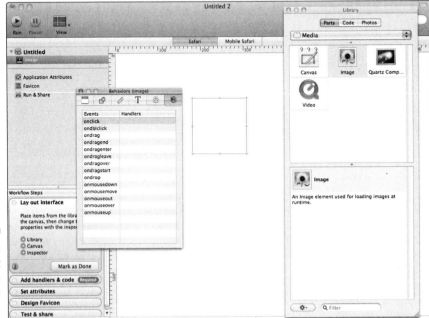

Figure 6-1: Check out the events for an Image part.

Events all begin with `on` to emphasize the fact that their handlers run when the specific event occurs — or *on* that event.

Programmers often talk about the fact that handlers *fire* when their events occur. Fire means that their handler code runs.

Controlling the Interface with Buttons

The interface rules for buttons are pretty clear for users and developers. The distinction is that developers may be able to refer to documentation to remind them how a button behaves. Users simply have internalized what those interface rules are. As you start using buttons in your interface, you have to be a bit more aware of what those interface rules are so that you use buttons in ways that users expect. It's not just the expectation that's important: It's the fact that with those expectations, users not only know how to use your app but also what it can do.

What is a button?

"What is a button?" may seem like a trick question, but think about it for a minute. What is a button in a graphical user interface? You can describe its appearance because you know what buttons look like on graphical user interfaces. The popup menu on the Library window has a section for buttons, so by looking at that section, you can see what buttons are available for you to add to your app or widget.

Another way of describing a button is by its behavior. A button is something that does something when you click it. And there's where the trick question comes up. In Figure 6-1, you can see the events in the Behaviors inspector for an image part. onclick is one of those events. Assign a handler to onclick, and it does something when you click it — but it's an image.

It's OK to have an onclick handler for an image because clicking an image isn't such a far-fetched idea. But just about everything on the interface responds to an onclick event. The only items that do not respond to onclick events are Indicator parts in the Library, as shown in the figure. The Indicator parts display information and have no reason to respond to any clicks or taps. (The exception is the Activity indicator which might respond to a click canceling the operation.) Other interface elements, such as sliders, display information and also respond to clicks.

If you want to be precise, a button is an object that looks like a button and that responds to the onclick event. The only time when it is very important to distinguish between buttons and other interface elements that respond to mouse clicks is when the user may be confused. Remember, responding to a mouse click requires not only the onclick handler, but it also requires that the object be enabled in the Attributes inspector (Buttons are enabled by default.) A button in the interface that isn't enabled won't respond to a mouse click. To keep your users from being frustrated (and angry with you), do something to indicate that the button isn't usable at that moment. Graying items out is a common strategy. For example, use the Fill & Stroke inspector, shown in the next figure, to reduce the opacity down to 25 percent. When you're done, have someone else look at it or look at it yourself the next day. When you've been staring at it while you work, you may be more attuned to slight differences than most people would be. As a result, when you come back and look at it, you may want to bump the opacity up a little bit so that the effect is more noticeable.

Buttons for your app or widget are available in the Library. Each comes with a brief description that reminds you when and how to use it.

The consistency of the user interface for widgets, Safari Web pages, and Safari Web applications is what makes them easy to use; the fact that this consistency extends in many cases through Mac OS X itself just increases the number of people who understand what these elements are and what they do.

Working with the basic buttons for Safari

The Library buttons vary for each type of Dashcode project. Figure 6-2 shows the buttons for Safari Web pages. These buttons are the most basic in the Library; you can find them in the other types of projects. Although their appearance is customized, these buttons are all basic HTML form elements.

Figure 6-2: Library buttons for Safari Web pages.

The basic button types are the push button and the lozenge button (both are shown in Figure 6-2). Push buttons are also referred to as rounded buttons, but for most people, they're just the standard buttons. The interface guidelines from Apple don't differentiate between the uses of these buttons. You can use one or another depending on the look of your project, or you can make a subtle differentiation in their purposes or contexts.

How users learn to use an interface

A frequently told story demonstrates how users can learn to use an interface . . . and how they can be wrong. A number of years ago, researchers apparently asked users how to create a new document in an application. Most people would answer that the way to create a new document is to choose File⇨New or to use the keyboard shortcut ⌘-N.

One person in the study provided a different answer. Quit the application, relaunch it,

and you'll have a new document. While these instructions are absolutely true, they are far from the easiest steps to create a new document.

The moral of this story is that people constantly search for patterns. If they can find a pattern, reproduce it, and find that it achieves the desired result, they have learned. Your job when you develop apps and widgets is to use the interface to point them toward finding a simple, easy-to-use pattern that works.

In the Finder, for example, you can use lozenge buttons to show or hide the toolbar as shown in Figure 6-3. (The lozenge button is in the upper right corner of the window.) Compare that button to the rounded buttons elsewhere in the toolbar: The lozenge button is slightly smaller, and its shape is different. Although users may not think much about the shape of these buttons, this distinction helps pinpoint the different functionality of the two shapes of buttons in this context. The rounded buttons perform actions on the Finder data — its windows, files, and so on. The lozenge button performs actions on the interface itself. (Apple uses small lozenge buttons in other places in its software for this purpose.)

Users are remarkably good at finding these subtle patterns in the interface. Your job is to create those patterns; part of that job is to decide what that pattern is. If you mix and match colors and styles for your interface elements, you'll make it harder for people to figure out what is going on and how they can use your interface most effectively.

Figure 6-3:
A lozenge button shows or hides the toolbar in the Finder.

Changing the look of the basic buttons

These basic buttons have four variants, two each for rounded buttons and lozenge buttons. These variants are the left and right sides of the buttons. At first, you may look for a middle part of the button so that you can construct one yourself, but you can just select the handles on a rounded button or a lozenge button and enlarge it to the size you need (usually you widen it). The left and right variants are there in case you need only part of a button.

Using the inspector, you can change the colors of your buttons. Keep your eyes open as you use Apple's own software (it goes through many review steps for the interface) as well as when you use apps and widgets from third parties. In most cases, the color of buttons rarely changes. The most frequent change is to change the color to red, such as when you edit an event in Calendar on iPhone or iPad. The Delete Event button is just like all the other buttons except that it's red as a caution to you.

The identifiable look of a button is created by default for all the Library buttons. Figure 6-4 shows the settings, but be careful about changing them: They help users see that this is a button. In fact, if you change these settings, the button will look a little strange. In extreme cases, users may decide that your altered button isn't a button at all and will never click it. Changing a button's color doesn't carry these risks.

You may also want to note that the height of buttons by default is 30 pixels. Most people react to larger buttons by thinking that they're a little strange, and in the context of apps and widgets, space is so precious that you don't want to waste any of it. Reducing the height of a button is fine if you have a consistent reason to do so, such as the Show/Hide Toolbar button in the Finder.

Four other buttons appear in the common set of Library buttons for all types of projects.

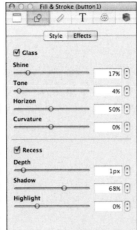

Figure 6-4:
Fill & Stroke
effects for
buttons
make them
button-y to
users.

Check boxes

You can use check boxes in two ways. You can use a group of check boxes to let people choose zero or more options. You can place the check boxes within a Library shape so that it's clear that they're all related. The second way of using check boxes is to use them alone. In that case, you use the check boxes as on/off indicators.

Radio buttons

Radio buttons always appear in groups of at least two. You can only turn a radio button on; it automatically is turned off when you select another radio button in the group. For this reason, you can never use a single radio button. (How would you turn it off?) Also, if you want an interface that allows people to select more than one option, you have to use check boxes.

You can create an interface that presents people with a set of radio buttons that are all off. Then, users can select and reselect the one that they want to choose. This setup isn't really a great type of interface because users have no way to get back to the initial state in which all the radio buttons are off.

Pop-up menus

Pop-up menus let users choose among several options. The pop-up menu list starts with placeholders (Item 1, Item 2, and so on). Customize your list by selecting your pop-up button and using the Attributes inspector to add or remove items. Double-click an item to change its name or value, as shown in Figure 6-5. The name is what the user sees; the value is what the program receives from the pop-up menu. This structure is exactly the HTML `select` element; the list in the Attributes inspector is the `option` elements located inside a `select` element.

Figure 6-5:
Set your
pop-up
menu's list
with the
Attributes
inspector.

Also note in Figure 6-5 that you can set images for buttons both in their normal and clicked states. You can choose how the image is positioned within the button. This applies to all buttons.

The maximum number of choices in a pop-up menu is a matter of some discussion: Most designers think that no more than a dozen items is best. More than that number means that people have to scroll through a lengthy list. This viewpoint may be a lost cause, because the Web is littered with pop-up menus that let people choose the U.S. state in which they live (more than 50 with territories and the District of Columbia) or even worse, the country in which they live (more than 250 countries appear in that list). For people in Alabama or Albania, a long list isn't a big problem. For people in Wyoming or Zimbabwe, it can be an annoyance. The keyboard can let you jump a specific item in a pop-up menu's list, but because you have to open the pop-up menu with the mouse, you have to take your hand off the mouse and move it back to the keyboard, which is an extra step or two.

Chapter 7 describes some navigation features that can substitute for lengthy pop-up menu lists.

Slider

The slider lets users select any value from a range. You see the range in the Attributes inspector, shown in Figure 6-6.

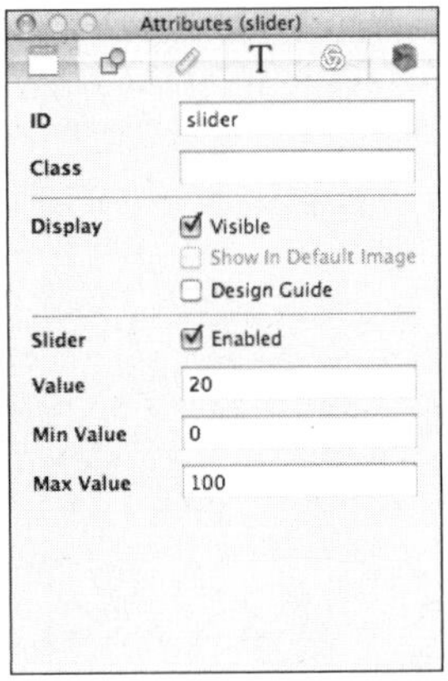

Figure 6-6:
Set a slid-
er's values.

If you don't enable a slider, users can't change its value. A slider that isn't enabled for input can be a good way to display data in a simple graphic way.

Working with the buttons for Mobile Safari apps (iPhone)

Figure 6-7 shows the Library buttons for iPhone apps.

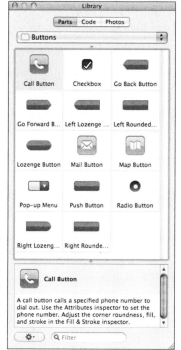

Figure 6-7:
Buttons
for iPhone
extend the
basic
buttons.

When compared to Safari, the iPhone (mobile Safari) has several new buttons, and one (the slider) is removed. The changes reflect the size and capabilities of iPhone. For example, the slider is problematic on a small touchscreen. Also, iPhone introduces a navigation structure that is very efficient for touchscreen navigation (see Chapter 7).

Here are the buttons that are specific to iPhone apps:

✔ **Call:** This button initiates a call. You can customize the image on the button using the Attributes inspector, shown in Figure 6-8. The default image is the phone icon that people are used to, so you may not want to customize it. Note that you can embed a phone number at the bottom of the button. (You can see how to dynamically adjust that number in Chapter 10.) You don't have to implement events and handlers for this button; it has only one function, which is programmed into it.

✔ **Map:** This button maps a specific address. It, too, requires no special coding after you've set its attributes. The settings are the same as the call button shown in Figure 6-8, but instead of a phone number, you provide an address.

✔ **Email:** This button sends an e-mail message. Its Attributes inspector interface is the same as call and map buttons except that at the bottom, you provide both a recipient address and a subject. If either one is missing, a blank e-mail message is created, and the user can fill in the address and subject.

✔ **Go Forward, Go Back:** These buttons help users navigate through a structure navigation tool (see Chapter 7).

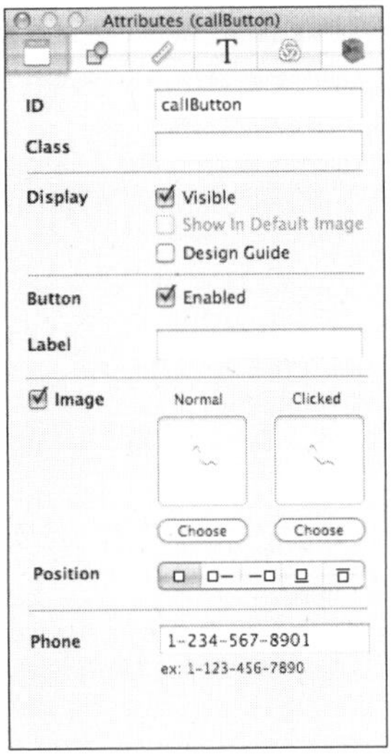

Figure 6-8: Set attributes for a call button.

Working with widget buttons

Figure 6-9 shows the buttons available in the Library for Dashboard widgets. This set of buttons is larger than the sets of buttons for Safari and mobile Safari.

The biggest variation is an alternate style for a number of the interface elements. For the Safari-based projects, buttons have a rich appearance. You can still use those buttons for widgets, but you can also use grayscale and less three-dimensional buttons. These buttons are earlier versions of interface buttons, and even today, they make a good deal of sense for Dashboard widgets where space is as much an issue as it is on a small iPhone screen. The reason for these differences in appearance is that Dashboard widgets appear on Mac OS X, and they live in an environment that doesn't involve touch. Objects that you manipulate with a tap can't be as small as objects that you manipulate with a click of the mouse; the tip of the pointer of a mouse is much smaller than a fingertip, and the positioning of the pointer is much more precise than the positioning of a fingertip. As a result, you can use much smaller objects on widgets than on iPhone or iPad.

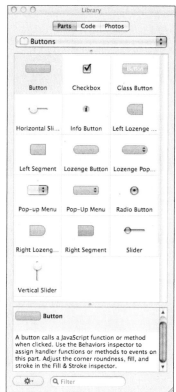

Figure 6-9:
Explore
buttons for
Dashboard
widgets.

You have a set of grayscale buttons that function just as their richer versions do in other projects. The grayscale buttons are

- **Button:** Similar to push button except for appearance. Widgets don't have push buttons.

- **Pop-up Menu:** Similar to pop-up menu. The richer pop-up menu also exists for widgets.

- **Lozenge Pop-up:** Controls a pop-up menu. It functions just as the pop-up menu button does.

- **Right Segment, Left Segment:** Similar to left and right rounded button. These buttons don't appear for widgets.

- **Horizontal Slider, Vertical Slider:** The horizontal slider is similar to the richer version; the vertical slider is available for widgets only.

In addition, two buttons that are specific to widgets and have a front and back:

- ✔ **Info Button:** This button's built-in behavior flips the widget from its front to its back. This button is designed to fit in a small space and to be as visible as possible. For those reasons, you can customize its appearance but only within limits. You use the Attributes inspector, shown in Figure 6-10, to set the foreground and background to white or black.

- ✔ **Glass Button:** This button is the backside version of an info button; it flips the widget to its front.

Figure 6-10:
Configure
an Info
button.

Understanding the Behavior Structure

To get into the details of behaviors, you can work with buttons that manipulate data in your app or widget. (This section is an expansion and revision of the basic structure described in Chapter 4.)

What you do here is initiate the transfer of data from one field to another when the user clicks a button. (In Chapter 4, that transfer was done automatically when that project launched.) The right place to put that code is into a handler that is invoked by a click on a button, but buttons weren't introduced yet, so they weren't able to be used. Start by understanding how the button behaves straight out of the Library with no customization and then figure out how to customize that behavior.

Looking at a button in action

To observe how a button behaves without customization, add a button from the Library to a new project.

You use this process over and over as you add code to your Dashcode project, so this example is very detailed.

To add a button to a new project:

1. **Create a new Custom project.**

   In order to experiment with several features, select both Safari and Mobile Safari, but work in the Mobile Safari environment for now.

   Your new Dashcode project looks like Figure 6-11.

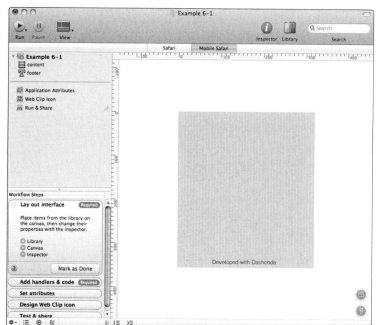

Figure 6-11:
Create a
new Custom
project for
Safari and
Mobile
Safari.

2. **Add a button to your canvas from the Library.**

   It doesn't matter what kind of button you choose or where you put it. In Figure 6-12, you can see that I used the lozenge button for this example. Guidelines appear when the button is centered or aligned with other interface elements.

You'll notice that the button clings to the top of the view. Remember that you can choose document flow for positioning elements (that is, top-to-bottom with lower elements being automatically pushed down if higher-up elements are resized to be larger) or absolute positioning. By default, buttons go into your product with document flow positioning. You can change that later, but for now, leave it as is so that you can see exactly how a button behaves with no customizations.

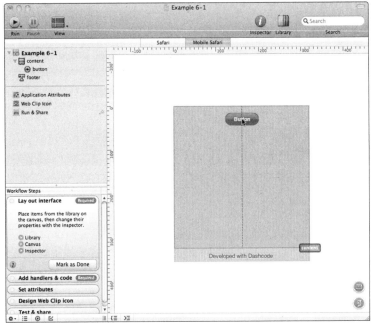

Figure 6-12:
Add a button.

3. **Click Run in the upper left corner of the Dashcode window.**

4. **If you're asked if the simulator application should accept incoming messages, as shown in Figure 6-13, click Allow.**

   If you've previously run the simulator application since the last time you logged in, you don't see this message.

Figure 6-13:
Run the project in the simulator application.

5. Click the button to see the visual feedback.

To further investigate the feedback, click and hold the button so that you see the effect that remains until you release the mouse button. All this functionality is built into the button objects. You can use the Library to drag a photo into your project. Run the simulator application and click the photo, and you see that you get no visual feedback: it's not a button, but you're able to add a behavior to it so that it performs a function. The built-in button feedback is specific to the button objects.

Making the button useful

Now you can implement behavior to move content from one field to another when the button is clicked. (I discussed this behavior in Chapter 4 without the use of a button.)

1. **Select the button you added to the project in the preceding section.**

2. **Using the Metrics inspector, change the button's Layout positioning to Absolute so that you can move it wherever you want on the canvas.**

3. **From the Text parts in the Library, add a text field to the canvas.**

   Using the Attributes inspector, change its name to `source`, as shown in Figure 6-14.

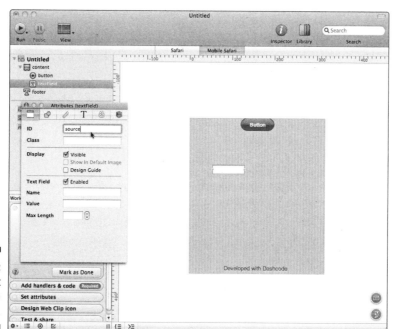

Figure 6-14:
Add a text field to the canvas.

TIP

4. Add another text field and name it destination.

You can speed up the process if you select the first text field and use Edit⇨Duplicate or ⌘-D to duplicate it. Then just change its name.

5. Rearrange the fields and button, using the guides to align them.

REMEMBER

If you have any problems, check the Metrics inspector to see whether any of the objects has Document Flow positioning set. If so, change it to Absolute. As part of the cleanup, you can double-click the button and change its name from Button to Switch (or anything else you want). You can also select the button and use the Attributes inspector to change its label. Both have the same effect.

The canvas should look like Figure 6-15 at this point.

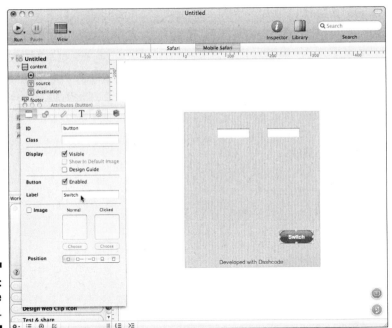

Figure 6-15:
Clean up the interface.

6. Show the Behaviors inspector by selecting the button on the canvas, as shown in Figure 6-16.

7. In the Handlers column, double-click next to the onclick event.

In the editable field that appears, type the name of the handler that will respond to this event, as shown in Figure 6-16. A good name is switch-ButtonHandler. The conventions are as follows:

- Handler names begin with a lowercase letter.

- Words that make up the name are in camel case (capitals at the beginning of each word except the first and no embedded blanks).

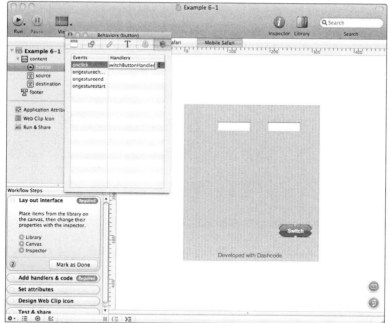

Figure 6-16: Create the handler.

When you click out of the text field, the handler is created. You see a right-pointing arrow next to the name; clicking it shows you the code. If the Code pane at the bottom of the canvas isn't visible, drag it up from the bottom, as shown in Figure 6-17.

Dashcode has created a JavaScript function for you that shows you where to insert the code. Don't worry about writing the code: You can drag the code in from the Library.

8. **In the Library, select Code from the tabs, choose Text from the menu, and then locate Get Text Field Text from the snippets, as shown in Figure 6-18.**

9. **Using the icon for Get Text Field Text in the upper pane of the Library, drag the code snippet into your code and place it just below the `Insert Code Here` comment, as shown in Figure 6-19.**

10. **Using the same process, drag the Set Text Field Text code snippet into your code and place it beneath the Get Text Field code.**

    The code will probably need some reformatting, but don't worry. Just make sure that you drag each snippet below the previous one, as shown in Figure 6-20.

11. **Clean up the code.**

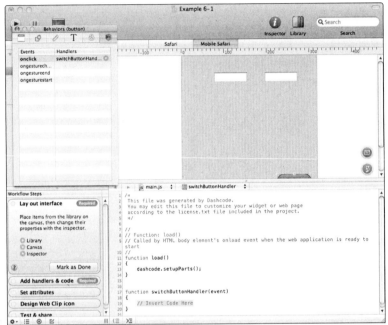

Figure 6-17:
Go to the
code.

Figure 6-18:
Locate Get
Text Field
Text from
the code
snippets in
the Library.

Figure 6-19:
Drag the code snippet into the project.

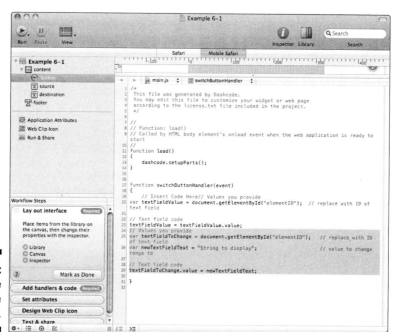

Figure 6-20:
Add the other code snippet.

The easiest way is to notice that the two slashes (//) introduce a comment. In the code snippets, these slashes often appear at the right-hand side of a line of code, but when you drag them into your project, the lines may be too long. Just insert a return character before each //, and the code looks like it does in Figure 6-21.

12. **Replace the variables in the snippets: change the source field ID.**

    Take a look at those comments, and you see what you have to change. The first comment you deal with is `replace with ID of text field`. It follows this line of code:

    ```
    var textFieldValue = document.getElementById("elementID");
    ```

    This code gets the value of the text field that you want to move to the destination. Change `elementID` to `source`. (It's part of the first code snippet, Get Text Field Text.)

    To avoid confusion, remove the comment after you've made the change.

13. **Replace the variables in the snippets: change the destination field ID.**

    Look for the next `replace with ID of text field`. It follows this line of code:

    ```
    var textFieldToChange = document.getElementById("elementID");
    ```

    This code gets the text field that you want to use to receive the value. Change `elementID` to `destination` and remove the comment.

    Because you're combining two snippets, a certain amount of duplication occurs. You can simplify matters a bit. In the first snippet, the value of the source field is stored in a JavaScript variable called `textFieldValue`. In the second code snippet, the destination field is set to a variable called `newTextFieldText`. You already have that value in `textFieldValue` from the first code snippet so you can simplify matters.

14. **Delete the following:**

    ```
    var newTextFieldText = "String to display";



    // value to change range to
    ```

15. **Set the destination field to the value of the first field:**

    Change

    ```
    textFieldToChange.value = newTextFieldText;
    ```

    to

    ```
    textFieldToChange.value = textFieldValue;
    ```

16. **Save the project.**

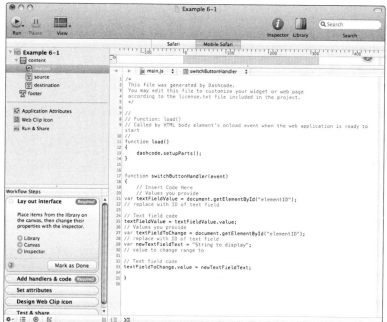

Figure 6-21:
Clean up the code.

17. **Run the project in the simulator application with the Run button in the upper left corner of the window; click in the first field.**

    Because the first field is a text field that can receive data, the keyboard appears (see Figure 6-22).

18. **Click Done to hide the keyboard.**

19. **Now click Switch.**

    The data moves into the destination field.

Taking stock

You have implemented a button to switch the text in two fields. This type of process is repeated over and over with buttons and handlers. Here it is in summary form:

1. **Create the fields you need to act on such as the text fields, giving them unique and meaningful IDs.**

Figure 6-22:
Enter text.

Dashcode ensures that the IDs are unique, but you have to make them meaningful rather than just `textField1`, `textField2`, and so on.

You need to create these objects and give them IDs so that you can customize the code.

2. **Create the button to perform the action and give it a unique and meaningful ID.**

   Also, give the button a label that makes sense to users. You must create the button before you can provide an `onclick` handler for it.

3. **Select the button and in the Behaviors inspector, double-click next to `onclick` to create a handler, and give it a name.**

   Use the right-pointing arrow to show the shell of the handler in the Code pane of the window.

4. **Drag code snippets from the Library into the handler you created in Step 3.**

   Look for comments in the areas you must customize. The most frequent customization is replacing something like `elementID` with the ID of the elements that you created in Step 1.

5. **Clean up and run the simulator application.**

Chapter 7

Viewing the Interface

The Library provides you the parts and code snippets you need to build powerful apps and widgets. You have additional tools to help make the interface more attractive and easier to use. Looking at the interface critically and improving it is what this chapter is all about.

Aligning, Distributing, and Setting Layers for Objects with Graphics Tools

The graphics tools are your guides for placing objects and help you get and keep things organized.

Dashcode gives you five primary graphics tools for arranging objects on your canvas:

- ✔ **Autoguides**
- ✔ **Front-to-Back Arrangement**
- ✔ **Alignment and Distribution**
- ✔ **Locking**
- ✔ **Guides**

Autoguides

Autoguides are the dotted blue lines that appear as you move objects on the canvas. When an object you're moving is aligned with other objects at their center, top, bottom, or one side, these guides appear. As you continue to move an object, the autoguides may disappear, and new ones appear. Figure 7-1 shows autoguides in action.

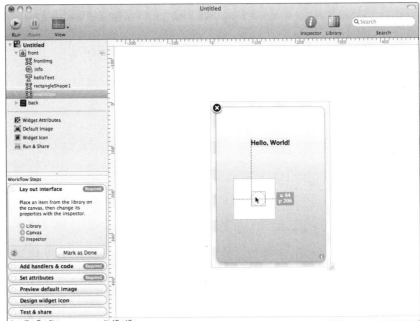

Figure 7-1: Autoguides help you place objects on the canvas.

You can turn autoguides on and off by choosing View➪Show/Hide Autoguides.

Front-to-Back Arrangement

In addition to autoguides, you can use layers to arrange objects in two dimensions on the canvas. The canvas has layers from front to back. Unless they're transparent, objects in front of other objects hide all or part of the objects behind them, just as in the natural world.

The Arrange menu provides you with four commands that work on any objects you select:

- ✔ **Bring Forward**
- ✔ **Bring to Front**
- ✔ **Move Backward**
- ✔ **Move to Back**

These commands let you construct sophisticated interfaces, but, as you do so, you may outsmart yourself. How do you select an object that is behind another one in order to move it or change other settings?

The answer is the navigator at the left of the Dashcode window. Whatever is selected on the canvas is selected in the navigator. On the canvas, an object may be hidden behind another one (or may even have its settings configured so that it's invisible), but in the navigator, the object is right there with its label and an icon indicating what type of object it is.

Watch the navigator as you use the front-to-back commands from the Arrange menu, and you'll see that within a set of objects, the last one in the list is the one in the front. With this object selected, choose Arrange⟹ Move to Back, and the object jumps to the top of that section.

You can drag objects in the navigator (see Figure 7-2). Be careful because you can position these objects inside other objects or above and below, as shown in Figure 7-2. If you just want to reorder an object, make certain that you move the object between two others and not inside one. If you do make a mistake, remember the Undo command!

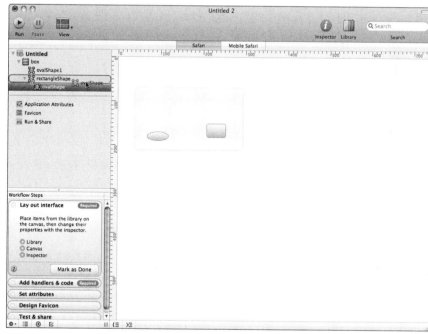

Figure 7-2: Manage front-to-back arrangement from the navigator.

Alignment and Distribution

Sometimes letting Dashcode do the work for you is easier than doing it yourself. Select two or more objects on the canvas and use the Arrange menu commands to align or distribute them.

If you select two or more objects on the canvas, you can use any of the commands in the Arrange⇨Align submenu:

- ✔ **Left**
- ✔ **Center**
- ✔ **Right**
- ✔ **Top**
- ✔ **Middle**
- ✔ **Bottom**

The selected objects move as you require.

A companion command, Arrange⇨Distribute, spreads the horizontal or vertical spacing of the centers of selected objects.

Locking

You can choose Arrange⇨Lock to lock one or more objects on the canvas. (If a selected object is locked, the command changes to Arrange⇨Unlock.)

Here's how you can assemble a set of objects, such as the horizontal sliders that are shown in the Fill & Stroke inspector Effects tab, shown in Figure 7-3:

1. **Add four horizontal sliders to your canvas for Shine, Tone, Horizon, and Curvature.**

2. **Position the top left object (Shine, in this case) exactly where you want it and lock it by choosing Arrange⇨Lock.**

   Now the object won't move.

3. **Drag what will be the lowest slider to what will be the bottom of the set of sliders.**

4. **Select all four sliders.**

5. **Choose Arrange⇨Align⇨Left.**

   Because the top slider is locked, the others move horizontally to be aligned under the top slider.

Figure 7-3:
Creating
aligned and
distributed
objects as
in the Fill
& Stroke
inspector
interface.

6. **Lock the bottom slider by choosing Arrange⇨Lock.**

7. **Select all four sliders.**

8. **Choose Arrange⇨Distribute⇨Vertically.**

   With their left edges aligned and the top and bottom sliders locked,
   the other two are distributed in the space between the top one and the
   bottom one (refer to Figure 7-2).

9. **Lock all the sliders to prevent accidentally moving them.**

Guides

In addition to automatic guides, you can create your own guides to help you
arrange items on the canvas. Simply click anywhere in a ruler at the top or
side of the canvas and then drag onto the canvas. A horizontal or vertical line
appears. Drag that line to the location you want the guide, as shown in Figure 7-4.

You can position objects against the guide. Sometimes this positioning is
easier than aligning the objects directly. When you finish with a guide, you
can drag it back to the ruler, and it disappears.

You also can show or hide guides by choosing View⇨Show/Hide Guides.

If you don't see the rulers, you can't drag a guide from them onto the canvas.
Choose View⇨Show/Hide Rulers to control the rulers' visibility.

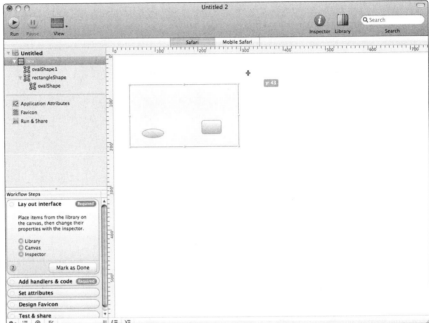

Figure 7-4:
Use your
own guides.

Packing Up Your Interface in Containers and Groups

If you want to organize information, you can use graphic, groups, and containers.

Using graphics to organize information

One of the time-honored ways of organizing information is to use graphics, such as separator lines or enclosing boxes. You can use these to indicate groups of items that belong together. If you really want to be fancy, you can add a color to the box so that the items within it stand out as a clear group.

As you see in the Library, you have shapes that you can use in this way. Just place them on your canvas and position other elements, such as buttons or text, within them to make a logical and attractive whole.

Grouping objects to organize information

Many programs let you *group* objects together so that you can drag them around as a whole. A standard way of grouping is to take a shape, add your buttons or text, and then group them all together with a group command.

Grouping is the graphics-oriented way of doing things. Remember that in Dashcode, everything that you're dealing with is an object, and every Dashcode object can have events and behaviors associated with it so that you can call JavaScript into play as needed.

Using Dashcode containers to organize information

In Dashcode, you can also use containers to organize information. Unlike a purely graphics-oriented approach of grouping things together, you actually place buttons, fields, and other elements *inside* containers. Then, when you move the container, the objects inside it move. You don't have to do any grouping: The objects are truly inside the container in the same ways that eggs are in an egg carton.

Dashcode provides a variety of containers for the different types of products that you can create. Figure 7-5 shows the Library containers for Dashboard widgets. These containers are available for most of the other product types, and the other product types also add their own containers to the basic set.

The two most basic containers in Figure 7-5 are the box and rounded box. The box and rounded box look very much like the rectangle and rounded rectangle shapes in the shapes pop-up of the Library. In fact, if you drag the rectangle and rounded rectangle shapes from the Library onto your canvas, you can make them look exactly like those containers.

Comparing containers and shapes

The following steps demonstrate the difference between a shape and a container. These steps use the Custom template for Dashboard widgets, but they work with any template.

1. **Drag a shape, such as a rounded rectangle shape, from the Library onto the canvas.**

   The shape is selected as soon as you release the mouse button.

2. **In the Fill & Stroke inspector Style tab, change the Fill from Gradient to Solid, as shown in Figure 7-6.**

3. **Click in the color well beneath the Fill pop-up menu to open the Color Picker and choose white.**

4. **In the Stroke section at the bottom of the inspector, change the color to black by clicking in the color well.**

   Now the shapes look exactly like the container.

5. **Drag an ellipse shape from the Library onto the canvas and change its Fill & Stroke settings in the same way.**

6. **Drag this shape inside the rectangle.**

   Notice how guidelines appear so that you can position the shape in the vertical center of the rectangle and align it with the edge of the text. As you drag the ellipse around, different guides appear relative to other objects on the canvas.

7. **For the grand finale, drag the rectangle away (like a magician pulling a tablecloth out from underneath a plate).**

   Actually the same thing happens as with the magician: You can drag the rectangle wherever you want, but that ellipse is going to stay where it is.

Now repeat the process with a box container (not a shape) and the same ellipse. When you drag the container away, the shape stays within the container.

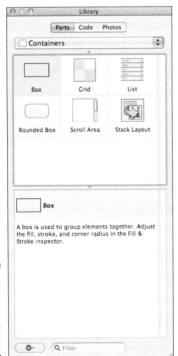

Figure 7-5:
Use basic containers from the Library.

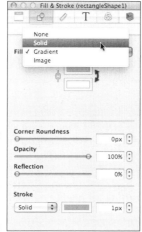

Figure 7-6:
Make a
shape look
like a
container.

Using runtime containers

You can create other widget containers by dragging them from the Library and setting their attributes just as you would any other parts. However, most of the time, you actually populate the containers at runtime using JavaScript code that you write or drag from the Code section of the Library.

For widgets, these additional containers, shown earlier in Figure 7-5, are

- ✔ **Scroll Area:** This container can have a horizontal or vertical scroll bar (or both). Use the Attributes inspector to automatically hide the scroll bars. Depending on the size of the scroll area's content, this behavior is the default.

- ✔ **Grid:** This container is a grid of cells, each one of which contains an image and a title.

- ✔ **List:** This container is in many ways a grid that has only one column to it.

- ✔ **Stack Layout:** This container is a complex set of views that provides navigation tools for users and organizational tools for you.

The following section describes the basics of using these containers. You can find out more about using them at runtime in Part III.

Organizing Information with Scroll Areas, Lists, and Grids

Lists, grids, and scroll areas are all about making data easier to understand:

- ✔ **Provide visual organization for data:** Particularly when you're working in a limited space, such as the screen of iPhone or even iPad or a Dashboard widget, anything that provides visual organization is helpful to you and your users. The problem, of course, is that almost every visual element itself takes up space, which is what you're trying to conserve. (The primary exception is a background color or pattern that can indicate that the data placed in front of it is all organized together for some reason.)

- ✔ **Facilitate dynamic data placement:** You're not laying out data the way a page designer does for a printed page. In the case of a printed page, the designer knows what is going to be presented on that page. For apps and widgets, you frequently need to use code to automatically lay out dynamic data that is retrieved from a data source or generated by a calculation. I talk about this issue in this section.

Any organizing elements group similar items together. What that similarity is may not be obvious at first glance. For example, if your widget is displaying a list of movies and show times for a specific theater or city, or if your app is showing mail messages, you're dealing with like items (movie listings or mail messages), but you don't know how many items you have when you're laying out the interface. (You can create artificial limits by deciding to show only the first three movies or the last five messages, but those limits are work-arounds.)

Thus, runtime containers provide an answer to this question: Where do I (or my app) place the next item? These dynamic containers provide a structure that always answers that question, while each object provides a slightly different way of answering that question.

Scrolling forever with a scroll area

Just as on a desktop, the scroll bars in a scroll area or window let you look at an object that is larger than the scroll area or window itself. For Dashcode, the scrolling terminology is the same as it is for most interfaces. The scroll area itself can have horizontal and/or vertical scroll bars. The content that appears in the scroll area is a view (a *scrolled view*, if you want). If the view is the same size or smaller in either dimension than the scroll area, the scroll bar in that dimension is hidden or just not usable.

Although your interface layout arsenal has some very useful tools, you need to watch out for some issues that apply to all uses of scroll bars and not just to apps and widgets:

> ✔ **Scroll bars aren't helpful for small sizes of scrolled views.** If you have a scroll area with a view that is slightly larger than the scroll area, you have to scroll a short distance in order to see half of the first or last line of text. This extra scrolling isn't convenient: it's annoying.

> ✔ **Scroll bars are vague except for their ends.** You can quickly use a scroll bar to get to the top of the scrolled view or the bottom. If the view is displaying a 300-page document, good luck getting accurately to page 194. That's why many interfaces provide a number of additional feedback mechanisms. Unfortunately, as with everything in the world of apps and widgets, these feedback mechanisms take up space, and you're back where you started.

Despite these drawbacks, scroll areas can be very useful in many circumstances. For example, when the scrolled view doesn't contain separate objects but a large image, scroll bars are perfect. Who cares if you're a little bit off in positioning the scroll bars if you just want to see the part of the image with your dog in it?

Here's how to create a scroll area that contains several shapes. In real life, you wouldn't just use ellipses as in this example, and you'd lay out the scrolled view dynamically (probably using code snippets from the Library). Your real-life scroll area may contain a large image, or a good deal of text or, as is the case here, a variety of individual objects. However, these steps provide you with an overview of the techniques and issues for scroll areas.

To create a scroll area:

1. **In a Dashcode project, drag a scroll area from the containers section of the Library Parts pane to the canvas.**

   In this example, I used a Dashboard widget.

2. **Resize the scroll area so that it takes up a good part of the canvas.**

3. **From the Library, drag a shape, such as an ellipse, into the scroll area.**

   Make certain that the shape is inside the scroll area. Use the Navigation pane at the upper left corner of the Dashcode window to confirm that the shape is inside the scroll area.

4. Drag a few more objects into the scroll area, as shown in Figure 7-7.

Make certain that one of them is slightly outside the visible part of the scroll area. Don't worry if the object appears to be on top of the scroll bar; just make certain that it's contained in the scroll area, as shown in Figure 7-7.

The names for the various parts in Figure 7-7 are the default names generated by Dashcode. Note that the Metrics inspector shows that the selected ellipse is below the bottom edge of the scroll area — that's why its vertical coordinate is a negative number.

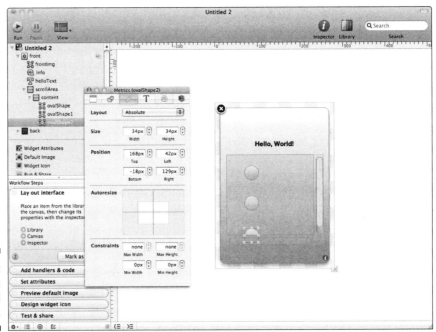

Figure 7-7:
Add a shape to the scroll area.

5. Run the project in the simulator using the Run button in the upper left corner of the Dashcode window.

You can use the scroll bars to move the partially-hidden object into and out of the scroll area. Compare Figure 7-7 with Figure 7-8, which shows the simulator in action.

That's all you need to do to create a scroll area. All the behaviors are built into the parts that you use from the Library, and you can wind up displaying much more information than the scroll area could display if it didn't have scroll bars.

If you're placing separate objects into the scroll area, you can do it at run-time with code snippets, but you will need to keep track of the coordinates of the last item you added so that the next one will be in the right place. (This is that "where do I put the next object?" issue.)

Making a list

A list provides an answer to the question of where to place the next object because the list itself contains more structure than a scroll area does. Experiment by dragging a List part from the Library onto your canvas. (You may want to either begin a new project or delete the scroll area or other parts you may have on the canvas.) Figure 7-9 shows a List part added to a widget.

Figure 7-8:
Experiment with the scroll area in the simulator.

The Attributes inspector lets you select the type of data displayed in the list. *Static data* is data you can create before the app or widget runs. Most often, you use an inspector to create static data. *Dynamic data* uses data sources (see Part III), and the data is generated or retrieved at runtime.

At the bottom of the Attributes inspector are the default values for labels and values. (These values are just like an HTML selector; if you're not used to selectors, don't worry.) As always with Dashcode, the interface responds to your changes. If you double-click the label for the first row in the list, you can edit it — perhaps changing Item 1 to My Item. Whether you change the label in the inspector or in the List part visible on the canvas, as soon as you click out of the field, the data changes in the other location, too.

By default, the labels and the data values are identical. So if you change the label `Item 1` to `My Item`, the corresponding value also changes to `My Item`. This process doesn't work in reverse. If you go on and change the value from `My Item` to `My Other Item`, the label is unchanged.

For example, when you choose from a list of choices for your hometown, you may want to select the item labeled Akron, Ohio. By separating the labels from the values, you can create a label called `Akron, Ohio` but give it a value of `327`. On the code side of things, `327` is easier to manipulate than the text for a city name, and by keeping the label (visible to the user) meaningful, you can then work with the numeric or other value.

This logic carries over into Dashcode. You can add or delete rows in the list by using the + and – buttons in the lower left corner of the Attributes inspector.

Notice in the navigator that the List part has a disclosure triangle to its left. Open it to disclose the parts it contains, as shown in Figure 7-10.

You see a `listRowTemplate` and a Text part called `rowLabel`. Both of these concepts are going to reappear in the context of other parts.

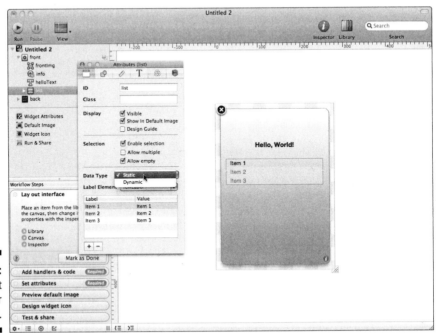

Figure 7-9:
Add a List part to your project.

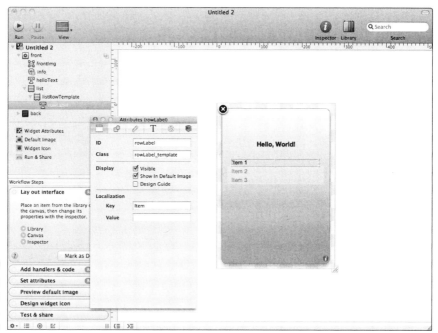

Figure 7-10:
Look inside
the List part.

The template provides settings that apply to every row in the list. For example, select the `listRowTemplate` and use the Fill & Stroke inspector to change its color. Every row in the part now changes color. Use the + to add another row to the list (it's on the Attributes inspector when the List part itself is selected), and that new row has the same color.

Now select `rowLabel` and examine it in the Attributes inspector, as shown in Figure 7-11. You can change its name by double-clicking it in the part or by changing the value of the Key field in the Attributes inspector.

Note that when you select `rowLabel` in the part, you can see the outline of the label field within the boundaries of the list row. Note, too, that you can select and change only that value for the first item in the list. To change other items, you need to write code.

The reason this field in the inspector is called Key is that you can use it for localization, a topic Chapter 18 explores. Once again, you can have a parallel structure of data that the user sees and data that you manipulate. If you use the localization tools, you can identify the row label as Name. If a user runs it in French, the key (Name) can be translated into *Nom* (the appropriate French word). The localization process is narrowed down to a list of keys that are basically the words in the original language and values for each translated language. This localization process means that you can give the list of keys to a translator who may not know JavaScript from a cup of tea but who does know the target and source languages.

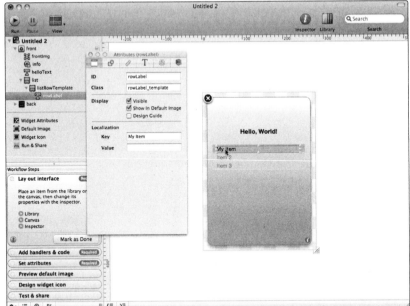

Figure 7-11:
Change the
attributes
for `row-
label`.

If you put all these pieces of the puzzle together, here is what you have inside the List part from the Library:

✔ **You set the outside boundaries and the location of a List part.**

✔ **You can use the Attributes inspector to set static data in a list:**

• Set the number of rows in the Attributes inspector.

• Set labels and values in the Attributes inspector. The values may be the same for each row, or they may be different with, for example, a human-readable label and a program-readable numeric or other value.

✔ **You can use dynamic data to set the number of rows and their values.** You can find out more in Part III.

✔ **Use the Fill & Stroke inspector as well as other inspectors to customize the `listRowTemplate` part within the list.** Each row has these settings.

• **You can customize the label for each row in the Attributes inspector with the `rowLabel` part selected.** You can also use these customizations to translate those labels (see Chapter 18).

Not bad for a single part in the Library!

Moving to the next dimension

A grid is basically a list in two dimensions. When you first drag it from the Library, the grid contains three cells. As you see in Figure 7-12, the grid may even be wider than your canvas.

Don't worry if the grid is too wide. Just resize the Grid part, and the cells automatically rearrange themselves within it, as shown in Figure 7-13.

Look in the navigator to see that you have the same basic structure as in the List part described in the previous section with a `gridCellTemplate`, `gridLabel`, and `gridImage`. The arrangement of grid cells in the two-dimensional structure is automatic based on your resizing of the grid, so you can place an image in a grid cell without any further ado. In fact, you can place two images in a grid cell.

Most of the time, you populate grids and lists dynamically, but you can customize the first cell to see how it will look. Take an image (perhaps a photo from the Library's Photos pane) and drag it into `gridCellTemplate`. (You may want to drag the image into the navigator because it gives you more precise control than the canvas.) As soon as you drag the photo into `gridCell-Template`, it appears as the background of each cell in the grid.

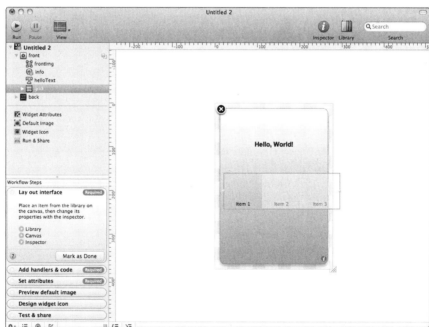

Figure 7-12:
The Grid part may be larger than your canvas.

`gridImage` is a separate field. When you start populating the grid with a script, you can set a different image for each cell. The position of the image is the difference between the template and the individual cells.

The Library contains more container fields, and they all work in basically the same way as the other examples throughout this book.

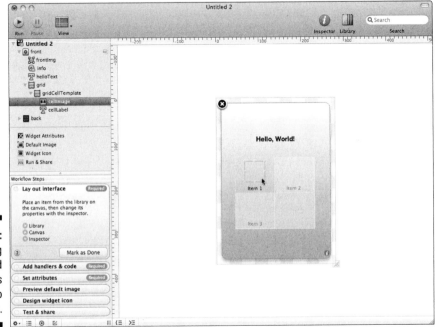

Figure 7-13:
Resizing
the Grid
part causes
its cells to
reflow.

Chapter 8

Finishing Up in Style

A lot of Dashcode's power comes from the fact that it helps you assemble all sorts of parts and components from the Library (your photos, Dashcode parts, and code snippets from both you and Dashcode; data from online and files you create); and — most important of all — your unique approach to the data, interface, and information that makes the final result useful to yourself and others.

Often the difference between a Dashcode project that looks, feels, and works with the best of them all comes from the tools and techniques I discuss in this chapter. Some of these items are finishing touches — the cherry on top of the wonderful dessert. Many of these tools and techniques are simple and require as little effort as putting that cherry on the ice cream sundae, but they often require a little planning and foresight. You need to plan ahead so that your Dashcode project gets the applause it deserves.

These tips and techniques focus on the project itself. In almost every case, the single most important aspect of a Dashcode project that determines its success is its basic idea. The old saying, "You can't make a silk purse out of a sow's ear" applies to Dashcode projects, too. If you don't have a clear idea of what you want to do and the benefits that it can provide to users, all the decoration and user interface elements can't disguise that fact (and, if they can, it's only for a short time).

It's Your Own Fault if You Don't Use Defaults

The first two parts of this book cover some of the settings and options for your Dashcode projects. Many of these settings come with default values, which, in many cases, are excellent choices.

At least at the beginning, avoid the temptation to change default settings until you've experimented with them. Create an uncustomized application or widget from a template and see what you have with the defaults. Often, you find that the default settings provide functionality that you haven't even thought of — and you get it for free.

After you're more experienced, you'll probably develop a preference for certain settings that you often use with your apps and widgets. You don't want everything to be the same, but you receive a definite benefit when you set guidelines and standards for the look and feel of your Dashcode projects. (If nothing else, these guidelines make it easier for people to learn how to use them and even what features they can find in your projects.)

The workflow steps in the lower left corner of the Dashcode window help you keep track of what you've done on the project. (You may have to show the list from the View menu or from View in the toolbar). Even if you have your own way of working and keeping track of your status with another tool, make it a habit to keep the Steps list up to date and to check it out from time to time so that nothing falls through the cracks.

The following sections describe the attributes and settings for each type of Dashcode project. Many of the attributes and settings (such as the project name) apply equally to Dashboard widgets, Safari, and mobile Safari. However, each environment often requires little tweaks, so make certain that you're looking at the right type of project as you're setting up your own Dashcode project.

Keeping track of projects with Bento

Apps and widgets are often connected to projects and tasks that you and others may be carrying out. You can keep track of a project's overall status in many ways ranging from pencil notes on a pad to arrows and diagrams on a white board — or, if you really want to be elegant, a Bento library. Bento from FileMaker (which is owned by Apple) is a terrific tool for keeping track of Dashcode projects and the related tasks that may be involved. You can find it at www.filemaker.com/bento in a version for Mac OS X ($49) or a version for iPad ($5). You can synchronize the two versions or use either one on its own.

Before jumping into the attributes, look at the navigator at the left of the Dashcode window, shown in Figure 8-1. You can use the View menu or View on the toolbar to show and hide various components, but the top of the Navigator always has the project's objects, and, below that, you always find links to parts of the project. The first item is always attributes — the label is Widget Attributes for Dashboard widgets and Application Attributes for Safari and mobile Safari. The final item is always Run & Share. The intermediate items depend on the type of project.

Figure 8-1: Set Widget attributes.

Setting Dashboard Widget Attributes

Dashboard widgets are where Dashcode got its start (as well as where iPhone Web apps got their start, too). These widgets are a good place to start looking at settings and attributes. (Refer to Figure 8-1 to see the attribute settings for a Dashboard widget.)

The attributes in Figure 8-1 are for the Maps widget template as it is when you first create a project from it. Dashcode attempts to fill in something for every attribute that is essential so that you can often run your app or widget as soon as you create it. Sometimes, you can't fill in every attribute. For example, with an RSS app, you need to specify the RSS feed to use.

However, the templates often have code to work around missing attributes. Take a look at the RSS widget template shown in Figure 8-2. If you haven't provided an RSS feed, the template can run and post an error message.

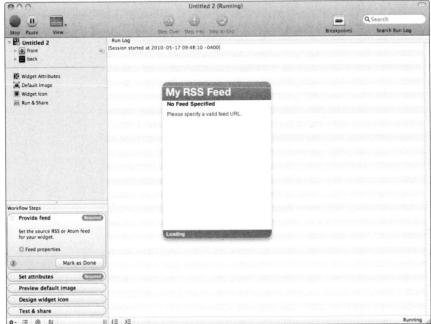

Figure 8-2: The templates try to work around missing attributes.

Creating a project from a template and deliberately leaving out data can be a worthwhile endeavor. Look at the error message that appears and then track down the code to see how that error message is created. These basic error messages provide good examples of how to handle runtime errors.

For example, in the Maps template, you need a key to the Google maps API in order to access it. An error message appears if you run an unmodified Maps project (see Figure 8-3).

Figure 8-3: Error messages can contain links so that users can correct problems.

Not only do you have an error message, but you also have a button that lets you deal with it. In this case, clicking the Get a Key button takes you to the appropriate Google page so that you can register for an API key.

Chapter 17 shows you how to find these built-in error handlers in your project code.

The attributes for all types of Dashcode projects are arranged in groups. The following sections describe the groups for widgets.

Identifying your widget

This section includes a unique identifier for your widget and a unique number for the specific version of the widget. The version starts automatically at 1.0.

The unique identifier for your widget has to be globally unique — that is, no other identifier in the world can be the same. This requirement exists because you can share widgets via e-mail and the Web. If someone installs your widget on a Mac in Peru, its name must be unique so that no matter where the widget is used, it's not confused with other widgets.

This problem has been around for a while and was addressed when Java was first developed. Java, too, required unique names for its components that could be developed anywhere in the world. The solution for Java and for many other uses including widgets is to use *reverse-DNS* notation.

Reverse-DNS notation starts with the assumption that you have a domain name or have access to one. (If you don't, see the suggestion in the sidebar "What to do if you don't have a domain name.")

Domain names are unique, thanks to a system of authorities and registrars, each of which is responsible for a set of names (the .com, .edu, or .org domains, for example). Registrars can assign names that are unique within their area. After someone registers a domain (mycompany.com, for example), he can assign *subdomains* at will. Thus, at mycompany.com, you may be responsible for assigning subdomains, such as marketing.mycompany.com and production.mycompany.com.

This process ensures that each domain and subdomain/domain combination is unique. This top-down process relies on delegated authority to ensure the uniqueness.

Reverse-DNS notation starts from a domain or subdomain and reverses it. Because mycompany.com is unique, com.mycompany is also unique. Whoever is in charge of mycompany.com can allow people to add their own extensions. Thus, you can create a widget called mywidget and give it a unique identifier that is `com.mycompany.mywidget`. The domain name is reversed for a number of reasons, including that reversed domain names can be sorted easily. In addition, the reversal makes it clear that the reversed-DNS names aren't domain names. Presumably, no one will type `com.my company` into a browser and expect to see a Web page.

The extension at the end of reverse-DNS isn't an address; it's just your widget name that is made unique be prefixing it with your reverse-DNS. Dashcode prepares a possibly unique identifier by taking your Mac OS X account name, prefixing it with `com` and adding `widget` to it. A variety of companies use this strategy of creating globally unique names in several contexts.

Figure 8-1, shown earlier in the chapter, shows a just-created widget project for a user running under the account name iWork. The widget is constructed with

- ✔ `com`
- ✔ `iWork` (the Mac OS X account name)
- ✔ `widget`
- ✔ `Untitled` (the name of the unsaved project)

The widget name that is constructed here is a best guess at a unique identifier. The name remains until you change it. If you save the project and rename it `mywidget`, the identifier doesn't change. It remains `com.iWork.widget.Untitled`. You can manually change the name to `com.iWork.widget.mywidget`, and you should do so at the first opportunity so that you have a unique identifier.

What to do if you don't have a domain name

Reverse-DNS starts from a unique domain name. If you don't have a domain name, you need to construct one. Fortunately, for many widgets, if the name isn't unique and you're not distributing your widgets, you can ignore the issue, but it's likely to crop up at the most inconvenient times.

One way to deal with the issue is to talk to someone who does have a domain name and ask whether you can use it as a prefix for your widgets. You can even arrange that the prefix will include your name or some other identifier. You aren't asking for actual Web addresses, so you really can't do any damage.

Many schools and other organizations have already set up reverse-DNS standards, so you may have access to a unique reverse-DNS-based prefix.

Allowing data access

Widgets can access data over a network (either a LAN or the Internet) as well as on disk. You need to indicate whether your widget uses either of these accesses. Either, both, or none are allowed. Widgets that don't use either type of access are those that use no external data — a calculator or game is a good example as long as scores aren't recorded and external data, such as a currency exchange rate, isn't needed.

Adding extensions to your widget

In Dashboard, you normally access widgets directly after you go into Dashboard itself (often with the default F4 or F12 key — you can set this setting in File➪System Preferences). However, you can allow an Internet plug-in, the Java programming language, or the command line in the Terminal application to access your widget.

Using plug-ins with your widget

You can also add plug-ins to your project. These plug-ins can be standard browser plug-ins, or you can build your own plug-ins using Xcode. If you build your own plug-ins with Xcode, you start from the Cocoa Bundle template.

Setting your widget's properties

Each template has its own set of properties, such as the RSS feed in the RSS templates and, in the Maps template the API Key, initial address to map, a URL for the mashup, and an option to reformat the map's marker descriptions.

In templates such as RSS and Maps, defaults fill in the essential properties. Properties needed to successfully run the widget may not be filled in, but error messages allow users to fill them in at runtime.

 The message you should take away from this structure is that your widget shouldn't fail. Somehow or other, the widget should allow the user to continue. (You find this refrain throughout this book.)

Localizing your widget

This section lets you associate localized terms for terms that you use in your widget. These terms are key/value pairs. The key is the term that you use in your widget's code. You provide a separate value for each key for each language. At runtime, the appropriate value is plugged into the interface. Chapter 18 talks about localization, which is available for apps as well as widgets.

Setting Safari Web Application Attributes

The attributes for a Safari Web application, shown in Figure 8-4, are much simpler than the attributes for a Dashboard widget — and also simpler than the attributes for a mobile Safari Web application. The basic setting is the page title, which is displayed just as any Web page title is displayed — in the browser's window frame.

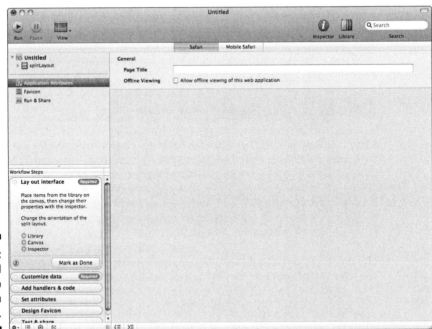

Figure 8-4:
Control
Safari Web
application
settings.

The option to view the application offline reflects Dashcode's support of the HTML 5 *manifest* specification. If your users don't have an Internet connection (or if they lose it as they're using your Safari application), they may be able to continue working if you select this checkbox. In a nutshell, what happens is that where possible, the files for your Web application are stored in the files that are deployed to your Web server. If the connection doesn't exist or is lost, HTML 5-compliant browsers know where to look for these files and can show them to the user on demand.

Obviously, files that include references to online databases or other dynamic data can't function without the Internet, but in many cases, static files allow you to implement much of your project. Dashcode automatically takes care of storing these files in the folder that you deploy to your Web server if this box is checked.

What's in HTML 5?

HTML (Hypertext Markup Language) is the language used for coding Web pages. HTML has evolved over time into a powerful and easy-to-use language that is implemented behind the scenes in Web design programs that use a graphical user interface.

In the olden days of the Web, many people learned how to write HTML by hand, and a lot of people still use the handwritten route for developing Web pages. (You, of course, are using Dashcode so you may never even see the HTML you're creating, but it's there helping Safari to display your applications and apps.)

During the 1990s, HTML evolved fairly quickly and implemented features, such as security, that most people now take for granted. Web designers and software engineers pushed the boundaries of HTML rapidly to provide ever-more-sophisticated Web browsing adventures. In fact, they often pushed right through the boundaries. For some types of functionality, such as displaying video in browser windows, the HTML standard was extended in various ways by various people, and these ways weren't always consistent and compatible.

Also, Web designers thought of features that would be useful in the next version of HTML, whatever it may be and whenever it may appear. The uncertainty was due to many things that were happening in the Web world. One major plan for moving on from HTML was to move to a related language called XHTML which was being designed to tighten up some issues that had emerged with HTML as time wore on.

Not everyone was ecstatic with XHTML, and the notion of simply moving to a new version of HTML gained traction. That notion turned into the plan to move to HTML 5, which is what is happening. Among the major changes in HTML 5 are the addition of storage features and a new way of handling embedded media, such as video. This new way of handling embedded media is built into the HTML 5 specification and doesn't require the use of third-party plug-ins such as Flash.

Apple is a firm supporter of HTML 5 and its associated technologies, which is one reason why Flash isn't implemented on iPhone or iPad. With Dashcode, your Safari Web applications will be ready for HTML 5.

Users must be using a browser that implements HTML 5 in order for this arrangement to work.

Setting Mobile Safari Application Attributes

Figure 8-5 shows the mobile Safari attributes. The page title and offline viewing options are the same as for a Safari application (see preceding section), but beyond that, you have settings that are specific to iPhone.

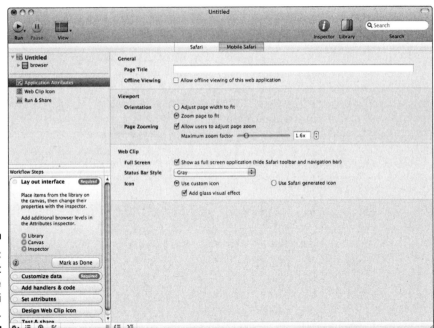

Figure 8-5: Adjust mobile Safari attributes.

Managing the Viewport

The *viewport* is the rectangle in which content is displayed (or is *rendered*, if you want to be technical). In a Web browser, you can adjust the size and shape of the viewport by resizing the browser's window.

On a device such as iPhone, you can't resize the window, so the viewport's size is fixed — that is, until you rotate your iPhone. The size of the viewport remains the same, but its height and width are swapped as the iPhone moves from a horizontal to vertical orientation.

What happens to the content of the viewport is up to you: The viewport orientation settings let you manage its behavior. You have two choices, as you can see in Figure 8-5:

✔ Adjust

✔ Zoom

The simplest way to demonstrate the difference between these two settings is to walk through an example of each one, showing how the content automatically changes based on the settings:

1. **Create a mobile Safari Web application using the Custom template.**

   The Custom template is the one with a totally blank canvas to start.

2. **Check that the orientation option is set to Zoom.**

   Zoom is the default for mobile Safari.

3. **Using the Library, drag a photo onto the canvas, as shown in Figure 8-6.**

   For the best demonstration of the viewport orientation options, choose a photo that is wider than the viewport. As you drag it over the viewport, it automatically resizes to the width of the viewport.

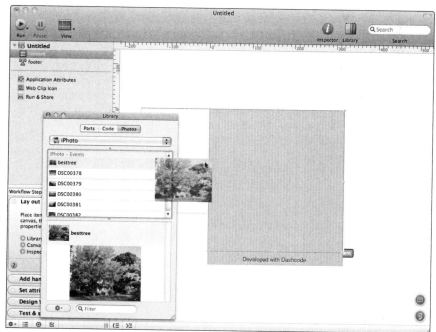

Figure 8-6:
Drag a wide
photo from
the Library
onto the
canvas.

You can drag a photo over the canvas, but you can place it only in the viewport. If you release the mouse button at any other place, the photo snaps back into the Library.

When you've placed the photo, the resized image appears (see Figure 8-7).

4. **Click Run in the upper left corner of the Dashcode window to start the simulator, as shown in Figure 8-8.**

The Dashcode window provides a good approximation of your app's appearance as you develop it. The simulator provides a much better approximation of your app's appearance, but nothing can substitute for testing it on an iPhone. At this stage, though, the simulator is just fine.

5. **Rotate the simulator by choosing Hardware⇨Rotate Right.**

Figure 8-9 shows the result. If you don't see the Hardware menu, click the simulator image to make certain that the simulator is the frontmost application. (You can tell the simulator is the frontmost application because the menu to the right of the Apple menu will be the iPhone Simulator menu.)

6. **Stop the simulator with the Stop button in the upper left corner of the Dashcode window.**

7. **Go back to Application Attributes and change viewport orientation to Adjust Page Width to Fit.**

8. **Rerun the simulator and rotate it to the right as you did in Steps 4 and 5.**

Figure 8-10 shows the result.

Two things are going on here. When you choose the Zoom option, the image zooms to fill the width of the screen, as shown in Figure 8-9. With Adjust Page Width, the image stays the same size it started as, and the page width is adjusted to reflect the new width of the viewport.

In either case, part of the image may be out of sight. Depending on the size of the image and the option you set, a different part of the image may be out of sight.

Figure 8-7:
The image is
resized.

Figure 8-8:
Use the
simulator.

The default setting is Zoom for a reason: Zoom makes your mobile Safari Web application look better for users. When you adjust the page width, the focus is on the page, and it seems to most users that they're looking at a Web page (which they are). When you zoom the image, most users think that they're looking at an iPhone app (which they aren't, but you usually want them to think that they are).

The simplest way to handle this issue is to leave the default setting and be done with it. One case in which you may want to change the default is if your content is text or a table. Those items may look better if the page width is adjusted.

As you focus on rotation of the viewport, you're focusing in a way that most of your users won't. You can easily make a choice that isn't intuitive to your users. As you experiment, do reality checks with real people who haven't looked at your app for hours on end.

I discuss using the simulator in more detail in Chapter 18.

Setting Web clip options

The Web clip options help you refine your app's appearance. In most cases, you can start with the defaults and then customize them, if needed.

Hiding the Safari toolbar and Navigation bar means that users have less of the Web experience and more of the iPhone app experience. (If you also use Adjust Page Width To Fit as the orientation setting, you reinforce the app-ness of your project.) The default setting is Adjust Page Width To Fit, which works for most people.

To further differentiate your Web app from a Web page, you can create your own icon (see Chapter 18). If you let Safari generate an icon for you, it generates a small version of your first page. This generated icon isn't the default, but it's the fastest way of getting your project up and running.

One advantage of using a default icon at this point is that you can get the project up and running and then let a graphics designer look at it and work on a custom icon while you're refining the functionality.

Using Run & Share

After you've got your basic project started, you need to test it. That's where Run & Share comes into play. Deploying a Dashboard widget and a Safari application aren't the same process, however. The widget is deployed by installing it on your Mac, and the Safari Web application needs to be deployed on a server. In both cases, you can create a set of files that you can deploy manually and share with others.

Deploying your widget

When you're ready to test your widget, click Run & Share. Figure 8-11 shows your options.

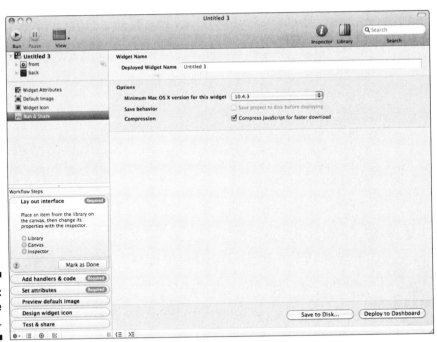

Figure 8-11:
Run & Share
for a widget.

If you haven't already, save your project. (If you haven't saved it, the Save Project to Disk Before Deploying option isn't available.)

TIP

You also should name your widget. You don't have to name it, but if you don't, you'll soon wind up with several widgets with various untitled names, which will be hard to track.

Do you want a package with that bundle?

A *package* is a directory that can contain files and folders but that appears in the Finder as a single file with its own icon. When you Control-click that icon, you bring up a shortcut menu that includes the Show Package Contents command. If you choose that command, the top level of the internal package directory is shown in a Finder window, and you can navigate through it just as you would through any files and folders. A *bundle* is a directory that contains files and folders for an application. The terms aren't synonymous, but they're very close. Because the command in the shortcut menu is Show Package Contents and not Show Bundle Contents, I usually use the word "package." Developers usually use the word "bundle."

In the lower right corner of the Run & Share window, you can save the project to disk or deploy it to Dashboard. Note that saving the widget to disk isn't the same as saving the project. The Dashcode project contains all the files within it; when you save it to disk, you wind up with a wdgt package that contains all the files. As always, the package appears as a single file, which you can send to other people via e-mail.

If you want to deploy the widget manually, drag the wdgt package to ~/ Library/Widgets in your root directory. If you want the widget to be available to all accounts and users on your Mac (unless they're prevented from having Dashboard access in System Preferences), drag it to /Library/Widgets at the root level of your hard disk. If you distribute your widget to others, they can install it the same way either for all accounts and users or for an individual user.

You can also choose which version of Mac OS X you want to use as a minimum for your widget. This choice matters if you're using new features of Mac OS X; you want to make certain that your widget is deployed only where it can run.

As with most settings, the defaults are fine except for the widget name.

Deploying a Safari application

Whether it's Safari or mobile Safari, you need to deploy your Dashcode project to a Web server. If you have a MobileMe account, you can easily deploy it there using Dashcode. You also can deploy it to the Sites folder in your Home directory on your Mac. That Sites folder is where you place the files that you want to place on the Web site that is automatically available to your account. You can access the Sites folder, of course, and other people on your network can access it. If you have an IP address that is visible to the outside world, anyone with that IP address can get to it.

You have to do some of this work only once. If you've already set up a local Web server (or if you have a local Web server or MobileMe account set up), refer to the section "Doing the Deployment," later in this chapter.

Setting up a local Web server

You use Sharing in System Preferences to enable Web Sharing, as shown in Figure 8-12. When you turn on Web Sharing, you see the two addresses that people can use to get to the Web site for your computer as well as for your own account. The difference is that the site for a specific account ends with `/~<accountname>`.

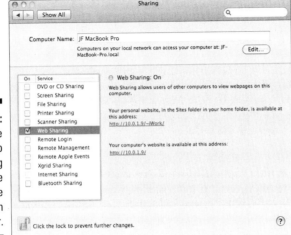

Figure 8-12: Use the Web Sharing preference to enable the built-in Web server.

These URLs may not work from outside your network. For example, an IP address that starts with 192.168 is reserved for a private network within another IP address; it can contain up to 65,000 unique IP addresses. You usually can't easily get to one of the 192.168 IP addresses from outside the network. Similarly, an IP address starting with 10 is also a private network; it can contain over 16 million unique IP addresses, but it, too, may not be easily accessed from outside the network.

Setting up a MobileMe account

If you have a MobileMe account, you configure it in System Preferences for MobileMe. (Chances are that if you have such an account, it's already configured.) All you need are your account name and password.

Setting up a Dashcode destination

Dashcode lets you create *destinations* to which you can deploy your projects. If you have a local Web server turned on or a MobileMe account configured in System Preferences, Dashcode automatically sets up destinations for them.

You can also set up a destination for your own Web server. Do so in Dashcode by choosing Preferences from the Dashcode menu and selecting the Destinations tab, shown in Figure 8-13.

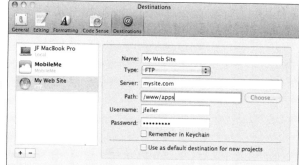

Figure 8-13: Configure your destinations.

The MobileMe and local server destinations are automatically configured, and you can't modify them here. (You modify them in System Preferences if you have to change them.) You can add as many other servers as you want. You can configure these servers using standard FTP settings (see Figure 8-13). Dashcode also supports WebDAV.

If you're using a Web server that someone else runs, all you have to know is these settings. You also may be relieved to know that these standard settings have nothing to do with Dashcode or the Mac. If your Web administrator talks only Windows or Linux, you should have no communication problem when discussing these settings.

Doing the deployment

After you set up your Dashcode destination, you can deploy your application to the Web. Figure 8-14 shows the Run & Share settings for Safari and mobile Safari applications.

Choose the destination from the pop-up menu. (An item at the end lets you create a new destination and opens the preferences shown in Figure 8-13, earlier in this chapter.)

You can type a pathname. The pathname shouldn't include spaces or special characters. Users may see it or need to type it as a URL, but most of the time, the pathname will either be displayed or used when someone clicks a link that goes to it.

You can save the files for manual deployment or shipping off to other people if you want, just as you do with widgets.

One option lets you send yourself an e-mail with the deployment address in it. Choosing that option is a good idea, particularly with MobileMe deployments. MobileMe converts certain URLs to internal addresses, and as a result, the URL that locates your file on your MobileMe site isn't the URL that you use to run the application. This e-mail prevents any confusion and is also handy if you want to let other people know about the application: You just forward that e-mail to them.

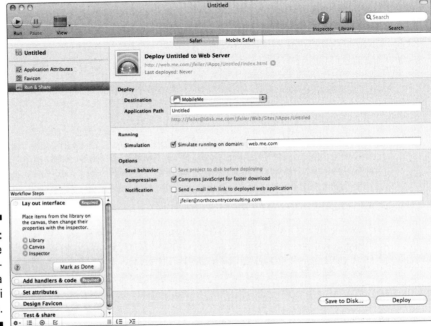

Figure 8-14:
Configure the deployment for a Safari application.

Part III
Integrating Data

The 5th Wave   By Rich Tennant

In this part . . .

Data provides the power for a set of Dashcode construction components. Data sources and data model views provide graphical user interfaces to data that you specify using JSON or XML (or that's created for you as output from programs, such as FileMaker Pro). You can also access these data sources and data model views dynamically over the Internet whenever you need to use them.

This part shows you what the tools are and how you can use them to power your Dashcode projects. Dashcode's tools for integrating data with your projects are based on a pretty simple concept: If you want data from a data model view to appear in an interface field, draw a line from the data model view to the field. Just one line. This part shows you what's behind that single line that binds data to your interface.

Chapter 9

Working with Data Sources

*Y*ou can create very impressive and useful Dashcode projects that incorporate both your own photos and a wide variety of graphics from the Library. The various inspectors let you adjust interface elements so that they look and work exactly as they should in your particular product.

Typing data into the interface as you're developing your app or widget is great; letting the user type data into a modifiable field at runtime is even greater. But how do you get data into your app or widget from the Internet or a file? Do you have to type everything that will appear in the interface? Or can you retrieve data and automatically put it where you want it in your app or widget? Yes, you can, and I talk about it in this chapter.

Even if your eyes glaze over at the mention of data and databases, it's a critically important component of many apps and widgets. The Mac OS X operating system now has a very robust core of data components, which Dashcode is built on top of. Much of what you may "know" about how to work with data doesn't apply to Dashcode, and you may be very pleasantly surprised at how easy it is to manage data for your apps and widgets.

Introducing Data Sources and Data Models

Just as Dashcode structures the user interface, it also structures the data that it uses. That structuring process has four phases, and there's nothing particularly complicated about them:

✔ **Data "out there":** The first phase of data is raw data, such as the data you encounter every day: the population of Ecuador, what you had for lunch yesterday, an errand you have to run, and so on. Not to use too technical a term, but most of the data that you deal with every day in the real world is a mess.

✔ **Formatted data:** Whether your data is a single item (Ecuador's population or that errand you have to run) or a whole list of items, you can format it. Formatting your data is usually the first step in preparing data for computers. You can format your data by putting it into a spreadsheet or any structure with rows and columns. (The smallest spreadsheet has one row and one column — a single piece of data.) Sometimes the formatting does involve a spreadsheet; sometimes it involves separating the items with quotes, commas, tabs, or a combination of them. Those characters make it easy for computers to parse the data; if the audience for your data is people, you can also separate the data items with paragraph marks, bullets, dividing lines, or even varied colors and typefaces.

When data is formatted for use by computers, it's often stored in files. Data can also be located on the Internet. When you access data over the Internet, you may be downloading a file, but you also may be accessing a computer at the other end of your Internet connection that is calculating and formatting the data. When you receive data over an Internet connection, you can't easily tell whether it's a file that is transmitted to you or the results of dynamic calculation: It's all data, and it's all formatted.

Formatted data — whether it's in a file or presented dynamically — is a *data source* in Dashcode terms. Dashcode accepts data using JSON formatting as well as XML. These are defined and discussed in Chapter 10.

✔ **Structured data:** You can structure formatted data into something more complex than cells in a spreadsheet row. For example, you may have a list of things to do today. Within your To Do list, you may have several that are grouped under Urgent, a number grouped under Work, still more under Fun, and so on. Urgent may have subcategories for different projects; the same is true of Work and Fun. This setup is a structured form of your data.

Structuring data generally requires you to know something about it. You don't have to know the population of Ecuador, but if you're structuring demographic data, you need to know that the population of Ecuador is a data item that has something in common with the population of Brazil as well as with the population of Peru. You can do much of that structuring automatically with a computer, but it often requires human intervention to structure the data in such a way that the population of Ecuador has something in common with the population of Ecuador 100 years ago, the population of South America today, and the state of Illinois (which has a similar population).

For Dashcode, structured data is a *data model*. Dashcode has tools to convert formatted data into structured data as you see in the following section. (XML data can be both formatted and structured in a hierarchical way. Sometimes XML data is used simply as formatted data, and you can structure and turn it into a data model using Dashcode tools.)

✔ **Bound data:** In Dashcode, you can bind parts of a data model (that is, structured data) to elements in your app or widget.

Viewing Data Sources and Data Models in Dashcode

With the built-in templates, you don't have to start a project at the beginning. The template provides you with a head start, and that head start often includes a data source and a data model. In order to customize a project template with its own data source and data model to use your own data, you merely need to replace the built-in data with your own data. Because you're often starting from a template with these features, this section helps you find your way around. In the next chapter, you see how to put data into your project and how to create a data source and data model from scratch.

The navigator, located in the upper left of the Dashcode window, shows you the structure of your project. Figure 9-1 shows the Browser template with the Mobile Safari tab shown. The elements in the navigator have been expanded so that you can see all of them at once. Except for using the disclosure triangles, nothing has changed in the project. If you want, you can create a project based on the Browser template, and it will look like Figure 9-1.

Looking at data sources

The data sources for a project are just as structured as the elements of your interface. You can show the data sources for your project using the button built into the bottom frame of the Dashcode window, as shown in Figure 9-2. The View menu and View in the toolbar also let you show the data sources.

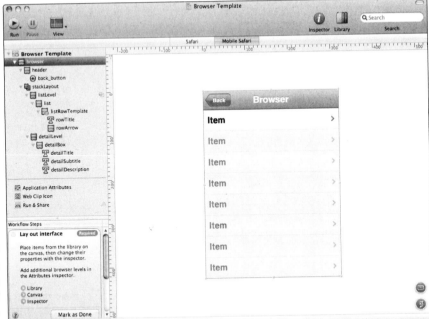

Figure 9-1:
Start from
the Browser
template.

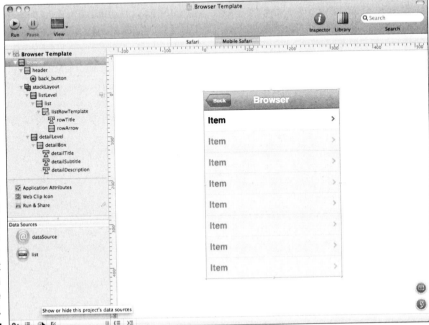

Figure 9-2:
You can
show
the data
sources at
the bottom
of the
navigator.

In the Browser template shown in Figure 9-2, you see two data sources (called `dataSource` and `list`).

A data source provides formatted data; the data model builds on that formatted data to structure it.

Looking at files

A data source is often a file. You can use the View menu, View in the toolbar, or the button in the lower left corner of the Dashcode window frame to show the project's files (see Figure 9-3).

In the Browser template, you have a file called `sampleData.js`. This file is the data for the data model that is used. If you click a file in the Files pane, you see its contents in the Source Code pane below the canvas, as shown in Figure 9-3. (You may need to move the splitter up to show it if the canvas is occupying the entire center of the Dashcode window.)

In the Browser template, the data is formatted in JSON. JSON uses JavaScript notation in its brackets, commas, and colons, but it's not actually JavaScript (or any other) code. Because the data uses JavaScript notation, you can use a wide variety of tools to read and parse JSON files. In addition, because these files have the `.js` suffix, they're recognized as legitimate data files, and they're not stopped by many firewalls and other security mechanisms.

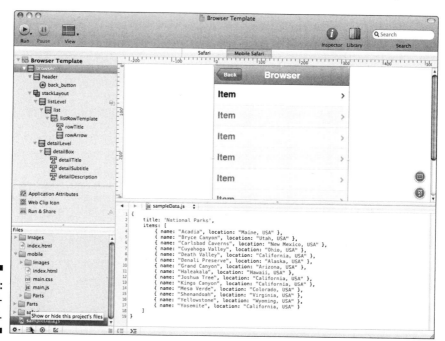

Figure 9-3:
View a project's files.

Looking inside a data model

When you select a data source and have the Source Data pane displayed, you see its structured data in the *data model view* (see Figure 9-4). This data model view is built automatically from the data you provide.

The first thing to do is to step through the data in the data model view. As you see in Figure 9-4, borders, shading, and indentation help you see the structure. You can even close up the entire content section so that you don't see anything within the data model.

With content open as it is in Figure 9-4, you have two high-level objects: title and items. In the sampledata.js file itself, these objects are easy to find in the code. Look for the underlined words:

```
{
    title: 'National Parks',
    items: [
        { name: "Acadia", location: "Maine, USA" },
        { name: "Bryce Canyon", location: "Utah, USA" },
        { name: "Carlsbad Caverns", location: "New Mexico, USA" },
        { name: "Cuyahoga Valley", location: "Ohio, USA" },
        { name: "Death Valley", location: "California, USA" },
        { name: "Denali Preserve", location: "Alaska, USA" },
        { name: "Grand Canyon", location: "Arizona, USA" },
        { name: "Haleakala", location: "Hawaii, USA" },
        { name: "Joshua Tree", location: "California, USA" },
        { name: "Kings Canyon", location: "California, USA" },
        { name: "Mesa Verde", location: "Colorado, USA" },
        { name: "Shenandoah", location: "Virginia, USA" },
        { name: "Yellowstone", location: "Wyoming, USA" },
        { name: "Yosemite", location: "California, USA" }
    ]
}
```

Each item of the items list has two subitems: name and location. These subitems are shown in Figure 9-4 with a navigation capsule. The navigation capsule shows that you're at item 4 of 14; you can use the arrows to step forward or back. (Here is where comparing the data source and the data model is useful.)

At the top of the data model view is the URL for the location of the data source. In this case, its relative path identifies the file within your project. If you move the file, you need to change the URL.

If you move the file or change the data, you need to reload the data model, using the circular reload arrow to the right of the URL.

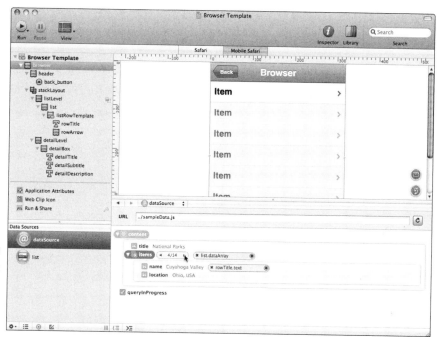

Figure 9-4:
Look inside
a data
model.

Binding Data Sources and your Interface

The data model lets you forge the connection between the data model and your interface. Think of it as the connection between two separate construction projects:

- ✔ **Interface:** Part II shows you how to assemble the interface from the Library and how to adjust it with the inspector. You may have elements within other elements (buttons within containers, for example), and the disclosure triangles in the navigator let you see this hierarchical structure. Although this structure can become complex, it's still a hierarchy of view elements that you arrange by dragging them up and down in the navigator and placing them inside another view, if needed.

- ✔ **Data:** In this chapter, you build from the data source (formatted data) to the structured data model.

All you have to do is put these two construction projects together, and you have your app or widget with all its data.

The Model-View-Controller pattern made simple

The construction projects referred to in the previous section suggest the basic structure of *Model-View-Controller* (MVC). The two construction projects (interface and data) are, in fact, what MVC refers to as a view and a model. In a nutshell, MVC is a paradigm (or *design pattern,* if you want to be geeky) that separates the structure of software into the *view* — what you see and interact with —and the *model* (the data). The two are linked by something called a *controller.*

The job of the controller is to mediate and translate between the model and the view. This mediation and translation has benefits in the development of software, particularly because the view needs to know nothing about the model, and the model needs to know nothing about the view. The only part of the system that knows about both the view and the model is the controller. Specialists can work on the view and the model without knowing much at all about what their colleagues are doing. This structure makes for some major benefits in development, not only because you can divide a project into subprojects that you can develop separately but also because the skills needed to design a user interface are often quite different from those needed to design a data structure.

After several decades of use, it has become clear to many people why MVC does pay off. The key element is the controller — the code that brings model and view together and that cleans up any ambiguities in the connections between the two. Some developers point out that working on a controller "feels" like working on a traditional program. The controller is where code is written.

You can complete the basic structure of your project by linking the model and view. You don't need to build a controller object. The controller functionality is built into Dashcode, and you implement it by connecting specific data elements in the data source to appropriate elements in the view (the user interface). This process is called *binding.*

How bindings work

In Dashcode, bindings work in the simplest way possible: You drag a connection from an object in a data model to an object in the user interface. When your app or widget runs, if it comes to a view that has a binding to a data model, it gets the data for that view by going through the data model to its data source.

Dashcode takes care of doing all these tasks: It reads the data source as needed, and, when needed, it gets the data needed for a view. If you think about it, this process works whether the data is stored in a file or whether it's retrieved dynamically over the Internet. After you specify the data source, Dashcode takes care of the rest.

Data is normally retrieved for a view (or an element in a view) when it's needed to be displayed. Retrieving the data just when it's needed makes for the most responsive possible performance.

Exploring a binding

The data model view shows the bindings that you create and that have already been created for you automatically in the template. The bindings are the gray capsules to the right of the data properties. In the center of the capsule is the name of the interface element to which it is bound.

The items in the data model are called *properties*. At this point, these properties have the names — like name and location — associated with them in the data source. It's useful to refer to them as properties because they are properties of the data model object, and that is the term used to describe them. You can bind properties of a data source to very specific *attributes* of an interface element (see Chapter 10). At this point, you're just interested in getting the value of an item in the data source into a field in the interface, but you can set many other attributes through a data model. Being precise about the terminology now helps you avoid misunderstandings later on.

As you slowly move the mouse over the data model, the bound elements in the interface are highlighted, and a small gray box appears (see Figure 9-5).

Figure 9-5:
Explore the
bindings.

Creating a Data Source

The Browser template has its files and data sources all created for you,
which puts you well on the road to completing a project of your own. But
where did they come from? If you have to build your own data sources, how
do you do it? You can't just live with the Browser template and its built-in
National Parks data forever. Here's how you create files, data sources, and
data models.

Start by showing the data sources and selecting the top data source (called
`dataSource`) — refer to Figure 9-5). Delete it by choosing Edit⇨Delete or by
using the Delete key.

When you select the data source, make certain that you select the data source
itself and not its title. If the text of the data source title is selected, when you
delete, that's all you'll delete — the text.

When you delete the top data source, any other data sources also disappear.

Choosing the data to use

When you're contemplating a Dashcode project that will include data, you have four choices:

- ✔ **File:** You can use a file as the Browser template does. The file must be formatted as JSON or XML. You should add the file to your project and specify that filename as the URL of the data source. (For more on this topic, see the next section, "Adding a file to your project.")

  Because the file is included in the project, any changes to the data require changing the project.

- ✔ **Dynamic:** You can access a Web service or other program on the Web via a URL. You specify that URL in the data source exactly as you do for a file. Dashcode expects exactly the same format of the data from an included file or a dynamic data source; it's up to you to ensure that happens.

  If you place a file somewhere on the Internet (or a local area network), that URL can point to the file. It's included as a dynamic data source because you can modify it outside the project even if it's a file. This technique — specifying the URL of an external file — is very useful for data that changes. Whoever is responsible for updating the data only has to make certain that the current file is available and is in the right format. If you begin with a file that you create, updating it may be as simple as just copying and pasting changed data into a copy of the file.

- ✔ **Static:** If the amount of data you need is relatively small and unchanging, you can simply type the data into your interface inside a text field, text area, or text part from the Library.

- ✔ **XMLHttpRequest:** You can use XMLHttpRequest to get a specific item of data when you need it. This request doesn't involve a data source because you're just retrieving data and displaying it somewhere. You can see how to make this request in Chapter 11.

Adding a file to your project

To add a file to your project, show the Files list (refer to Figure 9-3). Don't bother figuring out where the file belongs on disk: Use the Gear icon to bring up a shortcut menu and choose the Add File command, as shown in Figure 9-6. (The Files list must be selected when you use the Gear icon. Otherwise, you see commands that are relevant to another object in the Dashcode window.)

Figure 9-6:
Add a file to
the project.

You normally want to add the file at the highest level of your project rather than within the Mobile or Safari folders. If you add it at the top level of your project, you can have separate files for the two implementations of your project. From a user interface point of view, having separate files may be problematic because users will wonder why the data changes depending on whether they're using a mobile device or not. A much better choice is to display the same data but to modify the interface elements so that a different font is used or the text is wrapped differently.

Adding a data source to your project

After you have the file in place, you need a data source. Depending on which template you select, you may already have a data source in your project. If you don't have a data source, show the data sources list and use the Gear icon to add a new data source.

As with anything that you add to your project, your data source has a default name. This one is particularly catchy: `dataSource`. Renaming it to something more meaningful is a good idea. Remember that you may be building a small app or widget for your personal use, but over time, it may grow into something more; you may even share it with other people as you trade your apps, widgets, and techniques back and forth. A meaningful name can help.

Spaces within internal names are usually not a good idea, but you do want to somehow separate the components of a name. One technique that you can see used in Dashcode is what is called *camel case*. The first letter of each word except the first is capitalized. That technique gives you `dataSource`, but it also can give you `partsDeptDS`. It's useful to have a convention so that objects inside your project are identified by name and by type (DS for data source, as an example).

Make certain that the Source Code pane is visible. Now, select the new data source in the Data Sources list, and you see the Data Model view in the Source Code pane. Fill in the data source's URL. If the data source is being retrieved from the Internet, you need the full URL. If you added the file to your project, the Data Source pop-up menu above the URL field shows you all the candidate files (see Figure 9-7). This pop-up menu saves you from figuring out where the dots and slashes go. Remember that these possible data source files are actually text files. You also must have the source code pane visible below the canvas.

After you have selected a URL or file for the data source, click the circular Refresh button to the right of the URL, and data is actually retrieved from the file or URL. You see that data displayed in the Data Model view. If you get an error message, check your URL for missing or extra characters or other mistakes.

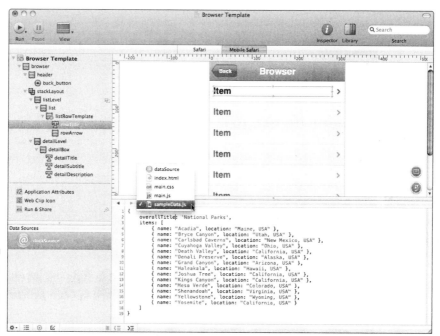

Figure 9-7:
Select the file for the data source.

Creating Bindings

Bindings bring structure and context to the data source based on the interface and your knowledge of the data.

Figures 9-4 and 9-5, shown earlier in the chapter, show the binding capsules for properties of the data source in the data model view. At the left of each binding capsule, you see an X that you can use to delete that binding.

You can have more than one binding for a property in a data source (see Figure 9-8). If you do have more than one binding, the first object is an arrow that can enlarge the capsule so that you see each binding. You can then delete the bindings individually, if you want to.

Figure 9-8: A data source property can have multiple bindings.

As you move the mouse over the properties in the Data model view, a small circle, called a *binding control,* appears to the right of each property name (see in Figure 9-9).

You don't complete the binding at this point, so feel free to experiment. Certain elements on the interface can be part of the binding for a data model property. As you drag from the binding control, these elements are highlighted. Release the mouse button over one of them (it doesn't matter which one), and you see a menu of the items that you can bind to the data model property, as shown in Figure 9-10. If you don't select one and click in the background of the canvas, the binding won't be completed, and you can explore again.

Figure 9-9:
Binding
controls
appear as
you move
the mouse
over data
source
properties.

Figure 9-10:
Choose
what you
want to
bind to.

You can bind a property of the data model (that is, data from the data source) to an interface. When you create an interface element, it always makes sense to give it a meaningful name, such as `title` or `location`. Then, when you see it on the canvas, and when you can see some data in the Data Model view, you can bind the title data to the `title` field. You can also bind data to attributes of elements as you see in Figure 9-10: The data you're using can thus determine at runtime whether the element is editable, visible, or enabled based on the choices shown in the pop-up menu of Figure 9-10. If you bind a complex property of a data model (such as the `items` array shown in Figure 9-10) to an interface element that can contain data in a `dataArray`, the multiple elements of the property are bound to an array. And that will create a new data source.

Your data file or URL is formatted into a data source with JSON or XML and then displayed as a data model and finally bound to interface elements. This process is pretty complex, but all you have to do is format your data properly with JSON or XML, create and name your files and data sources, and draw a few binding lines. (See Chapter 10 for more information on this process.)

Chapter 10

Binding Data to your Dashcode Project

....

In This Chapter

▶ Understanding XML and JSON formats

▶ Binding data properties to interface properties

....

*I*n the previous chapter you saw how you can use Dashcode to access a data source and display it in a data model view so that you can see its logical structure.

You can then bind a property in a data model to one or more elements in your project's interface by the simple method of dragging a line to establish the binding. This chapter explores bindings in more detail and gives you some examples from the built-in Dashcode templates and parts from the Library.

The best way to understand how bindings work is to look carefully at one. You need a data source and you need an interface that displays the data. That's what we start with in this chapter: the data source, the interface, and its bindings.

Although you still see the Browser template used in Chapter 9, this chapter adds a new Dashcode project that you can build from scratch. There's a big difference between working with a project where the data source, data model, interface, and bindings already exist and starting from scratch.

In real life, you often work with a combination of templates and from-scratch techniques. You need to understand the from-scratch techniques for those frequent occasions when you want to add functionality to a template.

You can download the files referenced in this chapter at www.dummies.com/go/dashcodefd.

Putting Data into Your Project with XML and JSON

The Browser template comes with its own built-in data source and data model, which is why it's ready to go as soon as you create it: It's got all the data it needs. The data lets you browse some information about National Parks in the United States. You can use and reuse that structure for other data. The Browser built-in data source and data model are the perfect place to begin looking in detail about how data gets into a project.

The sample data source in the Browser template and its functionally identical XML data source described here consists of the following major elements:

- ✔ **Container:** Everything is placed inside a container — the { and } in JSON, and a *document* in XML. (Note that the { and } delimit an XML document construct; it's not the document that you can edit, print, and move around on disk. That's a file-system document.)

- ✔ **Title:** This element's value is "National Parks" in the Browser template.

- ✔ **Items list:** In JSON, the Items list is enclosed in [and]. In the sample data, the Items list consists of the parks' names and locations.

- ✔ **Item elements**: These are the elements in the Items list. Each one is also delimited with { and }. In the sample data, each element consists of a park name and the name of its location.

Note that these terms (container, title, Items list, and item elements) are descriptions. They're not part of the JSON syntax, and you can name them anything you want.

The most important point to remember about both JSON and XML is that they're not just formats; they're structures for data. The data elements have names and values. You can combine the data elements into structures so that, for example, you can combine the names of committee members into a new element called *committee*. All the elements are combined into a single structure — a *document* in XML and a structure delimited by { and } in JSON.

Reviewing the JSON data source

The built-in data source for the Browser template is `sampleData.js`, a JavaScript file in the JSON format. Dashcode is equally happy using XML data. You can easily convert the JSON file to XML. Basically, you convert the quoted strings within brackets that are separated by commas into XML structures. (You can see that later in this section.)

The `sampleData.js` file shown in the previous chapter (and located in the Browser template) is repeated in Listing 10-1 for reference.

Listing 10-1: Browser Template Sample Data In JSON Format

```
{
    title: 'National Parks',
    items: [
        { name: "Acadia", location: "Maine, USA" },
        { name: "Bryce Canyon", location: "Utah, USA" },
        { name: "Carlsbad Caverns", location: "New Mexico, USA" },
        { name: "Cuyahoga Valley", location: "Ohio, USA" },
        { name: "Death Valley", location: "California, USA" },
        { name: "Denali Preserve", location: "Alaska, USA" },
        { name: "Grand Canyon", location: "Arizona, USA" },
        { name: "Haleakala", location: "Hawaii, USA" },
        { name: "Joshua Tree", location: "California, USA" },
        { name: "Kings Canyon", location: "California, USA" },
        { name: "Mesa Verde", location: "Colorado, USA" },
        { name: "Shenandoah", location: "Virginia, USA" },
        { name: "Yellowstone", location: "Wyoming, USA" },
        { name: "Yosemite", location: "California, USA" }
    ]
}
```

Structuring the data elements

When building software, some people like to work from the top down, but others like to work from the bottom up. Working from the top down means that you build the high-level interface and gradually get into the nitty-gritty. Working from the bottom up means getting the nitty-gritty of the data and functionality done and then combining it into the final product. Working from the bottom up has the advantage of letting you look at the simplest parts of the data structure first. Both methods have advantages, which is why many people use them both at different times. In the case of the Browser template, the bottom-level simplest parts are the individual data elements in the Items list.

For example, in the JSON file, the first item is coded as

```
{ name: "Acadia", location: "Maine, USA" },
```

In XML, it becomes

```
<item>
<name>Acadia</name>
<location>Maine, USA</location>
</item>
```

The data is the same. The structure defined in the JSON and XML files is logically the same, but it uses different names and syntax. For example, the name of the park (Acadia, in this case) is called `name`, and its location is `location`. The names really don't matter, because the user never sees those terms in the final project. The names appear in the data model views in Dashcode, but only you and other people who are working on the project see them.

Structuring the Items list

The list of items has a different structure in the two files. In JSON, the list is coded as

```
items: [
  { name: "Acadia", location: "Maine, USA" },
  ...
      ]
```

And in XML, the list looks like

```
<body>
  <item>
    <name>Acadia</name>
    <location>Maine, USA</location>
  </item>
  ...
</body>
```

In both cases, spacing doesn't matter except within quotation marks. And the names or labels are still irrelevant. The XML code works equally well if the individual parks are placed in an element called `<body>`, `<items>`, or `<stuff>`.

Adding the title

Each file has a title element. (Note that JSON and XML files often have title elements, but they don't have to.) The title element in this example is simply the title of the example.

In the JSON file, here's the title that's added before the list of items:

```
{
  title: 'National Parks',
  items: [
    { name: "Acadia", location: "Maine, USA" },
    ...
  ]
}
```

For XML, the structure is quite similar:

```
<heading>National Parks</heading>

<things>

  <item>
    <name>Acadia</name>
    <location>Maine, USA</location>
  </item>

    ...
</things>
```

Again, the spacing doesn't matter. What is more apparent in the XML file than in the JSON file is that everything has to be enclosed in some kind of outer container: You can't have a data element just floating around. In the JSON file, the container is marked by the [and] at the top and bottom of the list; in XML, it is the <stuff> and </stuff> tags that mark the beginning and end of the stuff element.

Tying up the container

Everything is tied up into a container: In JSON, the container is delimited by { and }, and in XML, it's delimited with tags for a user-defined element. In addition, the XML file has a standard identification line at the beginning of the file. Unless you're using another text encoding method (rare for English language text), you use the first line exactly as-is.

Because XML uses tags to delimit the container element, you need to name it. In this example, the container is called stuff, which is definitely not a formal part of general XML syntax.

Compare Listing 10-1, earlier in the chapter, which is the complete JSON version with Listing 10-2, which is the complete new XML version. (Listing 10-2 is available as a downloadable file at www.dummies.com/go/dashcodefd.)

Listing 10-2:   Browser Template Sample Data in XML format

```
<?xml version='1.0' encoding='ISO-8859-1'?>

<stuff>

  <heading>National Parks</heading>

  <things>
```

(continued)

Listing 10-2 *(continued)*

```
<item>
  <name>Acadia</name>
  <location>Maine, USA</location>
</item>

<item>
  <name>Bryce Canyon</name>
  <location>Utah, USA</location>
</item>

<item>
  <name>Carlsbad Caverns</name>
  <location>New Mexico, USA</location>
</item>

<item>
  <name>Cuyahoga Valley</name>
  <location>Ohio, USA</location>
</item>

<item>
  <name>Death Valley</name>
  <location>California, USA</location>
</item>

<item>
  <name>Denali Preserve</name>
  <location>Alaska, USA</location>
</item>

<item>
  <name>Grand Canyon</name>
  <location>Arizona, USA</location>
</item>

<item>
  <name>Haleakala</name>
  <location>Hawaii, USA</location>
</item>

<item>
  <name>Joshua Tree</name>
  <location>California, USA</location>
</item>

<item>
  <name>Kings Canyon</name>
  <location>California, USA</location>
</item>
```

```
    <item>
      <name>Mesa Verde</name>
      <location>Colorado, USA</location>
    </item>

    <item>
      <name>Shenandoah</name>
      <location>Virginia, USA</location>
    </item>

    <item>
      <name>Yellowstone</name>
      <location>Wyoming, USA</location>
    </item>

    <item>
      <name>Yosemite</name>
      <location>California, USA</location>
    </item>

  </things>

</stuff>
```

You now have seen the syntax for JavaScript/JSON and XML data that you can use in Dashcode. After you create the appropriate file in either format, it doesn't matter which format the file is in: Dashcode treats them both the same, and you use the Dashcode graphical representation exactly the same way.

Exporting XML or JSON from other applications

If you have data that you want to use in a Dashcode project, you may be able to export it from a database or spreadsheet in JSON or XML format. When you have your file, follow the steps in Chapter 9 to import it: Add it to your project and set the URL of a data source to the address of the file within your project (`../sampleData.js` syntax).

You can also deploy the file on a Web server and provide a URL to that location. As soon as you enter the URL, Dashcode may try to parse the file. If it doesn't, just click the Reload button to the right of the URL field.

If you get an error, open the JSON or XML file and compare it to the sample listings in this chapter. Often Export or Save As commands that create XML or JSON files save more information than you need, such as fonts, column widths for spreadsheets, and the like. Hunt through the listing for the actual data and then strip out any formatting instructions. This extra information on fonts, column widths, and the like is particularly an issue with sophisticated software such as Microsoft Excel and FileMaker Pro. Their XML exports are designed to allow the databases or spreadsheets to be easily exported and imported into other database or spreadsheet programs. You just care about the data.

In the case of FileMaker, writing a script to generate the XML that you want is often easier than relying on the more complete XML that is automatically generated. If you're a FileMaker Pro user, download `FM_XML.fp7` as described in the Introduction, which contains a simple table in which you can enter data (either in a form or table/spreadsheet view). The GenerateXML script (in the Scripts menu) turns your data into XML. The script doesn't bother fixing up spacing or things that don't matter: It's designed to move your data into an XML format that will run in Dashcode.

Using a New Data Source in the Browser Template

The Browser template comes ready for customization. You can create a remarkably useful Dashcode Safari Web application by using the template and merely changing the data in the data source. You can use `sample-Data.js`, which comes with the template, or you can use the XML version described in the previous section. Change the title from "National Parks" to whatever you want and then replace the name and location values in the data source.

If you reuse the template, chances are that your customized data source will have items with values for name, but you may want to redefine location. Perhaps you want to create a Safari Web application that lists people, places, or businesses. You still use the name, but perhaps instead of location, you provide an e-mail address. You can do that without changing anything except the data, but maintaining the Web app is easier if you changed the name of the data source `location` property to something like `email`.

The rules for naming objects in Dashcode are strict and are a little different from everyday use in some cases. That's why in this book I can talk about an e-mail field, but when it comes to an actual object in Dashcode, it has to be `email` because the hyphen (along with other special characters and spaces) is not legal inside Dashcode names.

Managing the development of a Dashcode project

Don't let the process described in this chapter mislead you: Most of the time, you don't start at the beginning and go through to the end when you're developing a Dashcode project. As you proceed, you'll see that you may need another data field — for example, the arrangements of data elements in the interface or in the data source makes it clear that something is missing. Or, as you see in this chapter, two data elements may need to be combined or split apart.

One of the great virtues of Dashcode and other such tools is that you can easily modify your project so that you don't have to start with an enormous amount of analysis and design up front. In fact, many people think that instead of doing a separate design process, it may be more productive and faster to jump in and create a Dashcode project. Even if you have to make a few revisions and back up a few times with your Dashcode project, that approach can be faster than working through a formal design process. If you do skip a formal design process, make certain that you constantly touch base with people who are potential users and who can help you decide what is a good idea and what isn't. Also, remember that someone on the project has to weigh the costs of new features and increased development and testing time against the benefits they can provide. Set aside a period of time for total exploration and experimentation of the project-in-progress. When that time is over, you freeze the design and simply focus on its implementation.

In the remainder of this chapter, you see how you can modify the template to provide more than just a single descriptive field for each item. You can modify the Browser template so that you can use it to browse a directory of data for public libraries. Each library has a name and a location, as in the Browser template, but you add an e-mail address, telephone number, and image to each one. When this project runs on iPhone, Dashcode automatically allows you to work with the iPhone features for telephony, e-mail, and mapping.

Figure 10-1 shows what the completed project looks like.

 The data is taken from the publicly available information about libraries in the Clinton Essex Franklin Library System (CEFLS) in northeastern New York State. You can find more about CEFLS and its libraries at www.cefls.org. This book's example uses only three libraries, but you can explore many more in person or at the CEFLS Web site.

To customize the Browser template and new interface elements with your data, follow these steps:

1. **Create a new data file.**

2. **Create a new project, remove the old data source, and add the new one.**

Figure 10-1:
Build a
project with
your data
and the
Browser
template.

3. **Add new interface parts for your data.**

4. **Test and deploy.**

The following sections examine each step in more detail.

Creating a new data file

After you've looked inside data source files in both XML and JSON formats, you can start to build your own. For starters, you can use the `cefls_libraries_brief.xml` file that you can download from www.dummies.com/go/dashcodefd. If you feel adventurous, you can create your own data source file from your own data right away.

Listing 10-3 shows the `cefls_libraries_brief.xml` file.

Listing 10-3: cefls_libraries_brief.xml

```xml
<?xml version='1.0' encoding='ISO-8859-1'?>
<body>

<rec>
<name>Akwesasne Library</name>
<address>321 State Route 37, Hogansburg</address>
<state>NY</state>
<email>mailto:akwlibr@northnet.org</email>
<web>http://akwesasneculturalcenter.org</web>
```

```
<telephone>555-555-5555</telephone>
<image>http://www.cefls.org/images/akwesasne.jpg</image>
</rec>

<rec><name>Altona Reading Center</name>
<address>3124 Route 191, Altona</address>
<state>NY</state>
<email>mailto:info2@cefls.org</email>
<web>http://www.cefls.org/altona.htm</web>
<telephone>555-555-5555</telephone>
<image>http://www.cefls.org/images/altona.jpg</image>
</rec>

<rec>
<name>AuSable Forks Free Library</name>
<address>9 Church Lane, AuSable Forks</address>
<state>NY</state>
<email>mailto:afbooks@charter.net</email>
<web>http://www.ausableforksfreelibrary.com</web>
<telephone>555-555-5555</telephone>
<image>http://www.cefls.org/images/ausable.jpg</image>
</rec>

</body>
```

Notice that the structure of this file is a little different from the XML file shown in Listing 10-2, earlier in this chapter. The overall structure of Listing 10-2 is

```
<stuff>

  <heading>National Parks</heading>

  <things>

    <item>
      <name>Acadia</name>
      <location>Maine, USA</location>
    </item>

    ...
  </things>

</stuff>
```

 A JSON or XML file has an outer container. In Listing 10-2 shown here, the container is `stuff`, and it contains two sub-elements: `heading` and `things`. In Listing 10-3, the outer container is `body`, and it contains the individual data elements that, in Listing 10-2, are contained in `things`. Without a title or heading element, you will have to hard-code the Safari Web application's title in Dashcode. In addition, the various `rec` elements are contained directly in `body`, which can have no other second-level element such as a title. If you add a `title` element, you need an element that corresponds to `things` that contain the `rec` elements.

If you want to create your own file, you can use any text editing program: TextEdit (built into Mac OS X), BBEdit (from Bare Bones Software — `www.barebones.com`) or Xcode, if you have it.

You may want to start with only a few records so that you can get your project up and running before adding more data. Add at least three records of data for your testing. Three records allow you to test going to a next and previous record. First, last, and single records in a list have special characteristics that make test results misleading, in some cases.

Creating the project and adding the data

The Browser template is ready for you to customize. The first step is to decide what you want to do with your customization. Figure 10-1, earlier in this chapter, shows you what the finished project looks like.

When you're working on another project, it's a good idea to have at least a sketch (even a mental one) of what your project will look like. You can modify and refine it as you proceed. Even if you wind up doing something completely different, having the initial idea down on the back of an envelope can make it easier to proceed.

Here's how you create the project and add the data:

1. **Create a new project from the Browser template.**

   The Browser template is available for Safari and mobile Safari. You can use either or both versions.

2. **Save the new project right away.**

   Naming and saving your projects immediately is a good habit to get into. Otherwise you can work on your project with the default name (`Untitled`, `Untitled 1`, and so on) and then, when you want to quit, you just save them and don't have a clue the next day what is what.

3. **Show the Files list.**

   You can use View in the toolbar or the Files command in the View menu. You can also use the button in the lower left frame of the Dashcode window.

4. **Select `sampledata.js` by clicking it once.**

   Notice where in the Files list `sampledata.js` is located. You need to know that location in Step 6.

5. **Use the Gear icon to delete the old file.**

6. **Add your new file to the project.**

   The file can be one you create or the downloaded file.

   Make certain that the Files list is shown. Choose File⇨Add File or use the Gear icon to choose Add File, as shown in Figure 10-2. Verify that the file is at the top level of the project (the same relative location where `sampleData.js` was in Step 4).

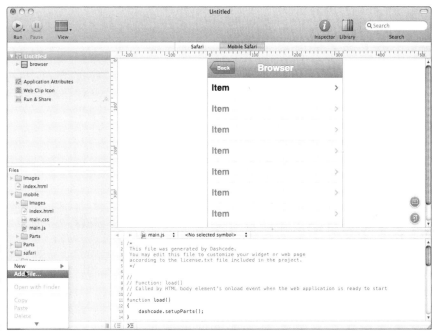

7. **Add a new data source.**

   Use the View menu, View in the toolbar, or the button in the lower left of the window frame to show the Data Sources list. Then choose the Gear icon's New Data Source command.

8. **Double-click the default name (`dataSource`) and give it a new name.**

9. **In the Source Code pane, type the URL for the new data source.**

   If you use the downloaded file and placed it where the `sampleData.js` file was, this URL is `../cefls_libraries_brief.xml`. As soon as you type the URL, Dashcode attempts to load it. If it doesn't, use the Reload button to the right of the URL. Figure 10-3 shows the loaded data source. You should recognize your data.

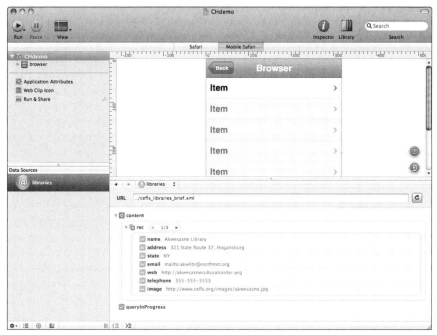

Figure 10-3:
Load the
new data
source.

Connect existing interface parts

The next step is to connect the existing interface parts to your new data source. Chapter 9 shows the basic technique but the next two sections talk about what is happening behind the scenes.

Binding a property to a view

Your data source (refer to Figure 10-3) has properties. (You might call these properties *fields* if you come from a database background rather than a programming background.) The elements in your interface also have properties. The binding process connects a property in the data model to a property of an interface element. This binding isn't a mechanical one-to-one connection, but as you work with the connection, you see how it works. As an example, if you have a property in the data model, such as the name of a library, you can bind it to a text element in the interface. Figure 10-4 shows how you can drag from the binding control to the right of the name field to the `rowTitle` view to bind them together. (The name is highlighted in the navigator.)

When you release the mouse button at the end of the drag, the menu that appears lets you choose which property of the interface element you want to bind the data source property to. For a simple item such as a name, you want to bind the property to the text property of the interface element.

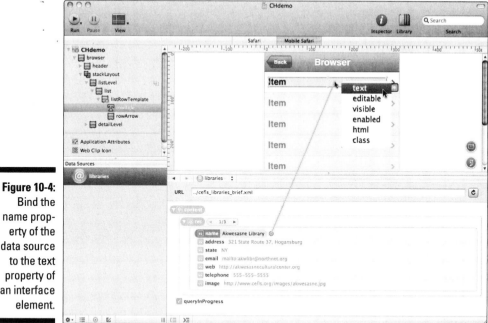

Figure 10-4:
Bind the name property of the data source to the text property of an interface element.

After you choose the property of the view to which you want to bind the data source property, the line and the menu disappear. The binding is complete (see Figure 10-5).

Binding a data source container to a Dashcode data array

After you create a binding, a lozenge (located to the right of the property in the data model) shows the name of the interface element to which it's bound, as well as the name of the property to which it's bound. This property is the one you choose from the menu at the end of the binding process (refer to Figure 10-4). Thus, when you look at Figure 10-5, you can see that the data source's `name` property is bound to `rowTitle.text`, which is the text property of `rowTitle`. The binding is actually from the data source property (the data) to both an interface element and a specific property within it. Not bad for just drawing a single line!

To the left of the name is an X, which allows you to undo the binding if you want. At the right is a binding control. Unlike the binding controls shown previously, this one has a solid center in its circle. A binding control without a solid center isn't bound; after you bind it, the center is filled in. You can bind a data model property to more than one interface element; if you do, the X to the left of the name of the bound property becomes a disclosure triangle, which reveals all the bindings.

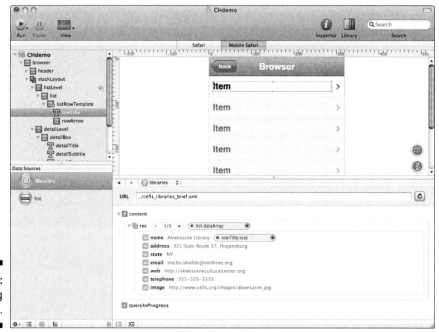

Figure 10-5:
The binding
is complete.

In addition to completing the binding of name to rowTitle, you have done a lot more. (Actually, Dashcode has done it.) A new binding has automatically been created for you from rec in the data source to the dataArray property of the List view. Because you frequently have a list of items in your data source, Dashcode builds in Library parts that specifically work on lists. You can bind a simple data source property, such as a name or number, to a simple property of a view (such as its text property), but for container parts in the Library, you can bind the lists or containers in your data source to those container parts. This binding takes place behind the scenes; you don't see a name in a text field, but the binding enables everything else to work. And, as you have seen with this binding, if you connect a field from a list or container in your JSON or XML file to a field that is contained within a containing view in your view hierarchy, Dashcode automatically binds that list or container in the file to the container in which the field exists.

If you want to understand the binding process for lists or containers to fields contained in view, you can try this experiment. Instead of doing the binding all at once, you can separately bind the rec XML element to the list interface element, as shown in Figure 10-6. The property of the list interface element to which you bind the rec XML element is dataArray.

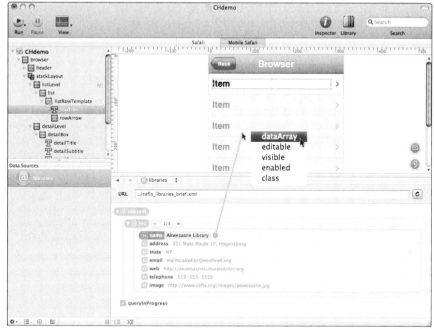

Figure 10-6:
Bind the
rec XML
element to
the list
interface
element.

The Edge-to-Edge List part in the Library is the part that provides the list, listRowTemplate, rowTitle, and rowArrow views. They all come into your project when you drag an Edge-to-Edge List into it. In the Browser template, the rowTitle and rowArrow views have been renamed for you. In the Edge-to-Edge List part, these views are called label and arrow.

This binding (XML or JSON list/container to a container part in the Library) creates a new icon in the Data Sources list. It has the name of the interface element to which it's bound, but you can change that name in the Data Sources list by double-clicking it. Changing its name doesn't change anything about the binding.

If you change the name of the interface element, the name of the data source icon automatically changes to match it. Even if you previously renamed the data source, if you change the name of the interface element, the icon in the Data Sources list changes to match the new name. Even so, nothing about the binding itself changes.

To change the binding, use the X at the left of the lozenge for the binding in the data model view to delete the existing binding and then draw a new one.

After you bind a container or list in your XML/JSON data source to a container from the Dashcode Library, you can then bind individual properties, such as name, to individual views that are contained within the row template for the container.

When you're binding to a view that is inside a template of a container, you must have a binding from your data source to the container. Instead of making you do this work, Dashcode notices when you try to bind a data source property, such as title to a view that's in a container template. If a binding to the container doesn't exist, Dashcode creates one, which is what happens when you followed the steps in this section. But nothing prevents you from manually binding the data source list or container to the container from the Library.

You can see your work in the simulator if you click Run in the upper left corner of the Dashcode window (see Figure 10-7). Dashcode properly retrieves all the data from the data source file and displays it in a list. Click an arrow to look at details for an individual library, and you see that you still have work to do.

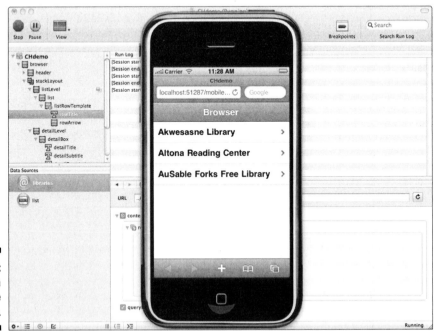

Figure 10-7:
See the data in the simulator.

When you're dealing with Dashcode containers and XML/JSON lists or containers, Dashcode manages the process for you. Sometimes, the process is confusing, so you need to understand what's going on.

For example, look at the detailLevel view. Use disclosure triangles where necessary to show it in the navigator. Now try to connect the name property in the data model view to the detailTitle view. (You can make the connection in the canvas, or you can use the navigator.) No matter what you do, you can't complete the binding. When you release the mouse button after drawing a binding line, you don't see the menu that lets you to choose the View property to which to bind. Instead, the line just disappears. Figure 10-8 shows the binding being drawn; it disappears as soon as the mouse button is released.

Figure 10-8:
Try to bind to detail-Title.

Because you're working inside a container or list in the data source, Dashcode can't figure out what data to use for the name property. This sample file has three values for name — one for each library.

That new icon in the Data Sources list is a *controller* binding the data source to a dataArray in a view. Click that icon, and you see the data model view change to reflect the binding created from the data source itself to a container in Dashcode. The first section of the data model view is for a single object in that binding — the *selection*. (The second section is for multiple selected objects; see Chapter 18.)

When your project is running and you click an item in an Edge-to-Edge List, it becomes the selection for the list it displays. When you have a view that expects to work with a single data value, you often want to bind the data value from the selection to that view rather than from the data source itself.

In Figure 10-9, you can see that the bound data model is selected in the Data Sources pane, and you can now bind `name` to `detailTitle`. You can also bind `address` to `location`.

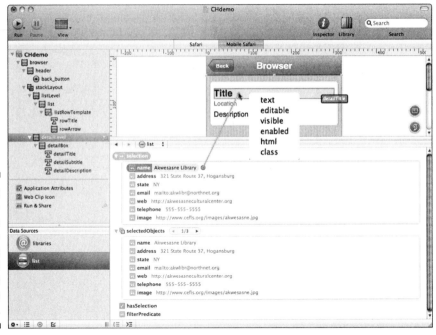

Figure 10-9: Bind a property from a selection in the data model rather than from the data source.

Figure 10-10 shows the project running in the simulator. You're almost done.

Most of the time, when the view displays a list of data, you want to bind from a property in the data source. For a view that displays a single data value, you want to bind from the selection in the bound data source.

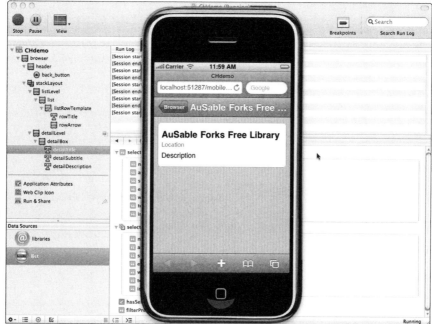

Figure 10-10:
You can
now display
data for an
individual
library.

Add and connect new interface parts

Finishing up this example is simple. All you need to do is add parts from the Library for a telephone number and an e-mail address, and you're done.

1. **Select `detailBox` in the navigator.**

   This box displays information about a selected library.

2. **Enlarge the box to take up most of the space.**

3. **Delete `location` and `description`.**

   The canvas looks like Figure 10-11.

4. **From the Library button parts, drag Call, Mail, and Map buttons into the box, as shown in Figure 10-12.**

   If you can't get them where you want them, use Absolute layout in the Metrics inspector rather than Document layout.

Figure 10-11:
Enlarge the
box.

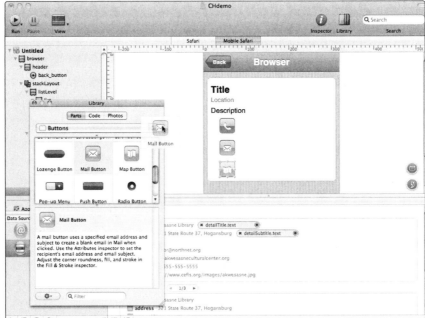

Figure 10-12:
Add Call,
Mail, and
Map
buttons.

5. Bind the `telephone` property to the Call button.

6. In the menu that lets you choose the property to which to bind it, choose `phoneNumber` as shown in Figure 10-13.

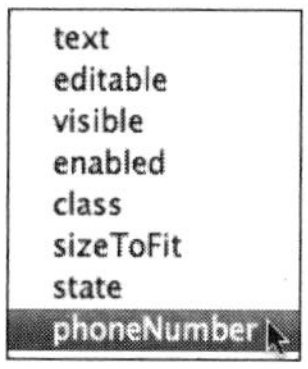

Figure 10-13:
Bind the
telephone
number.

text
editable
visible
enabled
class
sizeToFit
state
phoneNumber

7. Bind the `email` property to the Mail button using the `emailAddress` property, as shown in Figure 10-14.

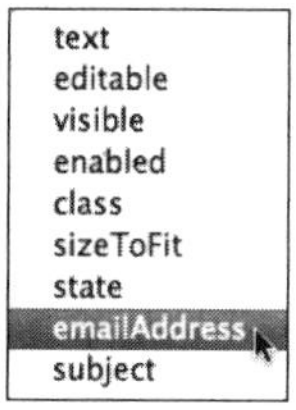

Figure 10-14:
Bind the
e-mail
address.

text
editable
visible
enabled
class
sizeToFit
state
emailAddress
subject

Note that among the other properties is the subject of the e-mail, which you can dynamically modify.

8. Bind the `address` property in the data source to the Map button using the `address` property in the button, as shown in Figure 10-15.

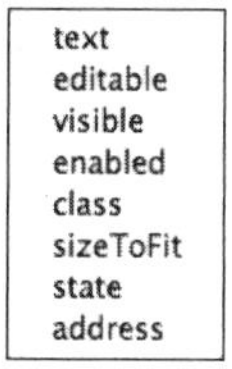

Figure 10-15:
Bind the
address.

text
editable
visible
enabled
class
sizeToFit
state
address

9. Test the results.

You should be able to test the Map button; the Mail button should work as far as creating the message — the simulator doesn't actually send e-mail. Similarly, you can't actually make a phone call from the simulator.

If you encounter problems with mapping, check the addresses directly on an iPhone. Sometimes, you find a discrepancy between the official names for streets and towns and the names that people use in real life.

Chapter 11

Using XMLHttpRequest to Get Live Data When You Need It

In This Chapter

▶ Exploring XMLHttpRequest

▶ Creating and sending a request

▶ Receiving and processing the results of a request

You can use data sources to provide data for your apps and widgets. That's great if your data is already in a file or at an Internet location where it's either stored as a file or created dynamically as if it were a file. (Dashcode really doesn't care whether you're downloading a file or downloading data in a file format that was assembled by a Web server in real time.)

This approach is a bit of overkill if you just need one piece of data. If that piece of data is the user's previous high score on a game, you can easily save it in Preferences or the built-in database, but what if the data is outside the user's area? What if it's anyone's highest score on the game? That information has to come from the Web because your app or widget knows only about its own data.

The XMLHttpRequest function lets you ask for a specific piece of information when you want it. The request goes to a Web server (sometimes the same server that provides the Web page or downloadable file you might be using), and the data is returned to you directly. This chapter explains XMLHttpRequest and shows you how to use it in Dashcode. You also see how the templates use XMLHttpRequest to get RSS feeds on demand.

Introducing XMLHttpRequest

If you think about it, the file-based model is inefficient in many cases. The data that's going to wind up in the files (or in the downloaded file-like data streams) often is stored in electronic form — either in a database such as FileMaker Pro or MySQL or even in a spreadsheet. (You can also extract data from a word-processing table and convert it into JSON or XML on its way into Dashcode.)

Why go through those conversions from database to JSON or XML and then, in Dashcode, from JSON or XML to JavaScript memory structures? Isn't that stroll through the land of JSON and XML a detour in some cases?

Yes, it is. If you can find a way to directly ask for data that is returned in a structure that Dashcode can use, you'd simplify your code and get rid of those intermediate files and file-like data streams.

Using the JSON and XML file-based formats is a bit easier for many people: After all, you can print the file and look at it as you're figuring out the data flow. XMLHttpRequest is a totally digital operation, so you have no file to look at. If you need to search through the step-by-step operations, you need to use the debugger. But XMLHttpRequest is worth it.

The main reason for using XMLHttpRequest isn't that it works (which it does, of course), but that it's now a standard Web protocol, so you can find lots of information and examples. (A Google search shows more than 1.5 million hits for "XMLHttpRequest example.")

A secondary reason to use XMLHttpRequest is that because it eliminates that intermediate structure (the file or file-based data flow), it's more robust and easier to maintain over time. You ask a source on the Internet such as an application server for specific information, and it transmits that information back to you. The format is digital, and you don't have to worry about quotation marks, brackets, and the like.

After the data is loaded into Dashcode, you're in the familiar world of data sources and bindings. The only difference when you use XMLHttpRequest is how the data is delivered to Dashcode.

If you're into buzzwords and terminology, you probably know that XMLHttpRequest is a key component of AJAX, one of the most important new technologies on the Web. AJAX stands for Asynchronous JavaScript and XML.

Understanding the XMLHttpRequest Structure

Even if you're used to traditional programming, XMLHttpRequest has two aspects that may be new to you: partial page loads and asynchronous processing. Fortunately, they're simple and easy to explain in relatively plain English.

Partial page loads

In the old days, you typed a URL into your browser, and it loaded that page from a Web server. The page could be large or small, but you couldn't load just a part of a page. That limitation changes with XMLHttpRequest, which is designed to retrieve specific pieces of information and display them as part of a page that has already been downloaded and displayed in a user's browser.

To implement this functionality, you need some programming logic built into a Web page. Most often, that logic is JavaScript, the programming tool at the heart of Dashcode.

When a page is loaded in a modern browser, its structure and content are displayed for the user in the browser, but the structure is also available to JavaScript code that is embedded on that page. The Document Object Model (DOM) is a set of conventions that many Web browsers use through HTML, XML, and JavaScript to access a Web page and its elements. The key feature of DOM that you care about is that it's the way that JavaScript accesses the Web page's data.

- **Properties:** Using JavaScript, you can access DOM properties. For example, the URL of the current page is document.URL, and its title is document.title.

- **Methods:** Methods, such as document.getElementById, are also built into the DOM.

- **Event handlers:** The handlers most often involved with XMLHttpRequest are handlers such as onclick and onmouseover. Those events can trigger a call to XMLHttpRequest. In Dashcode, handlers in the Behaviors inspector can fire off an XMLHttpRequest using JavaScript. (For more on this topic, see the section "Setting Up a Request," later in this chapter.)

These features fit together nicely with JavaScript. For example, you can locate a text field with the ID `textField` in this way:

```
myTextField = document.getElementById ('textField');
```

Having gotten that field, you can now get its value:

```
myValue = myTextField.value;
```

Or you can set it like

```
myTextField.value = 'some value';
```

Not all elements on a page have the `value` property, but text elements do. Most elements support a more general content property called `innerHTML`. Rather than containing information such as you find in a text field's `value` property,

```
some value
```

`innerHTML` includes the markup:

```
<p>some value</p>
```

As a result, after a page is loaded in a browser, you can use JavaScript to access each of that page's elements. You generally need to know their names, although you can access them in other ways.

You can access the DOM for any page using `document`. You can also get to the DOM by using `window.document`. The DOM exists only when the page is displayed in a browser (which means inside a window that contains a document). You can't access a DOM from an HTML file that isn't displayed in a browser.

Asynchronous processing

You can write JavaScript code that is activated by an event to send off an `XMLHttpRequest`. But then what happens?

This aspect of the structure may be new to you. Most people are familiar with traditional programming in which each line of code is executed in sequence:

```
a = 1;
b = 2;
c = 3;
```

Executing each line of code one after the other is called *synchronous processing,* and it's the common way in which code is executed — so common, in fact, that the term isn't used very often.

With *asynchronous processing,* you provide a function that is executed when something happens. So instead of executing code after the previous line is executed, with asynchronous processing, you execute code that starts the process running (such as an XMLHttpRequest). As part of the setup process, you provide the code that executes when the process finishes. (This code is sometimes called a *completion routine* or a *callback function.*) The sequence of events in between firing off XMLHttpRequest and executing the code that runs on completion of XMLHttpRequest is invisible to you.

You're probably wondering, "What happens if something goes wrong? How can I tell what's going on?"

The solution turns out to be quite simple. You can call the callback function for XMLHttpRequest many times. The callback function receives a status value that lets it know what is happening. Depending on the status value, the callback function can take data returned from XMLHttpRequest and put it into an element on the page, or it can display an error. If the status indicates that things are still chugging along, you can either ignore it or let the user know that it's just a matter of time before the wonders are revealed.

The only important point to remember in this type of asynchronous structure is that you don't query the XMLHttpRequest or any other variable to find out the status. You wait until your callback function is called to let you know what the status is.

Setting Up a Request

Code in the Library, shown in Figure 11-1, can help you set up an XMLHttpRequest.

Listing 11-1 also shows the code in full with spacing adjusted for readability. This default Library code is ready for your customization.

Because it's often used in retrieving RSS feeds (you can find variations on it in the various RSS templates), feedURL is used as a variable name. In fact, you can use any URL, so don't be misled.

Figure 11-1:
Set up an
`XMLHttp`
`Request.`

Listing 11-1:   Creating an XMLHttpRequest

```
// Values you provide

// The feed to fetch
var feedURL = "http://www.apple.com/";
// The function to call when the feed is loaded; currently calls
// the XMLHttpRequest load snippet
var onloadHandler = function() { xmlLoaded(xmlRequest); };
// XMLHttpRequest setup code
var xmlRequest = new XMLHttpRequest();
xmlRequest.onload = onloadHandler;
xmlRequest.open("GET", feedURL);
xmlRequest.setRequestHeader("Cache-Control", "no-cache");
xmlRequest.send(null);
```

When you use this code snippet, you must insert the URL of the location from
which you're retrieving data. That means that the first line will need to be

```
var feedURL = "http://yourwebsite.com/";
```

The `onloadHandler` line specifies the callback function, which is described
in the next section, "Loading a Response." The other code requires no customization at all, so you just need to change the URL and the callback routine.

The `XMLHttpRequest` is created as an object with `new XMLHttpRequest();`
on Internet Explorer up to version 7, `XMLHttpRequest` was implemented as an
ActiveX control. Since version 7, `XMLHttpRequest` is implemented in the way
shown here. (The ActiveX control is still supported.) If you're looking at reference material on the Web, you may see the ActiveX control code, but rest
assured that you don't need to worry about it today.

Loading a Response

There are two parts to the process of loading a response:

- ✔ Creating the callback routine
- ✔ Checking status and managing data inside the routine

Creating the callback routine

The Library has code for you to start with on your callback routine. Figure 11-2 shows the relevant code in the Library, and Listing 11-2 shows it with reformatting.

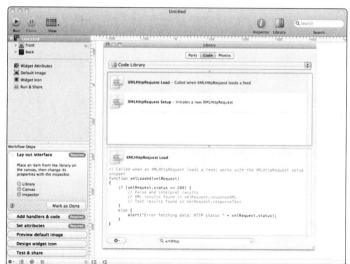

Figure 11-2:
Load an
XMLHttp
Request
response.

Listing 11-2:   Loading an XMLHttpRequest

```
// Called when an XMLHttpRequest loads a feed;
// works with the XMLHttpRequest setup snippet

function xmlLoaded(xmlRequest)
  {
    if (xmlRequest.status == 200) {
      // Parse and interpret results
      // XML results found in xmlRequest.responseXML
      // Text results found in xmlRequest.responseText
    }
```

(continued)

Listing 11-2 *(continued)*

```
else {
  alert("Error fetching data: HTTP status " + xmlRequest.status);
  }
}
```

You can structure the code you write in two ways. One way is to build on Listing 11-1. You can modify the code for `onloadHandler` with the code from Listing 11-2, as shown in Listing 11-3. The variable `onloadHandler` is set to the `function` operator, which includes the code for the function. Using the `function` operator to specify the code creates what is called an `anonymous` function because the function itself has no name: It's assigned to the `onloadHandler` variable.

Listing 11-3:   Structuring Your XMLHttpRequest (Function Operator)

```
// The function to call when the feed is loaded; currently calls
// the XMLHttpRequest load snippet
var onloadHandler = function() { if (xmlRequest.status == 200) {
    // Parse and interpret results
    // XML results found in xmlRequest.responseXML
    // Text results found in xmlRequest.responseText
  }
  else {
    alert("Error fetching data: HTTP status " + xmlRequest.status);
  }
};
```

Instead of the `function` operator, you can use the `function` statement. In that case, you declare the function, as shown in Listing 11-2 and refer to the function in Listing 11-1.

```
var onloadHandler = function() { xmlLoaded(xmlRequest); };
```

It doesn't matter which method you use. Some people prefer function statements, while other people prefer function operators. If your callback function is very short, the operator is often the easiest. Of course, "short" is a matter of debate, and it can lead to code in which you use both techniques, which can confuse people who are maintaining it. Which method you use is up to you.

Whichever way you declare the function (and whatever you happen to call it), the important line of code from Listing 11-1 still functions properly:

```
xmlRequest.onload = onloadHandler;
```

 `XMLHttpRequest` has several hooks for callback functions. The most commonly used are `onload` and `onreadystatechange`. You're often most interested in the end of loading (which may or may not include an error), but if the ready state changes, you can track the status of the handler as it proceeds.

Checking status and data

When your callback function is called, you first need to check its ready state and its status. status is the regular HTTP status code. (XMLHttpRequest is running over the HTTP protocol, which is one reason it's been so widely adopted.) Most people don't bother checking for all the status codes. (In fact, if you're using the onload event, you can probably bypass it entirely; for onreadystatechange, you should check its value.) The two status values you care about are OK (200) and Not Found (404).

The ready state values are specific to XMLHttpRequest. They are

- **0.** uninitialized
- **1.** open (processing has started)
- **2.** sent
- **3.** receiving
- **4.** Loaded

You're looking for status = 200 (OK) and ready state = 4 (loaded). This is done in this section of code in Listing 11-2:

```
if (xmlRequest.status == 200) {
  // Parse and interpret results
  // XML results found in xmlRequest.responseXML
  // Text results found in xmlRequest.responseText
}
else {
  alert("Error fetching data: HTTP status " +
    xmlRequest.status);
}
```

The ready state isn't checked because the code is invoked only for the onload event (which is 4).

When you have the 200/4 result, you can now access the data. As the code snippet shows you, you get XML results in xmlRequest.responseXML and the plain text version in xmlRequest.responseText. (Remember that xmlRequest is the variable into which you placed the XMLHttpRequest object. If you use another name, use it everywhere.)

When you're parsing structured data, such as an RSS feed, you can often find the code you need on the Internet. Take a look at how XMLHttpRequest is implemented in the RSS Dashboard widget templates.

You can find the relevant code in `main.js`. It's shown in Listing 11-4.

Listing 11-4: Getting an RSS Feed in a Dashboard Widget

```
httpFeedRequest = new XMLHttpRequest();

// Function callback when feed is loaded
httpFeedRequest.onload = function (e)
  {
    var feedRootElement;
    if (httpFeedRequest.responseXML) feedRootElement =
      httpFeedRequest.responseXML.documentElement;

      // Request is no longer pending
      // httpFeedRequest = null;

      // Process the loaded document
      processFeedDocument(feedRootElement);
  }
httpFeedRequest.overrideMimeType("text/xml");
httpFeedRequest.open("GET", feed.url);
httpFeedRequest.setRequestHeader("Cache-Control", "no-cache");

// Send the request asynchronously
httpFeedRequest.send(null);
```

In Listing 11-4, Dashcode-specific interface elements interact with common code that you can often find on the Internet to provide an effective user interface. This combination is common in Dashcode projects.

The `processFeedDocument` function does the parsing, which is standard RSS XML code you can find in many places. (You do have to add a couple of Dashcode-specific error messages to the standard code you can find on the Internet, but they're not necessary.) The data source has already been set up when you create it, so slipping in new content in the same format isn't a problem for Dashcode.

In order for this mechanism to work, you set up the data source when you're creating your widget or app by connecting to data in the format you're using later. After the data source is created and its properties are bound to interface elements, you can then use `XMLHttpRequest` to pick up new data in the same format.

Chapter 12

Navigating through Data

*W*hether your data comes from a file, a dynamic URL on the Internet, or from a call to XMLHttpRequest for the specific item you need, users have to find their way through the data to what they're looking for. Dashcode makes it easy for you to deploy tools to help them navigate through the data, and that's what this chapter is about.

Helping Users Find Their Way through Data

Data-intensive Dashcode projects tend to be built for Safari rather than Dashboard widgets. The main reason why is that navigating through data is something that people do very often on all personal computers. If you're running Dashboard, you can just as easily run Safari or data-specific programs, such as FileMaker Pro. Dashboard excels at quick lookups and calculations — conversions of units for times, temperatures, and currency; airline arrival and departure times; reference tools, such as dictionaries; and the like. The powerful data navigation tools of Dashcode are often not needed quite so much when you have your Mac right in front of you running Dashboard and anything else that you need.

On iPhone and in Safari, however, data navigation is a critical tool, and it's here that Dashcode's data navigation tools shine. Dashboard widgets can easily access the Internet and databases, but they truly excel at focused tasks. Safari running in a regular browser window on a PC or a Mac has the data resources and the space to provide sophisticated tools to navigate through them. In a strange way, the extreme limitations of the screen make data navigation easy on the iPhone; the designers at Apple knew from the beginning that space would be an issue, and they devised a variety of powerful interface tools to help manage the process. Many of these tools are built into Dashcode.

The data navigation tools build on the infrastructure I cover in the earlier chapters in this book:

- **Data sources and data models:** Dashcode structures format data automatically (see Chapters 9 and 10). When it comes to data navigation, perhaps the most important point to note is that Dashcode's data model support includes the ability to handle lists and containers of data elements. In the old days of handwritten code in languages such as C, FORTRAN, ALGOL, COBOL, and the like, it was usually up to the programmer to develop data structures and implement the code to step through them for every new project. It's now all in Dashcode.

- **Behaviors:** Dashcode behaviors can link interface elements, such as buttons, to code snippets that perform actions (see Chapter 6).

When you put these two sets of tools together, you have a powerful way to organize, structure, and navigate data. And on top of that theoretical benefit, you can find the combination of data sources and data models along with behaviors implemented in Dashcode templates so that right out of the box, you can provide powerful and data-rich projects that just need you to customize your data.

If you've ever built complex Web sites and applications, you may be surprised at what you can do with Dashcode. A great deal of what you had to code by hand in the past is now built into Dashcode so that you have less work to do, and it's a different kind of work.

Working with a List View

The most basic data navigation tool is a list view. The Edge-to-Edge list view (see Chapter 9) in the Browser template is available for mobile Safari; in Safari, it's just List. Mobile Safari also has a Rounded Rectangle list. All the lists behave the same way, and you set them up the same way. Figure 12-1 shows a Rounded Rectangle list being dragged to a Custom template in mobile Safari.

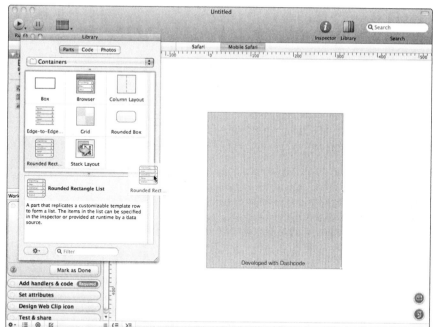

Figure 12-1:
Add a list to
a Dashcode
project.

Setting list labels and values with the Attributes inspector

Adding or deleting elements from the list in a Rounded Rectangle list or any of the other built-in lists is easy with the Attributes inspector. You can also change the labels and values, as shown in Figure 12-2.

Setting list labels and values with a data source

You can also use a data source for your list. Here's how to do it:

1. **Add a JSON or XML file to your project, as shown in Figure 12-3.**

   You use the `cefls_libraries_brief.xml` file from Chapter 10.

2. **Show the data sources and rename the default data source.**

   `listData` is used in the example.

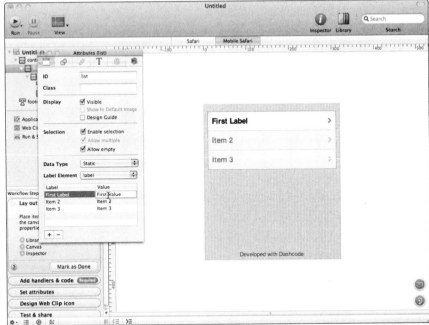

Figure 12-2:
Use the
Attributes
inspector to
change list
contents.

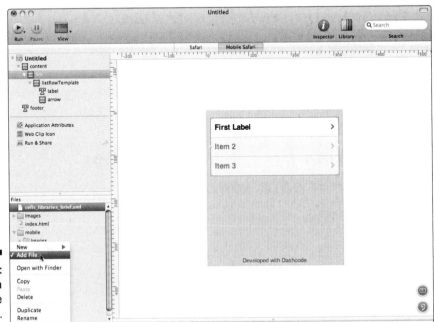

Figure 12-3:
Add a data
file to the
project.

3. **With the data source still selected, show the Source Code pane and set the data source URL, as shown in Figure 12-4.**

   The data model view is set up with data from the first item in the file. If it isn't, click the Reload button to the right of the URL.

4. **Bind the data source `name` property to the `label` property in the interface, as shown in Figure 12-5.**

   When you release the button, you see the binding for the `name` property as well as a new binding that Dashcode has automatically created from the data source `rec` element to the `list.datarray` property in the interface (see Figure 12-6).

   `rec` is the name of the list in the XML file. It stands for record, but you can name it anything. In the view hierarchy at the top of the navigator, you see the list view toward the top. It is created as part of the Library's Rounded Rectangle list. The list view is the highest level view inside `content`, and it contains `listRowTemplate`. You can rename any of those views, so you may wind up binding a `things` element in your data source to an `items` element in the interface.

5. **Run the project in the simulator, as shown in Figure 12-7.**

   Dashcode picks up the data from the file. To change the data, just change the contents of the file.

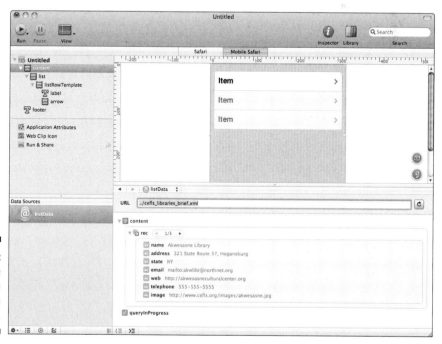

Figure 12-4: Name the data source and set the URL for it.

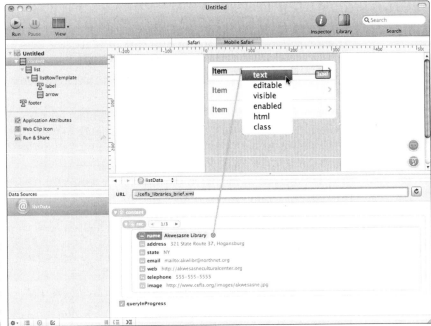

Figure 12-5:
Bind the
data source
to the list.

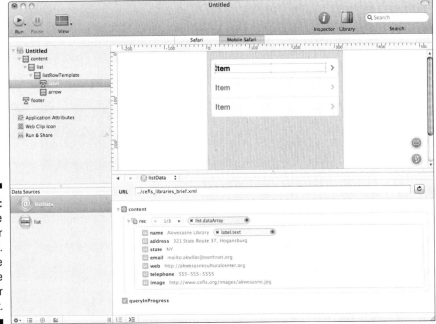

Figure 12-6:
Create the
binding for
the label.
Dashcode
creates the
binding for
the list.

Figure 12-7:
Test the
results.

Exploring with the Bindings inspector

You can format the interface using the inspector just as you always do: Adjust the color, size, and all the other attributes as you see fit.

As you're exploring the inspector, look at the Bindings inspector. You create bindings between the data model view and the interface elements by drawing lines between them. With the Bindings inspector, you can specify more details about the bindings you draw. Open the Bindings inspector and then select the list, as shown in Figure 12-8. The Bindings inspector is shown with the knot icon; it is the second from the right in Figure 12-8.

You want to click the list itself, so the easiest way to do so is to click the second or third item. The first item is the row template. If you click it, you see the binding shown in Figure 12-9.

The bindings between the data model view and the interface elements are bidirectional, but in the Dashcode data model view, you start from the property in the data model and look at the interface property to which it's bound. With the Bindings inspector, you start from the interface property and see the data property. After the binding is established, it doesn't matter which way you work.

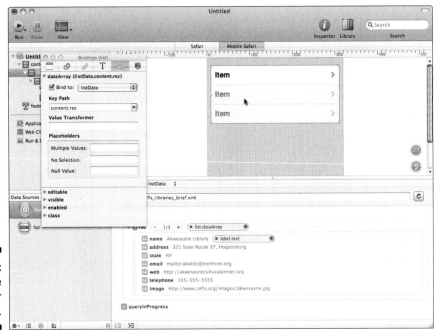

Figure 12-8:
Look at the
bindings for
the list.

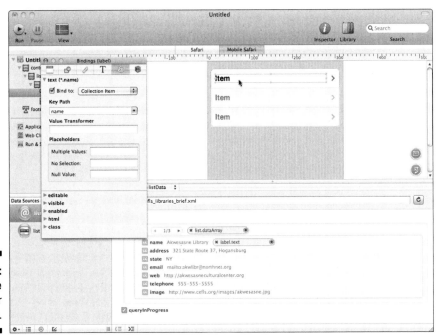

Figure 12-9:
Look at the
binding for
the first row.

The Bindings inspector can be very useful in sorting out what properties on either end can be bound. If you start from the data model view and draw the binding, you can't connect it to some interface elements. If you can connect it to interface elements, you see a menu letting you choose which particular properties you want to use. (Chapters 9 and 10 show you how to use some of those properties in bindings.)

Working with Multiple Controllers

You can use Dashcode to progress from formatted data in JSON or XML format to a data source that accesses the data from either a file or a dynamic source through a URL (see Chapter 9). The data file has a container at the top level that may contain a list of items, one or more single items, or a combination of the two. Conceptually, the following code is what such a file can look like. (The data is from the Browser mobile Safari template in Dashcode.)

```
{
    title: 'National Parks',
    items: [
        { name: "Acadia", location: "Maine, USA" },
        { name: "Bryce Canyon", location: "Utah, USA" },
        ...
    ]
}
```

In such a structure, you can bind the `title` element to any view in your project that accepts a text element. You can choose which particular property to bind the `title` element to, so you can bind it as a generic text property, but you can also bind it to specific text-based properties. You could even bind the title element of the data model view to a phone number field, although in that case, putting the title in a phone number field would not provide you with useful data — remember that you're adding context and your own knowledge to the formatted data in the file.

When you bind the `items` element, you normally bind it to a view that manages lists, and, in most cases, you bind it to a `dataArray` property. Doing so creates a new icon in the Data Sources list, and you can name it as you see fit. This icon is a *data controller*. The data controller keeps track of which element of a list is the current one. When you're working with a list that is bound to a `dataArray` property, you normally bind it.

Consider a situation in which you want to select two items from a data source. One of the most common is an interface in which you select the end-points of a route, such as the starting and ending location. Using the same library data that you've worked within "Setting list labels and values with a data source," you can select two libraries — one as a starting location and the other as an ending location. The data source is the list of libraries, so you don't need to have a second one. You will need two controllers, each of which can have its own selected library: one will be the start and the other will be the finish location. Using a single data source with two (or even more!) controllers is a common situation as you start working with data.

Here's how to use a single data source with two controllers:

1. **Create a new project from the Custom template, using the Safari option.**

   The completed project is downloadable at `www.dummies.com/go/ dashcodefd`.

2. **Add the `cefls_libraries_brief.xml` file to the project.**

3. **In the Data Sources list, rename the data source; in the data model view at the right, specify the file you added in Step 2.**

   Figure 12-10 shows the result with the data source renamed `libraries`. (Chapter 10 covers this technique in more detail.)

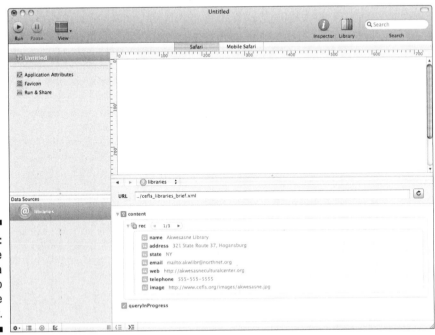

Figure 12-10:
Add a file and data source to the project.

4. **Add two List parts from the Containers section of the Library, as shown in Figure 12-11.**

   You have to add the parts one at a time.

5. **Add labels to the two List parts.**

   Name one label From and the other To so that you can select the appropriate libraries from the data source.

6. **Rearrange the labels and List parts, as shown in Figure 12-12.**

   The new List parts appear in the navigator.

7. **Change the List parts names to `from` and `to`, as shown in Figure 12-13.**

   Changing names of objects as soon as you create them helps keep your project organized.

8. **Bind the `name` property of the data source to the `rowLabel` view in the `from` view, as shown in Figure 12-14.**

   Don't worry if another view in the navigator is highlighted as in Figure 12-14. While you're binding a property, the highlighted view in the navigator isn't updated dynamically.

9. **When you release the mouse button, choose the `text` property.**

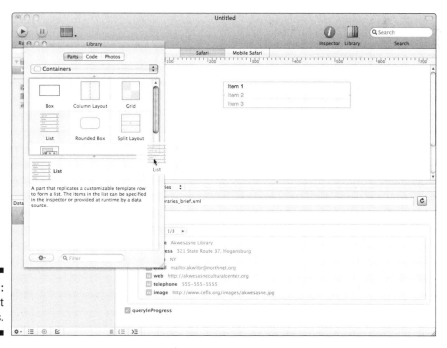

Figure 12-11:
Add two List parts.

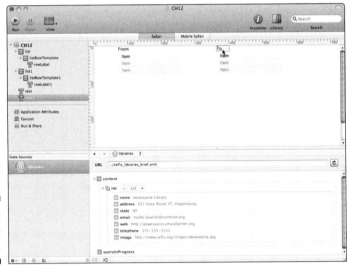

Figure 12-12:
Clean up the
interface.

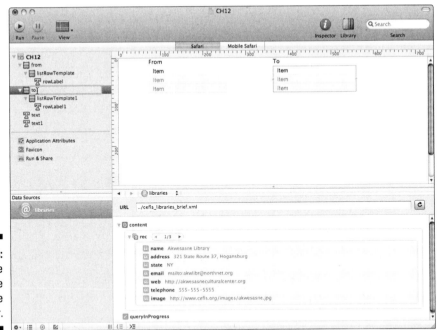

Figure 12-13:
Change the
name of the
views in the
navigator.

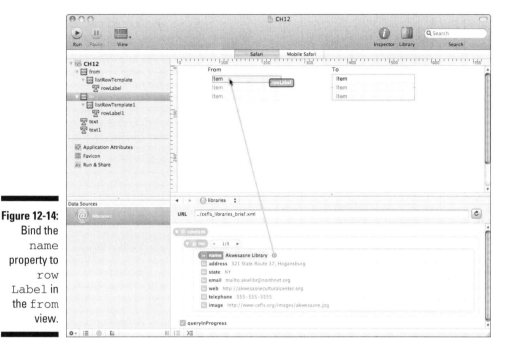

Figure 12-14:
Bind the
`name`
property to
`row
Label` in
the `from`
view.

A new controller appears in the Data Sources list. The controller has the name of the list view that contains the field to which the property is bound: `from`. Figure 12-15 shows the completed binding.

10. Bind the `name` property to `rowLabel` in the `to` view — the other view.

This step creates another controller, as shown in Figure 12-16. Use the disclosure triangles to view the multiple bindings for `rec` (the container) and the `name` property. Note that as you hover the mouse over a property with multiple bindings, the various interface elements to which it is bound are highlighted and identified.

11. Run the project, as shown in Figure 12-17.

Each of the List parts now can have a different library selected.

The ability to take a single data source and have several controllers, each of which has a different current record, vastly expands the possibilities of your project.

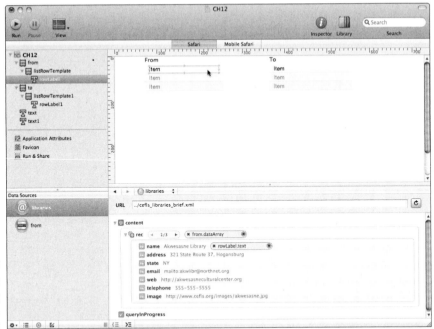

Figure 12-15:
The binding is complete.

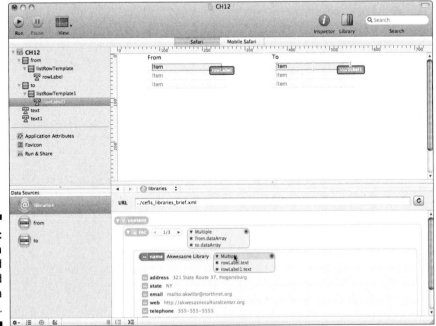

Figure 12-16:
Create a second binding and its data controller.

Figure 12-17:
Run the
project.

Working with Stack Layouts

The ability to select an item from a list that is drawn from a data source opens many doors. If you have several lists, you can have selections in each list that are based on the same data source but that are different from list to list. You can use those two lists and their own selections to select two types of items from the same data source (such as a `from` and `to` location).

Another common way of using a data source that is bound to a list is to drill down to specific information. The Browser template for mobile Safari implements this functionality. In Figure 12-18, the Browser template appears with the default data that is part of the template.

A stack layout provides a way to drill down through layers of data that is found in a data source. The stack layout and the views within it implement the functionality that works after you've connected the structured data source to the views at each level (see Chapter 10).

Figure 12-18:
Run the
Browser
template.

Chapter 13

Preferring Preferences for User Options and Saving Data

. . . .

In This Chapter

▶ Looking at data

▶ Understanding key/value pairs

▶ Storing data in different apps and widgets

. . . .

*W*hen you think about integrating data into your app or widget, you probably think of the traditional forms of data — files and databases. They often contain large amounts of data that your app or widget can process and display. Dashcode lets you build projects that interact with files and databases as data sources as well as projects that retrieve data on demand using XMLHttpRequest (see Chapter 11).

But as you can find out in this chapter, there's a lot more to data in Dashcode projects.

Whose Data Is It Anyway?

Other than the data that resides in databases and files and that is retrieved from the Internet, your project deals with two types of data:

✔ Data you put into your project

✔ Data users put into their copies of your project

You need to recognize these two types of data and manage them in different ways.

Looking at your project data

You can build all sorts of data into your project through its interface. If a field has a label next to it that says Name or Address, that's data. Dashcode provides a structure so that you can display these labels (and any other text in the interface) in various languages as long as you provide information in your project that says that "Name" in English should be displayed as "Nom" in French.

Automatically modifying the text in your interface is called *localization,* and it's not a word-for-word translation. Often, a single word in one language becomes two or more in another language. In addition, the word "Name" in one context may be translated to one word in certain contexts and to another word in other contexts. Each of these versions of the word *Name* is data, and the localization structure makes it possible to manage it properly with very little effort on your part. Data doesn't have to be text. Widgets and apps contain lots of data in their code. A Dashcode project with a button that converts temperatures from Celsius to Fahrenheit contains data; somewhere or other, the conversion formula appears in your project's code.

In other cases, your executable code can contain other data for its use, and sometimes that data isn't so specific as a conversion formula. A calendar app or widget may contain a button that computes the number of days between two given dates. If the date range is long enough, that calculation may make certain assumptions (or ignore certain situations) so that the formula may not match everyone's idea of what the date range should be.

The most common instance of confusion over the calculation of date range is the leap year calculation: Years evenly divisible by four are leap years unless they're also divisible by 400, in which case they're not leap years. But if they're also divisible by 1,000, they're leap years. And there are even some more wrinkles over very long periods of time extending many centuries out into the future.)

Apps and widgets, like all other types of programs, contain a wide variety of built-in data values. Developers learn to watch for them because eventually they can cause problems. If your project lets people keep track of restaurants and it has a limit of 10 (or 100, or 10,000), that's built-in data just as much as a conversion factor for a formula is. Somewhere you need to document this limitation because eventually you may need to change it or track down a bug when a user adds the 10,001th restaurant.

Looking at your users' data

The other kind of data is data that users store in your app or widget. This data can be what you often think of as data — facts and figures — but it also can be other data and information, such as a preference for the background color of your app or widget, the font to use to display text, and so on.

Making your users' data your data and vice versa

It's not always clear when you should code data for your project directly into the code (as is the case with a conversion factor) and when you should store it as a preference. You face the same issue with the choice of a font to display text: You can make that choice and code it into your project, or you can let your users make the choice.

Here's a tip that developers have used for years. Storing preferences in a database (the Dashcode technique) is a little bit more complicated for you than just setting a font with the Text inspector or using another technique to have your app or widget include the preferred value. If you hard-code a value, coming back later to turn it into a user-controlled preference means doing some rewriting. On the other hand, if you put the preference into the Dashcode structure that stores preferences, you can write your code so that it uses the stored preference. If you want to come back later and let the user choose, you just add an interface feature to let users set the value. For starters, you'll do the setting of the preference. The actual value of the preference is retrieved from the database that you'll use.

Because over time users want more and more control, implementing a structure that lets you support user-defined preferences in the future can save you time.

Note that it's not just users that often want more and more control. Whether you're building a Dashcode project for yourself, the public, or any other group, it can get tedious and boring (not to mention time-wasting) if every time a preference changes you have to modify your code.

From your point of view, data is data, but users make a distinction between the facts-and-figures type of data and the data that controls preferences and appearance. In fact, the tools that are most often used for storing preference information are different from those that store the facts-and-figures data. The two meet in cases where a user preference determines what data is stored. For example, a preference may allow your app to store data for 10 restaurants or 100 restaurants — or even to store an unlimited number or none at all.

Preferences are small snippets of data, such as the background color or the font to use for text displays. User data is often a larger quantity of data (the novel they're writing), but it can be a small amount of data, and in those cases, the tools used for storing preferences come into play. In reality, the tools you use depend on the quantity of data to be stored.

Using Key/Value Pairs for Preferences

The heart of Dashcode's architecture for storing small amounts of data, such as preferences, is a technique called *key/value encoding*. Key/value encoding is implemented using a data structure called an associative array.

Reusing key/value logic

The implementation of key/value storage in the Utility Safari app and in other Dashcode projects is very powerful. Not only can you store something like high-score or font-family along with its value, but you can use that same logic for several items in the project. Consider storing preferences for something such as fonts or colors.

The data that you store consists of a key that identifies each item, and the value that item has. For example, to store the preferences to use for displaying text, the key may be `font`, and the value may be `Helvetica`. You normally aren't limited to single words — the key may be font size, and the value may be 12. You can have multiple words for both keys and values.

Although you may have multiple words, most of the time the value in a key/value pair is a single value. If you want to store the high score in a game as well as the date it was achieved, the best way is to store two pairs: `'high-score'`-`'298'` and `'high-score -date'`-`'5/29/09'`. If you know a bit of programming, you can certainly pick apart a string consisting of both values, but there is relatively little cost in using two key/value pairs rather than having to pick the data apart with your own code.

You can store a key/value pair, such as font/Helvetica, or a separate pair, such as font/times. If you have several elements that you can styled separately, you can provide a key/value pair for each one using an `id` field in the database. If the name view has ID 1, and an address view has ID 2, you can store the key/value pairs as

```
1 (name) / font / Helvetica
2 (address) / font / times
```

Dashcode projects include the code that is needed for implementing key/value encoding, and it is slightly different for Dashboard widgets, Safari Web apps, and mobile Safari apps. In all cases, the following scenario happens.

A database built into Safari is implemented in SQLite, an implementation of the basics of the SQL database architecture. Unlike database applications, SQLite is code that you can add to applications to provide database functionality within them. For example, SQLite provides the database support for Firefox to store bookmarks, cookies, and other data; and various Adobe products as well as Mac OS X use it. It's also built into iOS for iPhone and iPad.

You don't need to go into implementation details. All you need to know is that a database is available to you for the purpose of storing and retrieving data for your Dashcode project. In its basic form, SQLite is designed for a single application to use: If you want to share data, you generally use a database application, such as FileMaker Pro or MySQL.

In the Dashcode templates, the database is created or accessed when the app or widget starts up. If it can't be created or the configuration doesn't support it, the widget or app just continues along using memory to temporarily store data. If you're interested in the internals of data management, that database table has two main columns: key and value. Because keys are unique, you simply request a key, and its value is returned. The process is simple, and it works well.

One environment where you often can't create a database is the simulator. To test the behavior of storing data, deploy it to an iPhone or the Web using the Run & Share pane in Dashcode. Try out the setting. Then leave the app or widget, and do something else. Then return to make certain that the settings have been retained. Then move one step further: Totally restart the Mac or iPhone to see whether the data has been preserved. A total restart on a Mac means choosing Apple⇨Shut Down and then powering the computer back on after ten seconds or so. On iPhone, use the Wake/Sleep button at the top right of the iPhone to turn it off. Wait ten seconds or so and then use the Wake/Sleep button to power it back on.

The architecture described in this chapter applies across Dashboard widgets, Safari Web applicationss, and mobile Safari Web applications, but the implementations are slightly different. For each implementation, you see how it works with one of the templates, and then you see how you can add your own preference using Library parts.

In all three implementations, the sequence of events for implementing key/value storage begins with creating or opening the database; it then continues with storing and retrieving preference values. That first step — creating or opening the database — usually consists of the default behavior in the Dashcode template, and you don't often modify it. You can skip over the steps of creating or opening the database if you want, but if you want to modify the way in which data is stored, they're essential.

Using Key/Value Preferences in Mobile Safari Apps

The basic architecture of key/value storage is provided in all the Dashcode templates for mobile Safari. In many cases, the code is commented out and not used. In other templates, the code is actually used. The Utility template is a good example of the use of key/value storage.

The Utility template uses some of the basic interface elements of a Dashboard widget, such as the concept of a front and back of the interface. As you see in Figure 13-1, the initial screen contains some text. If you tap it (or click it in the simulator), you can modify the text.

Figure 13-1:
You can enter and modify text.

Just like in Dashboard widgets, the *i* button flips the app over to the back, as shown in Figure 13-2.

If you create a new Dashcode project from the Safari Utility template, you can experiment with it.

The simulator often doesn't support database accesses. If you run the Dashcode project in the simulator, the settings for text and fonts will be lost when you quit from it. But deploy the project on an iPhone using Run & Share, and the settings are preserved even after you use the Wake/Sleep button to power the iPhone off and then back on.

The Utility app stores the following pieces of information:

✔ Text

✔ Font

✔ Font size

✔ Font color

Most people consider text as data and the other three values as preferences, but there is absolutely no difference in the way they are stored, retrieved, and set. Yes, the text is typed and the other items are selected with a tap, but in all cases, what is stored is the value of an element in the interface. The fact that it may be a text view or another type of element is immaterial.

Figure 13-2:
The back of the app lets you change settings.

Setting up the database

The first step to set up a database is to open or create the database when the app is launched. You rarely, if ever, need to change this default code.

Exploring the load function

The process of setting up the database begins in the `load` function in `main.js`. For any Dashcode project, the first place to look to find startup code is in the basic `index.html` file that is the first file loaded. For a mobile Safari project, control then passes to the `index.html` file in the `mobile` folder of the project. At the start of the body of that file, you find the key line of code:

```
<body onload="load();">
```

The `onload` event is triggered as soon as the page is loaded, and as a result, the `load()` function is called.

Listing 13-1 shows the code for `onload` in the mobile Safari Utility app; it's located in `mobile/main.js`. (Note that as in all listings, I changed some spacing from the template code to make it easier to fit on the book pages.)

Listing 13-1:   Setting Up the Database

```
// original message and settings, in case there is no
// client side database
var originalSettings = {};

//
// Function: load()
// Called by HTML body element's onload event when the
// mobile Safari web apps is ready to start
//
function load()
{
    var element = document.getElementById('message');
    if (element) {
        originalSettings.message = element.value;
        originalSettings.color = 'black';
        // We only have a limited set of color chips,
        // so use 'black' here.
        var fontSettings = getFontSettingsFromElement(element);
        originalSettings.fontFamily = fontSettings.fontFamily;
        originalSettings.fontSize = fontSettings.fontSize;
        element.value = '';
    }

    dashcode.setupParts();
```

```
var database = initDB(true);
if (!database) {
    element.value = originalSettings.message;
}
}
```

Whenever you're exploring a template, enlarge as many of the elements in the navigator as possible so that you can identify them. In Figure 13-3, you see that a click in the center of the canvas image highlights the text view there as well as in the navigator. (It's the `message` view.)

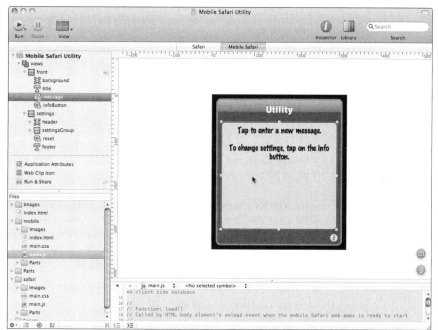

Figure 13-3:
Look at the views in the navigator and canvas.

This code not only shows the use of the database for preferences, but it shows a common structure for initializing many apps and widgets. Note that at the top of the listing, `originalSettings` is declared. The next chunk of code gets the message element and moves its properties into `original Settings`. The text you create in Dashcode (`element.value`) is moved into `originalSettings.message`, and `element.value` is emptied. The text you created in Dashcode will be overridden if necessary with data from the database — data entered by the user.

```
var element = document.getElementById('message');
    if (element) {
        originalSettings.message = element.value;
        originalSettings.color = 'black';
        // We only have a limited set of color chips,
        // so use 'black' here.
        var fontSettings = getFontSettingsFromElement(element);
        originalSettings.fontFamily = fontSettings.fontFamily;
        originalSettings.fontSize = fontSettings.fontSize;
        element.value = '';
    }
```

The next line is a call to `dashcode.setupParts`. This routine is located in `Parts/core/utilities.js`. It creates all the parts you've added to your project from the Library. This routine uses the list of those parts that Dashcode creates as you add them; it's stored in `mobile/Parts/setup.js`. These files are internal to Dashcode, so you almost never have to worry about them, but it doesn't hurt to know how Dashcode does its dynamic work.

Initializing the database with initDB

`initDB` is the routine that does the database initialization work. It's located at `Scripts/UtilitySupport.js`. You rely on the work done in `initDB` in the calls that you use later on as the project runs. The code is shown in Listing 13-2. Some portions of it are modifiable. Note that this JavaScript code uses the HTML 5 offline object storage API.

The `database` variable is declared and set to null. After that, the name of the database table your project will use is hard-coded (`SimpleKeyValueTable`). It's unlikely you'll want to change the name, but if you need to create an additional table or two, use that line of code as a template. In fact, what you very well might do is create a modification of `initDB` called `initMyDB` so that your changes are encapsulated.

Although you'll be running your Dashcode project on an iPhone, initially `__for_iPhone` is set to false. (The double-underscore at the beginning of the name means that it's an internal variable — keep out!) That setting is the default. When `initDB` is called from `load`, it will have `true` or `false` passed in, depending on whether it's to be used for iPhone. The parameter value always overrides the default setting.

Inside the function, the database opens. If the database isn't available, it's created. If you're modifying this code or copying it for another table, the line you need to change is

```
database = openDatabase("Message", "1.0",
    "MessageDatabase", 1000);
```

The name of the table is set in `DB_tableName` at the top of the `UtilitySupport.js` file

The four parameters are

- ✔ Name (internal)
- ✔ Version
- ✔ Display name (for users to see)
- ✔ Estimated database size

If the database opens successfully, it's returned from `window.open database` as an object that is stored in the `database` variable. The code then goes on to count the records. The structure of all database calls to SQLite in this API is the same.

Here is how you issue a database call using the database created by `initDB` and used throughout your mobile Safari project:

1. **Start from a database object, such as the one returned from `window.opendatabase` and stored in `database`.**

2. **Call the `transaction` method of that object as in `database.transaction`.**

3. **Pass in one to four arguments:**

   The first is the callback function that is executed. It contains your primary SQL.

   The second is an array of the parameters to be filled into the SQL. It often is empty as it is here — `[]`.

   The third is the callback routine that is executed if the call is successful.

   The fourth is the callback for an error.

In the code shown in Listing 13-2, you actually have nested calls. The basic call counts the number of records in the database that may have been opened. The call uses the value stored in `DB_tableName`, so the call is

```
"SELECT COUNT(*) FROM " + DB_tableName
```

or, with the variable filled in

```
SELECT COUNT(*) FROM SimpleKeyValueTable
```

If that call fails, the error callback assumes that the failure came about because the database wasn't there, so it goes ahead and creates the database with

```
tx.executeSql("CREATE TABLE " + DB_tableName +
  " (id INTEGER PRIMARY KEY,  key TEXT, value TEXT)",
```

A success callback follows, but there is no error callback in case the creation fails. You may want to add one, but in most cases, checking for failure on the first try is just fine.

Listing 13-2:   initDB

```javascript
var database = null;
// The client-side database
var DB_tableName = "SimpleKeyValueTable";
// database name
var __for_iPhone = false;

//
// Function: initDB()
// Init and create the local database, if possible
//
function initDB(foriPhone)
{
  __for_iPhone = foriPhone;

  try {
    if (window.openDatabase) {
        database = openDatabase("Message", "1.0",
        "Message Database", 1000);
      if (database) {
        database.transaction(function(tx) {
          // SQL to execute
          tx.executeSql(
            "SELECT COUNT(*) FROM " + DB_tableName,

          // SQL arguments
          [],

          // success callback
          function(tx, result) {
            var obj = result.rows.item(0);
            var rows = obj["COUNT(*)"];

            if (!rows){
              initContent();
            } else if((rows == 1) && foriPhone){
              initContent();
            } else if ((rows == 4) && !foriPhone) {
              initContent();
            }
```

```
          loadContent();
        }, //end (tx, result)

        // error callback
        function(tx, error) {
          // Database doesn't exist. Let's create one.

          // SQL to execute within error callback
          tx.executeSql("CREATE TABLE " + DB_tableName +
            " (id INTEGER PRIMARY KEY,  key TEXT,
            value TEXT)",

          // SQL arguments for SQL within error callback
          [],

          // success callback for routine called in
          // overall error callback
          function(tx, result) {
            initContent();
            loadContent();
          }); //(tx, result)
        }); // overall error callback
      }); //database.transaction
    } // if (database)
  } // if (window.openDatabase)
} catch(e) {
    database = null;
} // catch

  return database;
} // initDB
```

Finishing up the database calls

No matter whether you create a database or open it, you wind up calling two functions before returning from `initDB`: `initContent` and `loadContent`.

`initContent` does just what it says. It's called right at the beginning to set data in memory to default values or the values in the database. Listing 13-3 shows the code.

The `message` view is retrieved by ID and stored in a variable called `element`. Remember that in `load` (see Listing 13-1), the default settings were set for `message`, and the default message was stored in `originalSettings.message`.

Listing 13-3: initContent

```
function initContent()
{
    var element = document.getElementById('message');
    if (!element) return;

    // Clean inline styles so that external styles can be \
            // applied during init
    element.style.fontFamily = '';
    element.style.fontSize = '';
    element.value = originalSettings.message;

    insertValue(0, "message", originalSettings.message);
    insertValue(1, "font-family", originalSettings.fontFamily);
    insertValue(2, "font-size", originalSettings.fontSize);
    insertValue(3, "color", originalSettings.color);
}
```

In Listing 13-4, `loadContent` does the actual loading of values. (It's actually done in `retrieveStoredInfo`, which retrieves the data and sets up the key/value pairs.)

Listing 13-4: loadContent

```
function loadContent()
{
    if (!retrieveStoredInfo(setValueForKey)) {
        // Load defaults
        updateColorChip(originalSettings.color);
        updateSelectValue(document.getElementById('fontFamily'),
            originalSettings.fontFamily);
        updateSelectValue(document.getElementById('fontSize'), originalSettings.
            fontSize);
    }
}
```

These and other database calls are also located in `Scripts/UtilitySupport.js`. The various scripts let you insert data, update it (that is, modify existing data), clean out a table, and perform other utilities. The content of the scripts doesn't matter because you rarely go into them, but you may use them repeatedly. `initDB` differs from the other scripts in this file because you may go into it if you add another database or rename it.

Storing a key/value pair

After you set up the database, using it is simple, thanks to key/value encoding. For example, in order to change the font, here's what you do:

1. On the back of the interface, select the `fontFamily` pop-up button.

You can select the button in the canvas; it will automatically be selected in the navigator. Or, you can select it in the navigator, and it is automatically selected in the canvas, as shown in Figure 13-4.

2. Using the Behaviors inspector, go to the `fontFamilyChanged` handler.

If you were writing this code yourself, you'd type the name of the handler, and the shell to fill in the code would be provided for you. Figure 13-5 shows the code.

3. Review or write the code.

This process has three steps:

    a. Get the value of the interface element (the pop-up button, in this case):

```
var value = document.getElementById('fontFamily').value;
```

    b. Use that value to set the relevant property of the `message` element or any other element that needs to be changed now:

```
document.getElementById('message').style.fontFamily = value;
```

    c. Update the value in the database. You have to call one of the other routines in `Scripts/UtilitySupport/js` — `UpdateValue`:

Figure 13-4:
Implement font changing.

Figure 13-5:
The handler
implements
the
changes.

```
updateValue(1, "font-family", value);
```

Note that `updateValue` takes three arguments: the `id` number, which you use if you want to be able to specify a preference like font family for multiple objects, the key, and the value. `updateValue` is coded in such a way that it works no matter what the data you pass in happens to be.

These steps let you manage the preferences using interface elements, such as pop-up buttons. As soon as you call `updateValue`, the data is in the database and loads the next time you run.

Storing the text of the message view is slightly different from storing a font family, font size, or color. Select that view on the front of your project's interface, and, with the Behaviors inspector, go to the `messageChanged` handler, as shown in Figure 13-6. The difference is that because the interface element (the text view) already contains the data, you need to change it only in the database. You can leave out step 3(b) from the steps listed.

Using Key/Value Preferences in Safari Web Applications

The Safari Utility template is similar to the one for mobile Safari, although it looks very different. However, both of them are built on key/value encoding.

Figure 13-6:
You can
also store
the
message.

Instead of the small message area used in the mobile Safari version, you have a much bigger area, as shown in Figure 13-7.

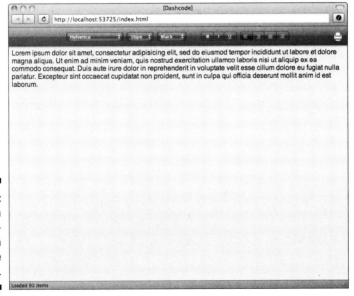

Figure 13-7:
You have a
larger mes-
sage area
and more
options.

In addition to options such as alignment and style, you also have a button that lets you print the document. Chapter 15 explores this template more fully; this chapter shows you the database interface and how it differs from the mobile Safari version of the Utility template.

The basic structure of key/value encoding is the same as you saw for mobile Safari.

Setting up the database

The database is set up in the same basic way for Safari as for mobile Safari. Once again, the process starts with the `load` function, which is the `onload` handler for `index.html` — just as it was for mobile Safari — only now the code is different. The code for a Safari Web application is located inside the `safari` folder in `safari/main.js`.

Exploring the load function

The Utility Safari Web application has a different kind of functionality from the mobile Safari Web application (see Chapter 15). This app isn't designed to run inside Dashboard nor on iPhone — both environments with serious constraints particularly with regard to size. As a Web app, the Utility template runs directly in a browser window, which means a larger and resizable window. Listing 13-5 shows you the load function for the Web app.

Listing 13-5:   Web Application load Function

```
var originalSettings = {};  // Original content and settings,
// in case there is no client side database

// Called by HTML body element's onload event when the
// Safari web app is ready to start
function load(){
  dashcode.setupParts();

  document.getElementById("leftJustifyButton").object.
    _setPressed(true);

    // enable editing
    doc = document.getElementsByTagName
      ("iframe")[0].contentDocument;
    doc.designMode = "on";
    Event.observe(doc, "keypress", updateContentDocument);
    Event.observe(doc, "mousemove", updateToolbarButtons);
    Event.observe(doc, "mouseup", updateToolbarButtons);
    Event.observe(doc, "keyup", updateToolbarButtons);
    Event.observe(doc, "keydown", updateToolbarButtons);


    doc.body.style.fontFamily = "Helvetica";
```

```
var placeholder = "Lorem ipsum dolor sit amet, consectetur
    adipisicing elit, sed do eiusmod tempor incididunt ut
    labore et dolore magna aliqua. Ut enim ad minim veniam,
    quis nostrud exercitation ullamco laboris nisi ut
    aliquip ex ea commodo consequat. Duis aute irure dolor
    in reprehenderit in voluptate velit esse cillum
    dolorefugiat nulla pariatur. Excepteur sint occaecat
    cupidatat non proident, sunt in culpa qui officia
    deserunt mollit anim id est laborum."

doc.body.innerHTML = originalSettings.content = placeholder;

initDB(false);
}
```

Chapter 15 describes some additional setup code. What you care about here are three familiar lines of code:

```
dashcode.setupParts(); //at the top
doc.body.stye.fontFamily = "Helvetica"; //towards the middle
initDB (false) // at the bottom
```

`dashcode.setupParts()` is the same function that is called for a mobile Safari app. It's located in `Parts/core/utilities.js`, and the `Parts` folder is at the top level of the file structure — next to but not within `safari` and `mobile`.

When it comes to initializing the database with `initDB`, once again, you're ahead of the game: The same code that is used for mobile Safari is used for Safari.

Finishing up the database calls

Finishing up database initialization for a Safari Web application is different from finishing up for a mobile Safari Web application. The content is stored in the database, so Listing 13-6 shows `initContent` and `loadContent`. The content includes the styling information (see Chapter 15). On iPhone, with its relatively small screen, setting the font for the entire text is fine. But on a Safari Web app, you can store the styling information as part of the content. Figure 13-8 shows the result.

Listing 13-6:   initContent and loadContent for Safari Web App

```
function initContent(){
    insertValue(4, "content", originalSettings.content);
}

// Load saved content and settings from the database. If there is
// no local database, we just use element's original properties
function loadContent(){
    if (!retrieveStoredInfo(setValueForKey))
        doc.body.innerHTML = originalSettings.content;
}
```

Figure 13-8:
You can store multiple styles within the content on a Safari Web app.

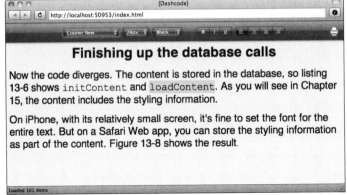

Storing a key/value pair

Although the implementation of storing a key/value pair is different from a mobile Safari app, a Safari Web app uses the same process. Because the preferences for fonts and styling are stored inside the content and apply only to sections of it (you can italicize one word, for example), you really only have to store one preference: the content itself containing the styles.

Safari Web applications use exactly the same mechanism as storing preferences in mobile Safari Web applications:

```
// Evaluate the key and update the corresponding element
function setValueForKey(key, value){
  if (key == 'content')
    doc.body.innerHTML = value;
}
```

Using Key/Value Preferences in Dashboard Widgets

Safari Web apps and mobile Safari apps run in the Safari browser; Safari processes all their code and then sends it to the browser on a Mac, PC, or a mobile device. That's why you and Dashcode have to be a bit involved in setting up the database, opening it, and managing it.

Dashboard widgets are different from Safari Web applications in that they run in Dashboard, which runs on Mac OS X. The code in a widget can access the application programming interfaces (APIs) of Mac OS X and Cocoa (the interface framework), as well as other APIs that may be installed for other software and hardware. This route is much more direct, which is reflected in this section. A widget that is running in Dashboard already has access to database storage courtesy of Mac OS X and Dashboard, so you have to get and set only the key/value pairs. Dashboard does everything else for you.

But you need to be concerned with one other issue, shown in Figure 13-9.

When you add Dashboard widgets to your Dashboard, you position them where you want them. The next time you go into Dashboard (most often with the F12 function key, the special F4 Dashboard key, or a keyboard equivalent on a laptop), your Dashboard looks the same as it did the last time you were there — at least with regard to where the widgets are.

You can add more than one instance of a widget. In Figure 13-9, you can see three instances of the built-in dictionary widget. One shows dictionary entries, and a second shows thesaurus entries. The third shows its back, where you can see a preference to set the font size. (Remember that preferences for widgets belong on the back of the widgets.)

If you look at the two forward-facing widgets, the font size setting clearly applies to a single instance of a widget: That's how you can have two copies of a widget each with its own data and settings.

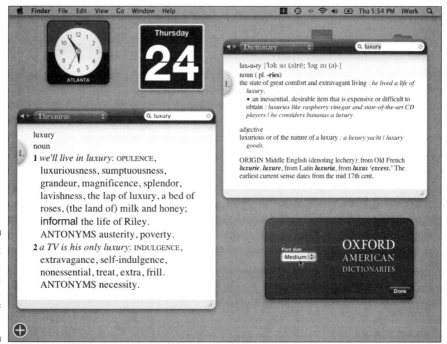

Figure 13-9:
You can
have
multiple
instances of
a widget.

You also can set preferences for all instances of a widget at once. For example, if the dictionary widget were programmed to use global preferences, the font size would be the same in each instance.

The distinction between global settings and instance settings also applies to data. If a widget's settings are stored in a preference (even if it's done without your explicitly setting it), the widget can open with the last data you looked at. Sometimes that's the right behavior.

Other times — for example, in a clock or calendar widget — you want the widget to open with data other than what appeared the last time. Perhaps you want a blank widget, but you may want appropriate settings. In order for all it to work, you distinguish between *global* and *instance* preferences. But the setting and getting of values is the same.

Setting a global preference

Here's the code from the Library to set a global preference for all instances of a widget:

```
// Values you provide
var preferenceKey = "key";
// replace with the key for a preference
var preferenceValue = "value";
// replace with a preference to save
// Preference code
widget.setPreferenceForKey(preferenceValue, preferenceKey);
```

As the comments indicate, you simply replace the key and value strings with the settings you want. The line of code then sets the global preference. You don't have to do any setup calls.

Getting a global preference

The Library also has code you use to get a global preference:

```
// Values you provide
var preferenceForKey = "key";
// replace with the key for a preference

// Preference code
preferenceForKey = widget.preferenceForKey(preferenceForKey);
```

You can compress this code so that instead of setting a variable (preference ForKey) to the key, you just use the string in the line of code. This version is slightly more verbose but easier to maintain for many people.

Setting an instance preference

If you want to set a preference for a single instance only (most typically the current instance), you can have the effect shown in Figure 13-9 where the font size applies only to one instance. Here is the Library code to set an instance preference:

```
// Values you provide
var preferenceKey = "key";
// replace with the key for a preference
var preferenceValue = "value";
// replace with a preference to save

// Preference code
widget.setPreferenceForKey(preferenceValue, widget.identifier +
    "-" + preferenceKey);
```

If you compare this code to the code for setting a global preference, you see that the key used is actually the identifier of the widget (see Chapter 14) concatenated with the actual key that you're using.

Getting an instance preference

Getting an instance preference works just the same way as setting one

```
// Values you provide
var preferenceForKey = "key";
// replace with the key for a preference

// Preference code
preferenceForKey = widget.preferenceForKey(widget.identifier +
"-" + preferenceForKey);
```

Dashboard automatically assigns the widget's identifier for the widget, so you don't have to worry about assigning it yourself. In the cases of both getting and setting instance preferences, the addition of the widget's identifier changes the key itself, so you're using exactly the same structure you used for global widget preferences as well as preferences for mobile Safari apps and Safari Web apps.

Part IV

Trying Out Each Environment

In this part . . .

This part lets you put tips and technologies together into practical projects. Part of the power of Dashcode is that you can write key sections of your projects once and then deploy those projects in various ways. For example, in this part, you see how to create and deploy a project based on the Browser template that can run on Safari itself, iPhone, and iPad.

Chapter 14

Creating a Browser Safari Application

In This Chapter

▶ Working with the Browser template

▶ Managing an iPad Safari Web application

▶ Using value transformers

▶ Using a browser behavior

The Browser Dashcode template is one of the most useful templates you'll find: It provides an efficient and compact navigation tool for browsing through hierarchical data. In this chapter, you see a start-to-finish guide on how to actually build and deploy a project based on the Browser template.

This chapter also shows you how to use the Browser template to build a Safari Web application that runs equally well on a desktop or laptop, iPhone, iPod touch, and iPad. This app uses different interface elements for each one so that users have an experience appropriate to the device that they're using.

Creating the Unmodified Browser Project

In this chapter, you modify the Browser template. Before you jump in, create your project from the template (whichever one it is), name it, and then test it. The purpose is to make certain that everything works in its unmodified state. It also tests your Dashcode deployment if this project happens to be the first one you've created.

Here's how you create and test the project before your modifications and improvements (and, if fate isn't with you, mistakes you may accidentally make):

1. **Open the New Project dialog by launching Dashcode or by choosing File⇨New Project (see Figure 14-1).**

Figure 14-1:
Create a
new project.

2. **In the left pane, choose Safari.**

3. **In the top right pane, choose Browser.**

4. **Check both the Safari and mobile Safari check boxes.**

5. **Click Choose to create the project.**

   Dashcode creates the project; it usually opens the Safari version as shown in Figure 14-2. If Dashcode opens the mobile Safari version, click the button just below the toolbar to switch to the Safari version.

6. **Click Run to test the project.**

   By default, your project opens in Dashcode's browser simulator, as shown in Figure 14-3. Click Bryce Canyon in the list at the left to show the details you see in Figure 14-3.

7. **Click Stop in the upper left corner of the Dashcode window to stop the browser simulator.**

   You can also just close the browser simulator; if you click in the browser simulator, you see its menu bar, where you can choose Browser Simulator➪Quit Browser Simulator. Just make certain that you're in the browser simulator and that you don't exit Dashcode!

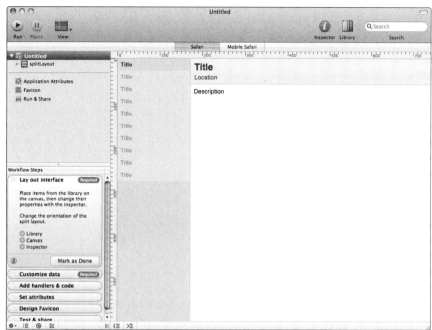

Figure 14-2:
Dashcode
creates the
project.

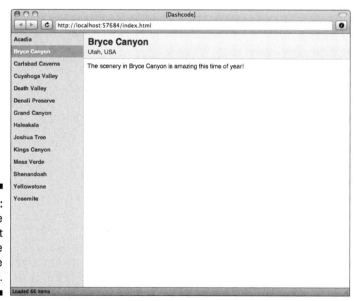

Figure 14-3:
Test the
project
in the
Dashcode
simulator.

8. **Back in the Dashcode window, click the mobile Safari button just below the toolbar to switch to that version of the project, as shown in Figure 14-4.**

9. **In the Dashcode window, click Run to test the product in the iPhone simulator, as shown in Figure 14-5.**

10. **Click Bryce Canyon to show the details you see in Figure 14-6.**

    The data is the same in the Safari and mobile Safari versions, but the smaller iPhone screen requires a slightly different sequence. You can't see the list at the same time as the details as in Figure 14-3. You have to use the left arrow (at the top left of the screen) to go back to the previous screen with the list of parks.

11. **Choose File➪Save to save the project.**

    Your life is somewhat simpler if you don't include spaces or special characters in the filename.

12. **Click Run & Share in the navigator.**

    The filename fills the Application Path field. If the name doesn't appear, fill it in.

13. **Set your destination.**

    If you need to create a new destination, see Chapter 3.

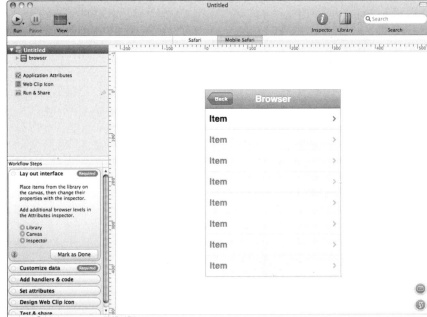

Figure 14-4:
Check out the canvas for the mobile Safari version.

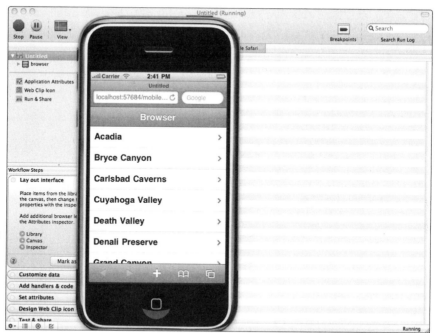

Figure 14-5:
Test the project in the iPhone simulator.

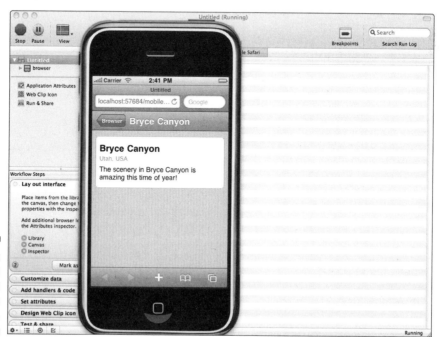

Figure 14-6:
Confirm the details on the iPhone simulator.

14. **Make certain that all three options are set, as shown in Figure 14-7.**

15. **Click deploy at the bottom right of the window.**

    As long as you click all three deployment options, you should receive an e-mail confirming your deployment, as shown in Figure 14-8.

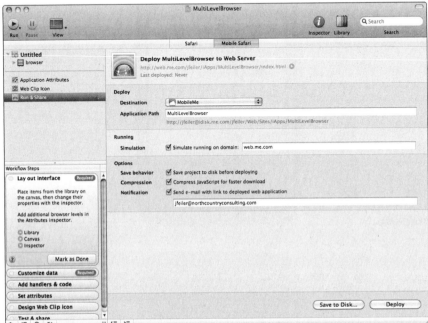

Figure 14-7:
Set
deployment
options.

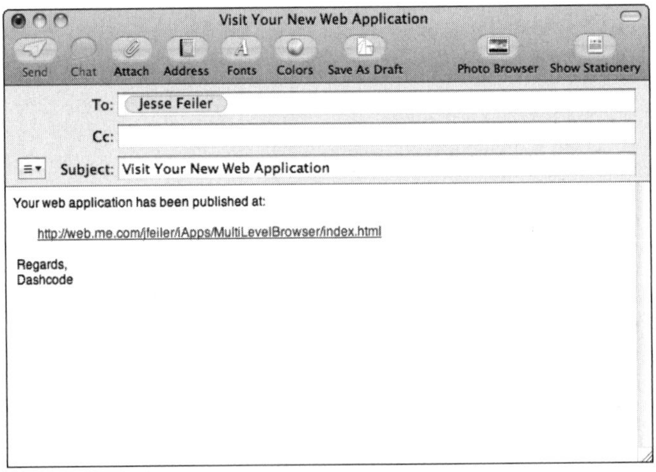

Figure 14-8:
You are
notified
of the
deployment.

If you followed these steps, you should have a successful deployment. If you don't, go back and redo the process. If you can't successfully deploy the unmodified template, any modifications you make to it are unlikely to succeed.

Testing the Project. . . for Real

Testing your project in both the Safari and mobile Safari versions using the Dashcode simulators is good for development, but when you finish up, you and others need to be able to run the project on your own browsers and iPhones.

If you want to be very, very careful, test on all the actual platforms as soon as you make any significant changes to the project. In reality, though, that approach is often overkill, particularly with a development environment such as Dashcode in which you're likely to be iterating through versions of your project fairly rapidly. You can often manage a decent level of quality control by doing a full test on all platforms at this step — the initial deployment of the unmodified template — and then at key points along the way. For a relatively simple Dashcode project, you might even go so far as to test at this point and then again when you finish your initial deployment.

For all the testing in this section, make certain that you have your project's deployed address at hand. Consider printing the confirmation e-mail you received when you created your project (see previous section). Every time you deploy your project, it overwrites the previous version, so the URL in the confirmation e-mail remains valid through the entire development process.

Testing the deployed Safari Web site on Mac OS X

Testing the deployed Safari Web site on Mac OS X is a simple test. Launch Safari on your Mac and then type the URL. You see the project looking very much as it did in the simulator shown in Figure 14-3, earlier in this chapter.

Bookmark the address of your project so that you can come back to it easily.

Testing the deployed Safari Web site on Windows

Your project should run in Safari wherever it can be deployed. If you have access to a computer running Windows (or if you have Boot Camp, Parallels, or other products installed along with a copy of Windows), try running your project in Safari on Windows (see Figure 14-9).

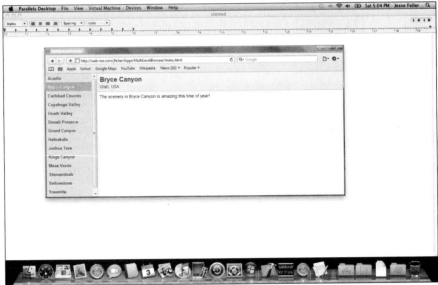

Figure 14-9:
Test in
Safari in
Windows.

Testing the iPhone version of the project

To test the project on an iPhone, type the address of your project into Safari on the iPhone you're using. Your project is displayed using the iPhone formatting that's built into the template (see Figure 14-10).

Just as in the simulator, you have to tap an item in the master list to show details, as shown in Figure 14-11.

Finally, tap the + at the bottom of the screen to bookmark this page. The easiest bookmark to create for now is to put this bookmark on the Home screen, as shown in Figure 14-12.

Setting up the Code for iPad

You need to modify the default code in the Dashcode project so that an iPad is identified properly as a mobile device and not as an iPhone (see Chapter 3).

Here are the steps. Put big stars and exclamation points next to Step 1: You don't want to jeopardize all your hard work so far.

1. **Save a copy of your project in a safe place.**

Figure 14-10:
Test on
iPhone.

Figure 14-11:
Check out
the detail
pages.

To be absolutely safe, choose File➪Save As to make this copy. Then, in the Finder, select the copy and choose File➪Compress to create a ZIP archive. You can then delete the unzipped copy. That way, you can't accidentally work in the copy because it's not visible unless you unzip the archive.

2. In Dashcode, choose View➪Stop Code Generator.

Although you don't see anything change, the code generator is turned off, which lets you change the JavaScript code in your project. When you're done, you turn the Code Generator back on (in Step 8).

3. Show the files in the navigator.

Refer to Figure 14-13 as you continue.

Figure 14-12:
Create a
bookmark.

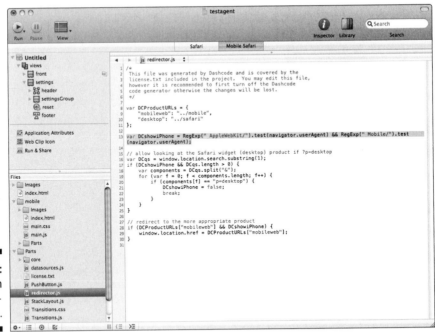

Figure 14-13:
Open
redirec-
tor.js.

4. Open the Parts folder to locate `redirector.js`.

5. Click `redirector.js` to view the code.

At the top of the function, you see this line of code:

```
var DCshowiPhone = RegExp(" AppleWebKit/").test(navigator.userAgent)
   && RegExp(" Mobile/").test(navigator.userAgent));
```

6. **Add && !RegExp("iPad").test(navigator.userAgent) at the
   end so that the code now reads**

```
var DCshowiPhone = RegExp(" AppleWebKit/").test(navigator.userAgent)
&& RegExp(" Mobile/").test(navigator.userAgent)
&& !RegExp("iPad").test(navigator.userAgent);
```

This step changes the test to look for both `Mobile` and not `iPad`. If
the environment is mobile and not an iPad, you use the `mobile` folder,
which is correct for iPhone and not for iPad.

7. **Save the file.**

8. **Choose View➪Start Code Generator.**

9. **Save your Dashcode project.**

10. **Deploy the project again.**

    On your iPad, tap Safari and type the URL. You see the Safari (not mobile
    Safari) version of the project, as shown in Figure 14-14.

Figure 14-14:
Check the
iPad
deployment.

To be really certain that you have correctly modified the code in the previous steps, double-check that the iPhone and desktop versions of Safari still function properly. The only change you should have made is causing the Safari (not mobile Safari) version to run on iPad.

11. **Make certain that the iOS features, such as rotation, work, as shown in Figure 14-15.**

    If rotation doesn't work, check that you haven't locked the screen.

12. **Bookmark the URL in your iPad with the +.**

    You see the pop-over shown in Figure 14-16.

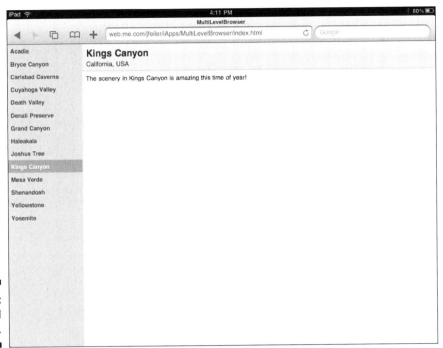

Figure 14-15:
Check iPad
rotation.

Checking Out the Template Behavior

The Browser template's default behavior has two parts to it:

- ✔ The data component that links data to fields in the interface
- ✔ The behavioral component that implements the navigation

Figure 14-16:
Bookmark
the page on
your iPad.

The data bindings

The default data (in `sampleData.js`) provides a list of parks and their locations. (`sampleData.js` is shown in Listing 14-1.)

Listing 14-1:   sampleData.js

```
{
    title: 'National Parks',
    items: [
        { name: "Acadia", location: "Maine, USA" },
        { name: "Bryce Canyon", location: "Utah, USA" },
        { name: "Carlsbad Caverns", location: "New Mexico, USA" },
        { name: "Cuyahoga Valley", location: "Ohio, USA" },
        { name: "Death Valley", location: "California, USA" },
        { name: "Denali Preserve", location: "Alaska, USA" },
        { name: "Grand Canyon", location: "Arizona, USA" },
        { name: "Haleakala", location: "Hawaii, USA" },
        { name: "Joshua Tree", location: "California, USA" },
        { name: "Kings Canyon", location: "California, USA" },
        { name: "Mesa Verde", location: "Colorado, USA" },
        { name: "Shenandoah", location: "Virginia, USA" },
        { name: "Yellowstone", location: "Wyoming, USA" },
        { name: "Yosemite", location: "California, USA" }
    ]
}
```

The location appears in the list of parks, and the detail views also use it — for example, as language shown in the small print below the park name in Figure 14-15.

In a case where you want to use an item such as location both in a list and also in information for a specific list element, you have two sets of bindings:

✔ The binding to the list of all parks from the data model view of the data source to the interface list element

✔ The binding to an individual, selected park in the data model view of the itemsList controller

The simplest way to see what's where is to expand all the views in the navigator and show the data sources. Hover the pointer above the data source, and you see where the bindings are (see Figure 14-17).

The items list in the data source is bound to itemsList.dataArray, which provides the data for the list.

The companion (named itemsList) that is based on the data source allows the selected item's name to be bound to detailDescription.text and detailTitle.text while subtitle is bound to detailSubtitle.text (see Figure 14-18).

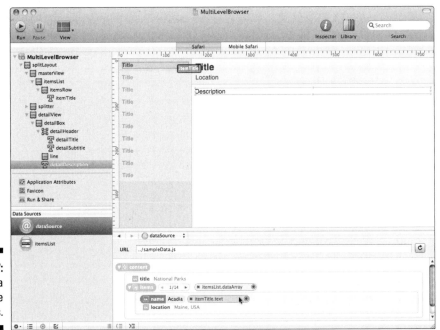

Figure 14-17: Look at data source bindings.

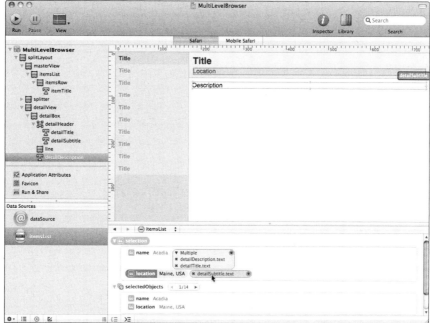

Figure 14-18:
Look at the
data model
view
bindings.

While `name` is bound to both `detailDescription.text` and to `detail-Title.text`, it appears differently in those two places. The reason is a transformer attached to `detailTitle.text` shown in the Bindings inspector (see Figure 14-19).

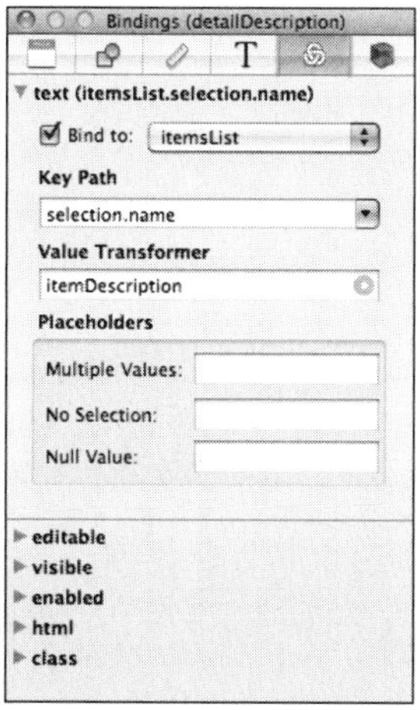

Figure 14-19:
Look at the
Bindings
inspector.

The Bindings inspector points to the `itemDescription` Value Transformer; the little arrow at the right of that field takes you to the code. Listing 14-2 shows how it adds the boilerplate text to the location.

Listing 14-2: itemDescription Value Transformer

```
// Function: itemDescription()
// This method is a value transformer that returns the
// appropriate description of the selected item in the
        list

itemDescription = Class.create(
  DC.ValueTransformer,{
    transformedValue: function(value){
      return "The scenery in " + value +
        " is amazing this time of year!";
        }

  }
);
```

The behaviors

The movement through the browser is implemented by basic Dashcode functionality. You need to unravel it a little (don't worry, it's not complicated) so that you can re-implement it with a multilevel browser. One difference in the behaviors of the mobile Safari and Safari projects is important here. For the Safari project, everything happens in one window. You just click a park, and it becomes the selected park; its data appears in the detail view.

In the case of the mobile Safari project, the detail view and the list view each takes up the entire smaller window on the iPhone. As a result, when you select a park from the list, a behavior has to come into play to move to the detail view. You can guess where the behavior is; a rather crude but effective method is to expand the views, open the Behaviors inspect, and just click down the views until you find the view that implements an `onClick` behavior. That view is `listRowTemplate`, shown in Figure 14-20, which uses the `itemClicked` handler.

Note that the behavior is attached to `listRowTemplate` and not to the arrow. You can verify that the behavior applies to the whole row and not just the arrow by running the unmodified template and clicking anywhere in a park row except for the arrow: The behavior is activated, and you go to the details for that park.

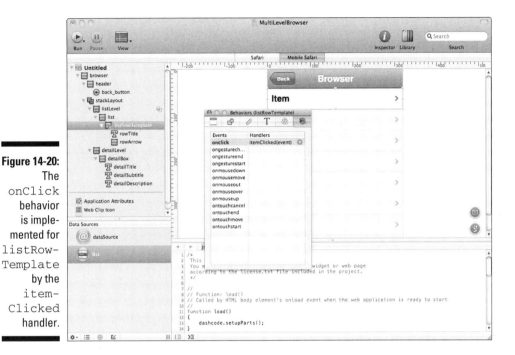

Figure 14-20:
The
`onClick`
behavior
is imple-
mented for
`listRow-`
`Template`
by the
`item-`
`Clicked`
handler.

Listing 14-3 shows the actual behavior.

Listing 14-3: onClick Behavior for listRowTemplate

```
function itemClicked(event)
{
    var list = document.getElementById("list").object;
    var browser = document.getElementById('browser').object;
    var selectedObjects = list.selectedObjects();

    if (selectedObjects && (1 == selectedObjects.length)){
        // The Browser's goForward method is used to make the
        // browser push down to a new level.
        // Going back to previous levels is handled
        // automatically.
        browser.goForward(document.getElementById('detailLevel'),
            selectedObjects[0].valueForKey("name"));
    }
}
```

The browser is an object that is built into Dashcode. All that matters to you is that the browser implements the go-back behavior without you doing anything; the go-forward behavior is implemented by a call to its `goForward` method. You must specify the view to which the browser goes as well as the value that appears at the top of that view. In this case, it is the name of the selected park.

Chapter 15

Creating a Multilevel Navigator for Mobile Safari

In This Chapter

▶ Creating complex data sources

▶ Creating complex navigation interfaces

*W*hile Chapter 14 shows you how to build on the Browser template for a Safari Web application and a mobile Safari Web application and modify the Safari app so that it runs on iPad, this chapter takes a different approach to navigation. It expands the Browser template for mobile Safari to allow for multilevel navigation. This means that instead of selecting an item from a list and then seeing its details, you can select an item from a list, then choose from a sublist, and then get to the details. That second step — the sublist — can be repeated over and over so that you can drill down to the data that you want. Particularly when you're dealing with the very limited screen size of the iPhone, this type of drilling down through levels of data is a very efficient way of providing functionality to users.

You can implement this type of structure in many ways. This chapter presents one of them. Feel free to expand and modify it.

Starting the Multilevel Navigator Project

The basics of the multilevel navigator project are the same as any Dashcode project, but, as always, you need to make a few little tweaks. Here's the quick summary checklist:

1. **Create a new project by choosing File⇨New Project or by launching Dashcode.**

2. **Choose the following options and then click Choose.**

   • In the top pane, select Browser.

   • In the left pane, select Safari.

   • In the center, select the mobile Safari check box.

3. **Choose File⇨Save to save the project.**

4. **Click Run & Share in the navigator.**

   Make certain that application path is filled in. (It should have been filled in automatically when you saved the project. If it's not, type the location of the application on your hard disk.)

5. **Choose a destination, such as MobileMe, or a location on your Web site.**

6. **Make sure all check boxes in the Options section are selected.**

7. **Save the project again and click Deploy.**

8. **Watch for the e-mail confirming deployment and then use the URL to try to run the project.**

   Alternatively, just click the small arrow to the right of the deployment address, as shown in Figure 15-1.

Quickly test both the projects. You should see blank windows in both cases. In this case, nothing is good.

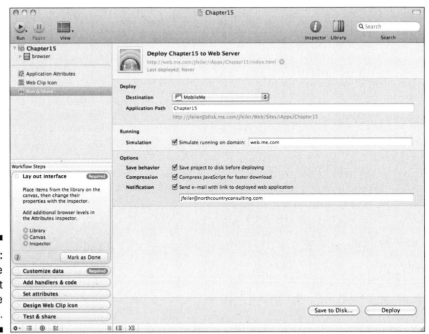

Figure 15-1: Test the project before proceeding.

For more details on starting the project, see the step-by-step guide in Chapter 14.

Planning Your Work

To build this project, you need to create data sources (described in the following section). After that, you need to wire up the interface as described in "Creating the Interface," later in this chapter. Then you need to test and tweak the project.

This sequence is the fastest way to build the project. If you haven't built a project (see Chapter 14), you may want to consider doing so now. Although this sequence of building the project is fast and efficient, the first time you get the project to actually run will be after you've done a good deal of work. (The process in Chapter 14 lets you test your project repeatedly as you build it.)

Creating the Data Sources

The multilevel browser lets you browse a list of National Park Service regions. When you select a region, its parks appear. When you select a park, you see its details. This appearance and behavior is exactly the same as the Browser template (see Chapter 14), with the regions list added on top of the list of parks.

The multilevel browser needs several data sources. In order to proceed, you need data for each level of navigation. You can download sample files from my Web site at www.dummies.com/go/dashcodefd. Note that this data is real, but it's not complete: More parks than those shown here are in the United States National Parks System (NPS).

For your actual project, you deal with additional data sources; they're most easily created programmatically as output in JSON or XML from a database program, such as FileMaker Pro, or a similar tool.

You can develop this type of project in a number of ways. This example uses the most flexible one with separate data sources for each navigation level. In addition to being the most flexible, this method also uses more data sources and views than is necessary if you can combine the data sources. A good way to experiment is with these view levels and data sources to get the feel of things. Then you can decide if you want to restructure the data to combine views and levels.

Creating the top-level data for all regions

In this case, it's easiest to work from the top down, so you start by creating top-level data for the regions.

A file called `regionData.js` lists the regions of the National Park Service, and, instead of a location, each region is followed by the name of another view. (You can download these files from www.dummies.com/go/dashcodefd.) The interface displays the region names. When one is selected, the Dashcode project shows the view for that project, which contains a list of parks in that region. You can then display a given park's details.

Listing 15-1 shows the `regionData.js` file.

Listing 15-1: regionData.js

```
{
  title: 'Regions',
    items: [
      { name: "Alaska",
        view: "alaskaRegion"  },
      { name: "Inter Mountain Region",
        view:"intermountainRegion" },
      { name: "Midwest Region",
        view: "midwestRegion"  },
      { name: "National Capital Region",
        view: "nationalCapitalRegion"  },
      { name: "Northeast Region",
        view: "northeastRegion" },
      { name: "Pacific West Region",
              view: "pacificWestRegion"  },
      { name: "Southeast Region",
        view: "southeastRegion"  }
    ]
}
```

This list has the same general format as `sampleData.js` in the Browser template: It's an array with a name (`Regions`) that contains a number of items. Each item has two fields: `name` and `view`. `name` is displayed; the handler function is then used to go to `view`. The list in `sampleData.js` contains `name` and `location`, but the structure is the same.

Creating the second-level data for specific regions

You can download data for two regions for testing. Listing 15-2 shows `northeastData.js`, and Listing 15-3 shows `intermountainData.js`. In both cases, you have a list of parks in the region. Each park has the same data elements as in `sampleData.js` (`name` and `location`) and a new field, `notes`. The new field contains additional information that will be used in the project. This is a standard way of extending the basic project template: add a field for new data and then connect it to the interface.

Listing 15-2:   northeastData.js

```
{
    title: 'Northeast',
    items: [
        { name: "Acadia", location: "Maine, USA",
            notes: "The first National Park east of the Mississippi River" },
        { name: "Shenandoah", location: "Virginia, USA",
            notes: "Home of the Blue Ridge Mountains" }
    ]
}
```

Listing 15-3:   intermountainData.js

```
{
    title: 'Inter Mountain',
    items: [
        { name: "Bryce Canyon", location: "Utah, USA", notes: "Not really a
            canyon, Bryce is carved by freeze-thaw cycles, not a river." },
        { name: "Carlsbad Caverns", location: "New Mexico, USA", notes: "117
            known caves - all formed when sulfuric acid dissolved the
            surrounding limestone"  },
        { name: "Grand Canyon", location: "Arizona, USA", notes: "There's
            nothing more to say." },
        { name: "Kings Canyon", location: "California, USA", notes: "The world's
            largest tress." },
        { name: "Mesa Verde", location: "Colorado, USA", notes: "Home to
            Ancestral Pueblo people from 600 to 1300" },
        { name: "Yellowstone", location: "Wyoming, USA", notes: "America's first
            national park." }
    ]
}
```

Notice one important architectural feature about this design. The lists of data for each region contain nothing about Dashcode: They're just names of parks and their data.

Only the top-level list (refer to Listing 15-1) refers to Dashcode internals — in this case, the names of views in the project. If you create additional levels (perhaps states within regions, with each state then having a list of parks, such as Listings 15-2 and 15-3,) only the levels above the lists of parks need names of Dashcode views. Leaving out the names of the Dashcode views makes the data as portable as possible. In fact, given these files, someone can build a full-fledged iPhone or iPad app from the data files. You can also use the data files to drive any number of other applications using any number of different development platforms.

You do need a way to properly dispatch the mouse clicks. To do this, the handlers bound to the interface elements inside Dashcode do refer to specific views, but the data — except for the top level — only contains the data, not references to the interface elements.

Adding the files to the project

After you create or download files for your project, add them to the project. Remember to use Dashcode to manage the files.

It's very important that the files be in a folder that is at the top level of the project's hierarchy — that is, not inside the `mobile` or the `safari` folder.

Here's how to add the files to your project:

1. **Show the Files list.**

   You can do so by choosing View➪Files, Views in the toolbar, or the button in the lower left of the window frame, as shown in Figure 15-2.

Figure 15-2: Show the files.

2. **Close the folders so that you're only looking at the top level of files.**

3. **Highlight `index.html`.**

   It's usually the only file in the Files list; the rest are folders in the Custom template.

4. **Use the Action menu to add a new folder, as shown in Figure 15-3.**

   The new folder's name is `Untitled` and is alphabetized under U at the bottom of the list with its name highlighted.

5. **Change the folder's name to `data`, as shown in Figure 15-4.**

   As soon as you click out of the field, the data folder moves to its proper alphabetical location at the top of the list.

6. **With the new data folder selected (it doesn't have to be open), use the Action menu's New File command.**

   Navigate to the files you want to add. By holding the shift key, you can select all of them with separate mouse clicks (see Figure 15-5).

7. **Verify that the files are all in the data folder (see Figure 15-6).**

8. **Delete `sampleData.js` from the project using the Gear icon.**

The downloadable files cover only two regions. If you create your own files, it makes sense to do a similar thing: Just add two regions (or whatever your categories are). Finish the project and test that it works for those regions. You can then add the other data. Just remember not to select regions that have no data yet.

Renaming the views

With your own data files in place, it's a good idea to change the default view names in the navigator so that you know what you're working with rather than having to convert from the default template names.

Here's how to rename the files:

1. **Expand all the views so that you can see the entire structure in the navigator, as shown in Figure 15-7.**

Figure 15-3: Add a new folder.

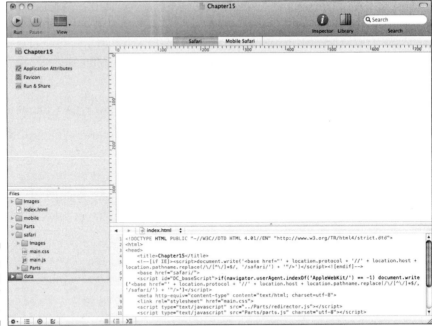

Figure 15-4:
Rename the
new folder
as data.

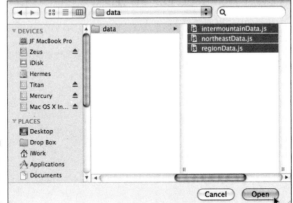

Figure 15-5:
Select the
files to add.

2. **Change `listLevel` to `nationalLevel`, list to `regionList`, and row-Title to `regionListTitle`, as you see in Figure 15-8.**

   This step implements the multilevel navigation. At each level (such as the national level), you have a list for the immediate subordinate level (such as the regions). If you were to add a third level, you might have a list of states within each region.

3. **Select `nationalLevel` and duplicate it using Edit⇨Duplicate.**

   By default, it is named `nationalLevel1`.

4. **Change `nationalLevel1` to `northeastRegion`.**

5. **If necessary, open `northeastRegion` to see its subviews.**

6. **Rename `regionList1` to `neParkList`.**

7. **Rename `regionListTitle1` to `parkListTitle`.**

   Each level thus has its subordinate levels identified properly. You can leave the other elements, such as the arrows, with their default names.

8. **Add a new Text part from the Library to `listRowTemplate1` and name it `location`.**

   This part is for the park's location. You may need to do some rearranging of the fields and reducing of the font size for location as shown in Figure 15-8.

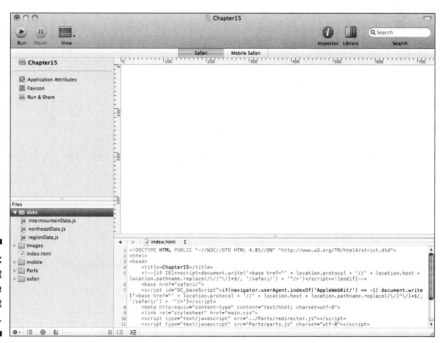

Figure 15-6:
Verify that
the files are
in the right
place.

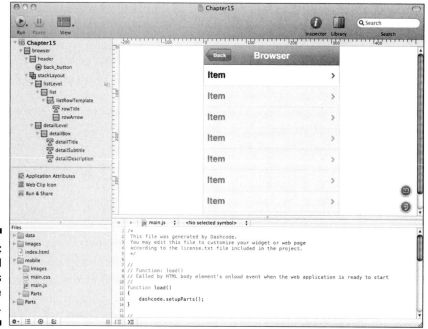

Figure 15-7:
Expand all
the views
in the
navigator.

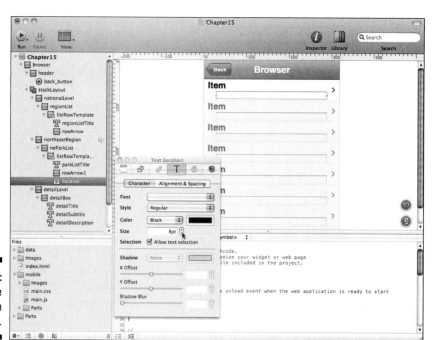

Figure 15-8:
Add the
location
field.

Creating the data sources

Once you have added the data files to the project, you can create the basic data sources. However, in order to work with the data model views, you need to create the interface. Still, finishing up your work with the basic data sources is a good idea. Which data source you work on first doesn't matter. (You'll have one for each file you've uploaded). After the first data source, you can work on the others in the same way. Whether you create the first data source in Safari or mobile Safari doesn't matter, either.

You can find out the details of this process in Chapters 9 and 10.

You can use more complex files and data sources so that you have fewer data sources to keep track of. This method is the simplest even though it may create a few more data sources than are absolutely necessary.

The Browser template includes a data source (called `dataSource`). Here's how you modify it for your own data:

1. **Using the View menu, View in the toolbar, or the button in the lower left of the Dashcode window frame, make certain that the data sources are visible (see Figure 15-9).**

   A single data source may be created as part of the template you're using.

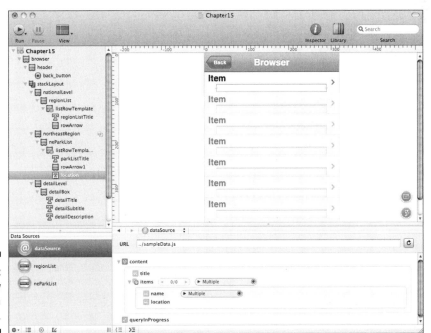

Figure 15-9: View the Data Sources list.

Dashcode has created data sources and controllers for you as part of the template and as part of your renaming. Click the first data source, and you see that it's still associated with sampleData.js, which was deleted.

2. **Rename datasource to nationalDS.**

3. **Change the URL of the data source file.**

The URL will be /data/regiondata.js if you followed the file structure described in "Adding the files to the project," earlier in this chapter. When you press Return or click the Refresh button at the right of the data model view, you see the data from the file as you see in Figure 15-10. If you don't, check each step. You may need to delete the new data source and recreate it. Don't continue until the data source is visible and its data is correct.

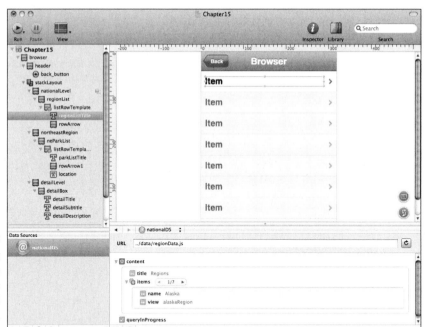

Figure 15-10: Change the data source name and its URL.

4. **Using the Gear icon in the lower left of the Dashcode window, create a new data source, as shown in Figure 15-11.**

This data source will be for the northeast region data. If you've experimented with other regions, add a data source for each one of them, but it's usually better to continue working just with a small amount of data until the project takes shape.

5. **Change the new data source's name to `northeastDS`.**

6. **Enter the URL — `../data/northeastRegion.js`.**

   Figure 15-12 shows what the window should look like now.

Creating the Interface

After you import the data files and create the data sources, you can create the interface.

Implementing the top-level navigation

To implement the top-level navigation:

1. **Bind the `nationalDS` data source to `regionListTitle`.**

   Show the Data Sources pane and select `nationalDS`. Connect `name` in the data model view to the `regionListTitle`, as shown in Figure 15-13.

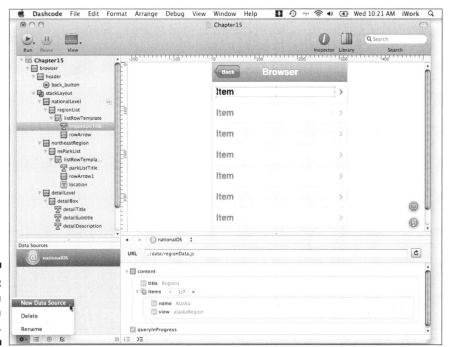

Figure 15-11:
Create a
new data
source.

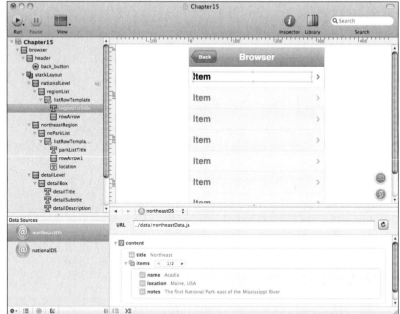

Figure 15-12:
Set the name and URL for the second data source.

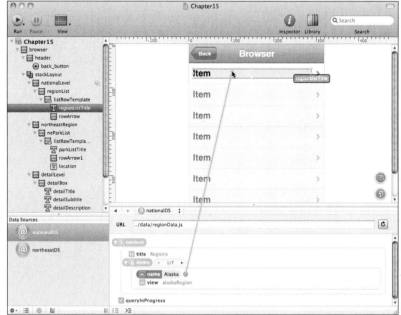

Figure 15-13:
Connect the data source array to the list.

2. Set the binding property of `regionsList` to `dataArray`.

When you release the mouse button, the pop-up menu shown in Figure 15-14 lets you choose the property of the list to which you want to attach the binding.

3. Bind `name` in the data source to the `text` property of `regionListTitle`.

Figure 15-15 shows the result. The binding of `name` to the `text` property of `regionListTitle` causes Dashcode to also bind `items` to the `dataArray` property of `regionList`.

4. Click Run and test.

You should see the result of the data source binding to the list (see Figure 15-16). Don't bother experimenting further: nothing except that list is now functional. Yet.

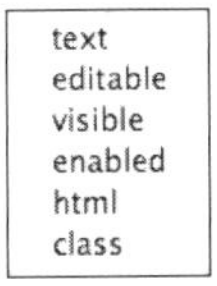

Figure 15-14:
Bind the list
to `data`
`Array`.

```
text
editable
visible
enabled
html
class
```

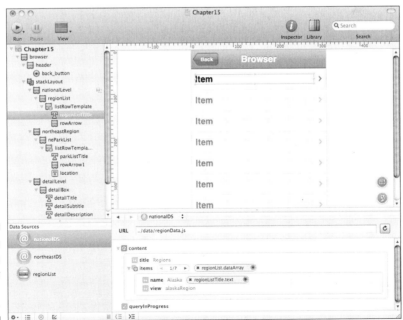

Figure 15-15:
Bind `name`
to `row`
`Label`.
`text`.

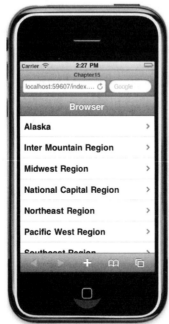

Moving to the second navigation level

After you implement the top-level navigation list, you need to implement the move to the second navigation level. Listing 15-1, earlier in this chapter, has a view for each name. You can implement the northeast region's data. (It's one of the downloadable files at www.dummies.com/go/dashcodefd).

```
Listing 15-1 associates the name Northeast Region with a view called
         northeastRegion.with this line of code:{ name: "Northeast Region",
         view: "northeastRegion" },
```

You need a handler to move from the list of regions to a specific region's data that is shown in its own view — northeastRegion, in this case. The basic version of that code is part of the Browser template. With the single-level implementation, it moves from a click on the top-level list to the detail view. You have to change it to move to the second-level list. From there, you can implement a third-level list. When you finish navigating the lists, the last click vtakes you to the detail data.

As you see in Figure 15-17, a small binding icon appears on listRow Template in the navigator. One also appears on listRowTemplate1 because you duplicated nationalLevel. Both those handlers need to be modified to accommodate your multilevel structure. Select listRow Template in the navigator and open the Bindings inspector, as shown in Figure 15-17.

Figure 15-17:
A behavior
is attached
to list
Row
Template.

View the code with the arrow at the right of the Bindings inspector. Listing
15-4 shows this default code.

Listing 15-4:   itemClicked Handler Code

```
function itemClicked(event)
{
    var list = document.getElementById("list").object;
    var browser = document.getElementById('browser').object;
    var selectedObjects = list.selectedObjects();

    if (selectedObjects && (1 == selectedObjects.length)){
        // The Browser's goForward method is used to make the browser push down
                to a new level.
        // Going back to previous levels is handled automatically.
        browser.goForward(document.getElementById('detailLevel'),
                selectedObjects[0].valueForKey("name"));
    }
}
```

You have to make adjustments to this code. Any time you implement an
onclick handler in a browser, you use a variation of this code, and you have
to make similar adjustments.

Here's how you implement that handler for second-level navigation.

1. **Rename `itemClicked` to `regionItemClicked`.**

   You need to change it in `main.js` as well as in the binding to `listRow-Template` in the Bindings inspector.

2. **In the first line of code, change `list` to `regionList` to reflect your renaming of the view in the navigator.**

3. **Instead of hard-coding the detail view where the handler will go, retrieve it from the data source.**

   Add this line below the last comment line (the comment line is repeated here so you can find the spot):

   ```
   // Going back to previous levels is handled automatically.
   view = selectedObjects[0].valueForKey("view");
   ```

4. **Change the last line to use the view picked up from the data source instead of a hard-coded view:**

   ```
   browser.goForward(document.getElementById(view),
       selectedObjects[0].valueForKey("name"));
   ```

   The full code for `regionItemClicked` is shown in Listing 15-5.

Listing 15-5:   regionItemClicked Handler

```
function regionItemClicked(event)
{
    var list = document.getElementById("regionList").object;
    var browser = document.getElementById('browser').object;
    var selectedObjects = list.selectedObjects();

    if (selectedObjects && (1 == selectedObjects.length)){
        // The Browser's goForward method is used to make the browser push down
            to a new level.
        // Going back to previous levels is handled automatically.
        view = selectedObjects[0].valueForKey("view");
        browser.goForward(document.getElementById(view), selectedObjects[0].
            valueForKey("name"));
    }
}
```

Building the second navigation level views

In "Renaming the views" section, earlier in this chapter, you change the name of `listLevel` to `nationalLevel`. You then duplicate it and change its name to `northeastRegion` along with renaming some of the interior views. You're ready to finish up the second navigation level views.

Here's how you build the second-level views and the handler to navigate to the third level.

1. **Select the northeastRegion view in the navigator.**

   If necessary, display all the interior views with the disclosure triangles.

2. **Select listRowTemplate1 and open the Bindings inspector.**

3. **Change the onclick handler for listRowTemplate1 to northeast-ItemClicked in the Bindings inspector and in main.js.**

   You perform this same process in Step 1 of the previous section.

4. **Change the code in main.js for northeastItemClicked to match the code in Listing 15-6.**

   This code is very similar to the code used in the second navigation level, except that the ultimate view (detailLevel) is hard-coded.

5. **Bind the location field you added to listRowTemplate1 to location in the neParkList controller.**

6. **Bind the notes field in the neParkList controller to detail Description in detailView, and bind the location field in the neParkList controller to detailSubtitle in detailView.**

   You may have to resize the fields.

7. **Run and test.**

   When you click Northeast Region on the first screen, you should move to the screen shown in Figure 15-18.

8. **Click one of the parks to go to the detail view, as shown in Figure 15-19.**

Listing 15-6: northeastItemClicked Handler

```
function northeastItemClicked(event)
{
    var list = document.getElementById("neParkList").object;
    var browser = document.getElementById('browser').object;
    var selectedObjects = list.selectedObjects();

    if (selectedObjects && (1 == selectedObjects.length)){
        // The Browser's goForward method is used to make the browser push down
            to a new level.
        // Going back to previous levels is handled automatically.
        //browser.goForward("northeastRegion", parkName);
        browser.goForward("detailLevel", selectedObjects[0].valueForKey("name"));
    }
}
```

Figure 15-18:
Check out
the second-
level view.

Figure 15-19:
Click a park
to find out
the details.

Chapter 16

Creating a Custom Web App/ Dashboard Widget for a Web Site

In This Chapter

▶ Figuring out how to build apps and widgets that interact with a Web site

▶ Building a Dashboard widget

▶ Creating a mobile Safari Web application

Many times, as you get deeper into a technology, the chapters get longer, and the topics more complicated. The reverse is true with a product like Dashcode: As you become more and more familiar with the basics, you can put them together quickly and easily to achieve impressive results.

This chapter shows you how to do something that's very simple: It lets you put an image or video into a Dashboard widget or a Safari Web app just by typing the name. You can use a browser to accomplish the same task, but by using Dashcode, you can set up a widget or Web application that's designed to show a video and photo at the same time, four photos, or any combination that you want. In other words, it's a really specific type of project that you can use for any purpose that comes to mind.

Because this project takes you very little time to do, you can produce a Dashboard widget for exactly what you want (maybe three photos and a paragraph of text) and then keep it around so that it's always there at the touch of a button (the Dashboard F4 key or the F12 key, by default).

Setting Up the Web Site

The first step in creating an app or widget to interact with a Web site is to identify a video or photo on a Web site that you can experiment with. The best way is to place your own photo or video on your own Web site. Not only does that approach eliminate the possibility of copyright infringement, but it also avoids the possibility of the photo or video moving as the Web site owner decides to rearrange things.

In this chapter, we use an image shown in Chapter 8: a spectacular maple tree in full blazing autumn colors.

You can download this image from the www.dummies.com/go/dashcodefd.

Whether you place an image on your own Web site or link to this one, type the URL you're using into a browser, as shown in Figure 16-1. Trying to get to the image through a browser makes certain that the image is where you think it is and that you can get to it. Any number of problems can arise, ranging from firewalls, security issues, and so on. Make sure that what you're starting from works.

Figure 16-1:
View the image in a browser.

Setting Up the Projects

Thanks to Dashcode's templates, setting up each of the projects is simple. You use the same basic code, but you need to accommodate each device you're working with, separately.

You can set up the projects in any order. The steps within each one matter with regard to sequence, but there's no sequencing to the various projects. (Nevertheless, the first project — the Dashboard widget — does have a few more details about general Dashcode techniques so you should at least glance at it.) The fact that you'll do basically the same thing for several similar projects should help you get the steps down and will make it easier for you to put these projects together in the future.

Creating the Dashboard Widget

The absolute first step in the Dashboard widget project is to make certain that Dashboard is installed and turned on. This step is true for all basic installations of Mac OS X, but sometimes people "improve" their system environment. Check System Preferences to see what the key is to launch Dashboard (by default it's F4 or F12), and make certain that you can get into Dashboard before you've done any programming.

To set up the widget, the first set of steps is basically the same for any new widget:

1. **Select the template.**

   In this case, you want the Custom template for Dashboard, shown in Figure 16-2.

Figure 16-2:
Create the
template.

2. **Before you do anything else, click Run and see whether you can run the unaltered template.**

   It should look like Figure 16-3.

3. **Set the basic attributes by clicking Widget Attributes in the navigator, as shown in Figure 16-4.**

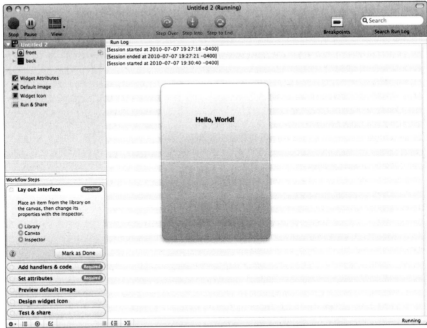

Figure 16-3:
Run the
unaltered
widget.

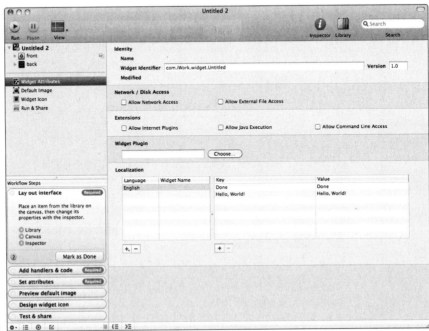

Figure 16-4:
Check the
attributes.

Here are the things you have to do:

a. The widget's name is `Untitled`. Save the widget and give it a name.

b. Change the widget identifier name to a meaningful name.

c. Because you're going to be accessing an image or video over the Internet, allow network access.

Figure 16-5 shows all these changes.

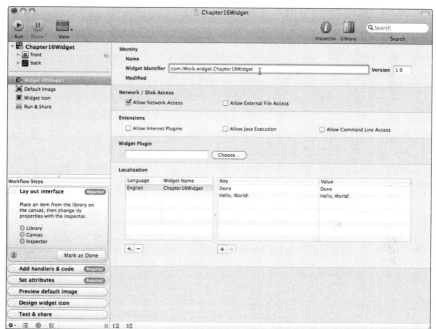

Figure 16-5:
Set attributes as needed.

Test each and every deployment

After you set up the widget, you need to go through the following a set of steps every time you complete changes or modifications to the widget:

1. **Click Run & Share.**

   You may want to save the project to disk, but that doesn't matter at this point.

2. **Click Deploy to Dashboard.**

   You're asked to confirm the deployment (see Figure 16-6). If you've deployed a previous version, you see the message in Figure 16-6. If you haven't, you see a different message.

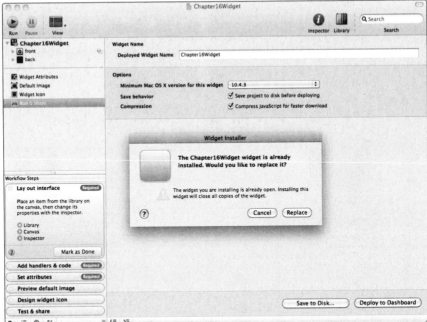

Figure 16-6:
Deploy the
widget.

When you okay deployment, you're launched into Dashboard, and the widget is almost ready to go. It has a frame around it, and you have yet another chance to change your mind, as shown in Figure 16-7.

3. Click Keep.

When you click Keep, the frame disappears, as shown in Figure 16-8.

4. Double-check that your data is correct and that your widget behaves as you expect.

For example, test that you can flip the widget to its back, as shown in Figure 16-9. As you continue to work with Dashcode, add to your list of things to check verifying that the data in the widget is correct and in the right place as well as any other behaviors that you expect the widget to display or actions that you expect it to perform. For now, flipping it from front to back (and back to front) as well as checking the text is all you can do.

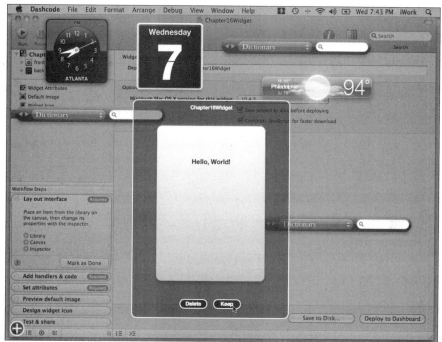

Figure 16-7:
Reconfirm
that you
want to
deploy the
widget.

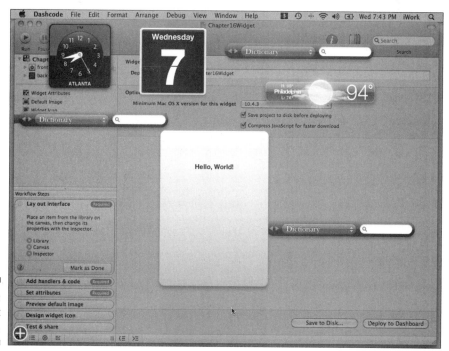

Figure 16-8:
The widget
is deployed.

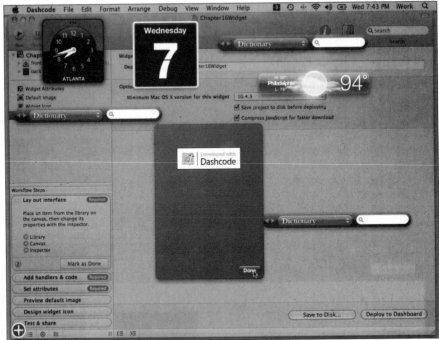

Figure 16-9:
Make sure
that every-
thing works.

Eventually, you'll get to the point that you can carry out these four steps for each deployment in less than a minute — unless, of course, something goes wrong. The fact that something can go wrong is a good argument for testing frequently and making a backup copy of your widget almost every time you test it. If something goes wrong, you may know what it is almost immediately. If you don't, just go back to the previous version and repeat everything you've done . . . very carefully.

Give yourself credit

After your project is working, don't forget to pat yourself on the back — you can give yourself credit for all your hard work. In the navigator, click the back view. From the Library's Parts tab, find the text part and drag it into the canvas, as shown in Figure 16-10.

Type the text you want to use and then set the character and alignment settings in the Text inspector. Because the back of the widget is dark, you'll probably want to use light-colored text. With the text field selected, you can click the color well and choose a color. (You can see that's been happening in Figure 16-11.)

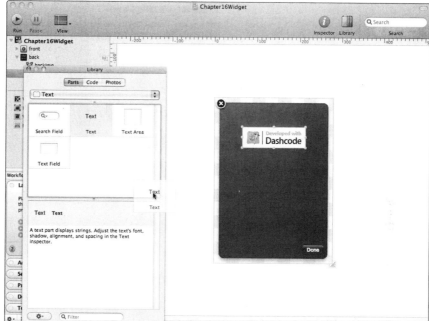

Figure 16-10:
Put your
credits on
the back.

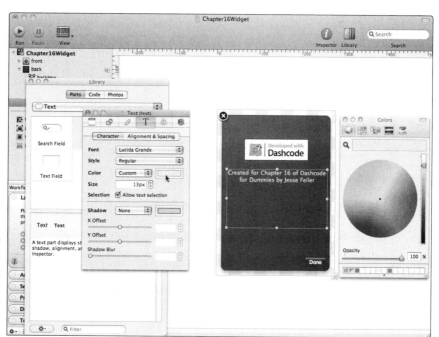

Figure 16-11:
Use the Text
inspector
to fine-tune
the text.

You may want to resist the temptation to use white text. Many people feel that a slightly off-white or light gray is more attractive.

Work on the front of the widget

Design the front of the widget by choosing the front view from the navigator. Delete the helloText field either from the navigator or from the canvas, as shown in Figure 16-12. Don't delete info (the info button that flips the widget) or the background image.

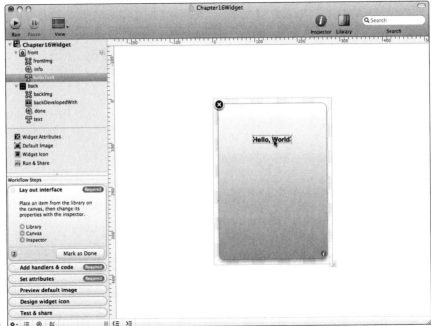

Figure 16-12:
Delete the
hello
Text field.

Now you need to add fields for the address of the image and the image itself:

1. From the Library, add a Text Area part, as shown in Figure 16-13.

URLs tend to be long, so a Text Field part, which is limited to one line, may not be big enough. (Remember that widgets are very constrained in size.) And don't use the Text part because it's not editable: It's for titles and information, such as your credits on the back of the widget. (See the preceding section for more on adding credits.)

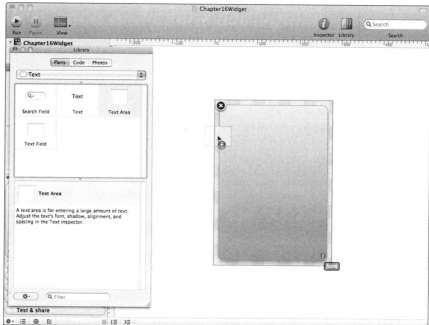

Figure 16-13:
Add a text
area for
the URL.

2. **From the Library, find the Image part in the Media section and drag it into your canvas, as shown in Figure 16-14.**

3. **Resize and rearrange the parts using the guide on the canvas.**

   Do this step (see Figure 16-15) whenever you add parts to your canvas. However, you may want to do the rearranging in batches rather than after each new part is added. That approach is faster for most people.

4. **Bind the data source to the text area.**

   The following steps sum up the process:

   a. Show the Data Sources pane and click the default data source, as shown in Figure 16-16. Don't worry that you see no URL.

   b. Bind the content in the data model display (below the canvas) to the value property of the text area, as shown in Figure 16-17.

   c. As soon as you release the mouse from drawing the binding line, a pop-up menu asks you which property you want to bind to. The correct choice is value, as shown in Figure 16-18.

5. **Bind the data source to the image.**

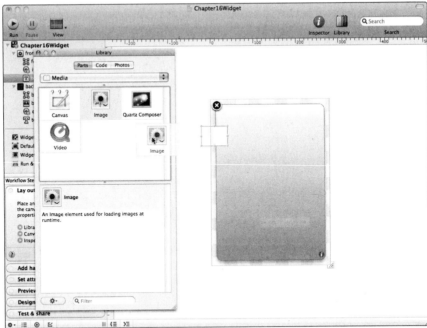

Figure 16-14:
Add an
image part.

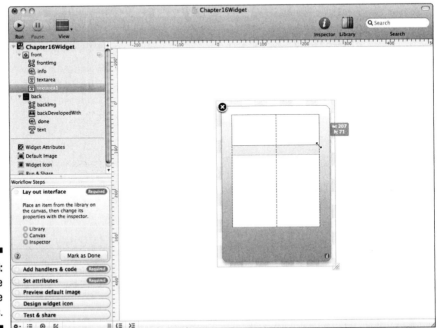

Figure 16-15:
Rearrange
and resize
the parts.

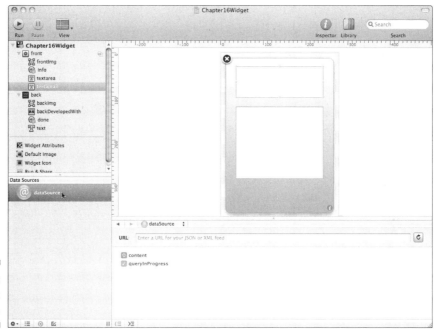

Figure 16-16:
Show data
sources.

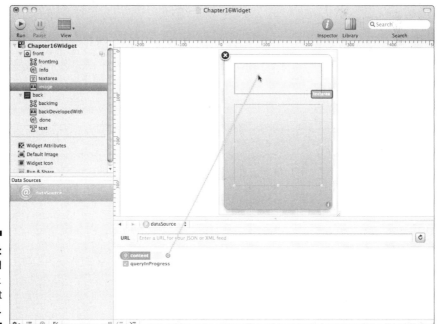

Figure 16-17:
Bind
`content`
to the text
area.

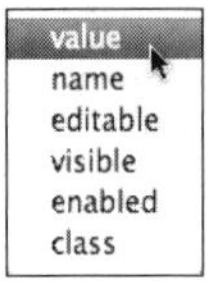

Figure 16-18:
Bind to the
`value`
property.

Note that the binding control for `content` already shows the binding to the text area. Go right ahead and add another, as shown in Figure 16-19. When you're asked to choose the property in the pop-up menu, choose `src`.

6. Check your bindings.

If you hover the mouse to display the bindings list items (use the disclosure triangle to open Multiple), you see the various bindings, shown in Figure 16-20.

That's it! You're done! Go through the deployment steps again and test the widget in Dashboard. You see the results shown in Figure 16-21.

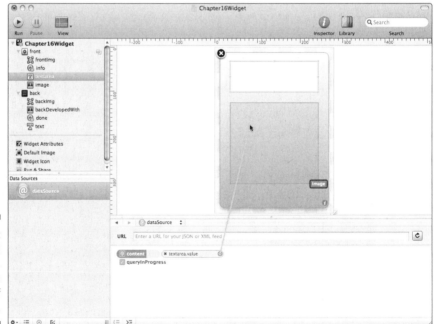

Figure 16-19:
Bind
`content`
to the `src`
property of
the image.

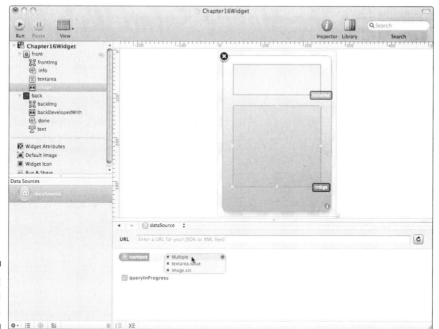

Figure 16-20:
Check the
bindings.

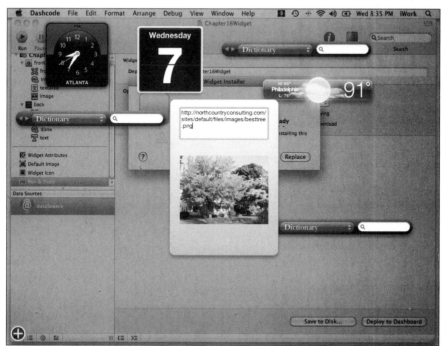

Figure 16-21:
The widget
is done!

Creating the Mobile Safari Web App

Creating the mobile Safari Web application is basically the same process. Here are the basic steps you follow:

1. **Create a new project for Safari using the Custom template.**

   You can save time by making sure that both check boxes are selected (unless you're certain you don't want both the mobile and standard versions of Safari). Figure 16-22 shows the new project dialog ready for this project.

Figure 16-22:
Create the
project.

2. **Set the basic attributes and names by clicking Application Attributes in the navigator.**

   a. Save the project and give it a name.

   b. If the page title isn't filled in, enter it. (You may want to check both the mobile and standard versions at this time.)

   c. Remember that the settings for mobile and standard Safari are different, so don't panic if Figure 16-23 doesn't match what you see. Just click the other tab to switch to or from the mobile version.

Test each and every deployment

Here's what you should do each time you revise a mobile Safari app:

1. **Save the project and possibly save a copy in case you have to revert to it after the next revision.**

2. **Click Run to test the project.**

   Remember that it can take a while for the simulator to launch. You should see the result shown in Figure 16-23.

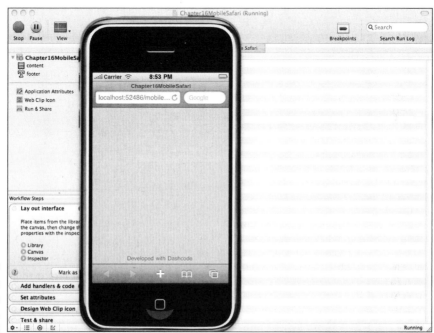

Figure 16-23:
Test the basic app.

Give yourself credit

Modify the footer text to give yourself credit, as shown in Figure 16-24. The process is exactly the same as the steps for the Dashboard widget; see the earlier "Give yourself credit" section.

Acknowledging yourself isn't just to make you feel good. One practical advantage to signing your work is that people know who you are in case they have suggestions or questions.

Finish the app

You can use the same steps as you did in "Work on the front of the widget" to complete the Safari Web application:

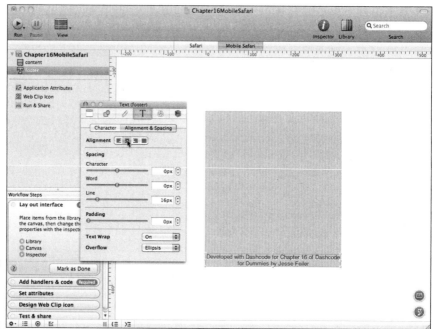

Figure 16-24:
Give your-
self credit.

1. **Add a Text Area part from the Library.**

   For the first element you add, use the Metrics inspector to set Absolute positioning, as shown in Figure 16-25. The absolute positioning setting carries over to the remaining elements.

2. **Add an Image part from the Media section of the Library.**

3. **Resize and rearrange interface element.**

4. **Show the Data Sources pane and select the default data source.**

   Your Dashcode window looks like Figure 16-26.

5. **Create the bindings.**

   a. Bind `content` to the `value` property of the text area.

   b. Bind `content` to the `src` property of the image.

   c. If you hover the mouse over the `content` binding control, you see all the bindings, as shown in Figure 16-27.

That's it! Try your new mobile Safari Web application on your iPhone. You see the results shown in Figure 16-28.

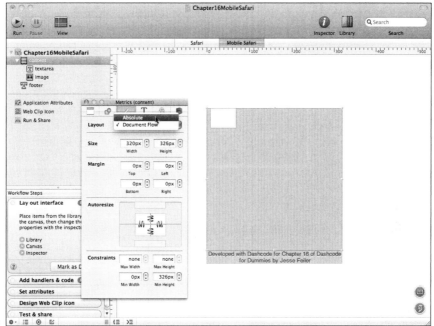

Figure 16-25:
Turn on absolute positioning.

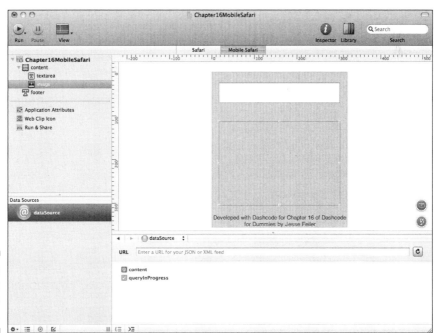

Figure 16-26:
The interface is laid out.

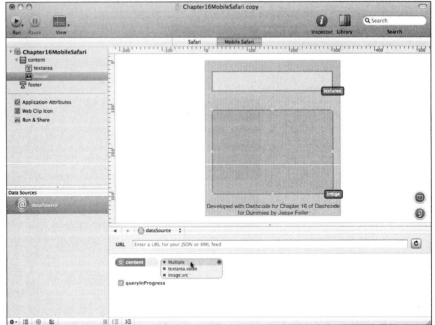

Figure 16-27:
Check the
bindings.

Figure 16-28:
Test the
mobile
Safari
Web app.

Part V
Refining Your Project

The 5th Wave   By Rich Tennant

"We're here to clean the code."

In this part . . .

With all the development time you save by using Dashcode, you have time to fine-tune your project. This part offers a guide to moving beyond the basics of Dashcode. You find tips on writing your own Library parts, improving your interface (including localization for multiple languages), and using the built-in debugger.

Chapter 17

Adding to Your Code

· ·

In This Chapter

▶ Working with Library code

▶ Writing transformers

▶ Creating handlers

· ·

*O*ne great feature of Dashcode is it offers you a Library of parts and code that you can add to your project. If you need to customize the resources from the Library, the inspector is ready for you to customize parts, and the Source Code pane of the Dashcode window is ready for your changes to the code. In this chapter, you see how to work with the code.

This chapter explores the general topic of working with code as well as two very common and specific cases in which you add code to a Dashcode project: value transformers and behaviors and handlers.

Comparing Value Transformers with Behaviors and Handlers

Value transformers convert data. This conversion may be as simple as converting one unit of measurement to another (miles to kilometers, for example), or it can be more complex so that a data value is presented in a sentence that is constructed by the transformer.

Behaviors and *handlers* are the sections of code that implement buttons and other interface elements.

In both cases, the inspector mediates between the data or the interface element and the result. In the case of value transformers, the data is transformed on its way to being displayed. In the case of behaviors and handlers, a click or tap on an interface element causes something to happen. In both cases, you write code and attach it using the inspector.

The code that's built in Dashcode is JavaScript. If you need a brief overview or a brush-up, take a look at Appendix A. You also can find a wide variety of tutorials on the Web by searching on JavaScript. On `http://developer.apple.com`, you can search the reference library for specific topics. You can also download a great deal of sample code, most of which is written in JavaScript for the Dashcode samples.

Using and Reusing Library Code

In order to get a feel for how you work with the code in the templates, the best way is to look at it closely. Start by creating a new project from the Utility template; target it for Safari and mobile Safari. To start exploring the files, show the Files pane of the project (see Figure 17-1).

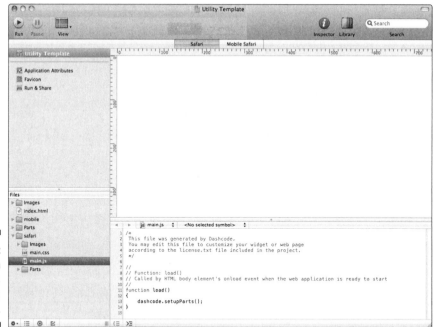

Figure 17-1: Start from the basic files in a template.

Before you start looking at (and changing!) the code, pay attention to two critical issues:

  ✔ **Watch the folders.** You may find several folders in a Dashcode project with the same or similar names. What you see in Figure 17-1 is a project targeted for Safari and mobile Safari. The `mobile` folder contains files for mobile Safari, and the `safari` folder contains files for Safari. Some folders have the same names — for example, a `Parts` folder is inside `safari`, another inside `mobile`, and one at the root level of the project. The one at the root level contains code used by both mobile Safari and Safari. The `Parts` folders inside `mobile` and `safari` are built dynamically by Dashcode as you add parts from the Library. It's very important that you don't touch these internal `Parts` folders. Dashcode builds them and relies on them.

✔ **Pay attention to formatting and comments.** The files in a Dashcode project include files you should modify, those that you should not modify, and those that you can modify if you know what you're doing. The formatting and comments at the beginnings of the files let you know which is which. The listings in the following section help you identify what you're dealing with.

Identifying files you can modify

You're absolutely safe in modifying files that contain an invitation to do so in a comment at the top of the file. `main.js` is one such file. It's the primary file in `mobile` and `safari`. Listing 17-1 shows the file.

Listing 17-1: **You Can Modify `main.js`**

```
/*
This file was generated by Dashcode.
You may edit this file to customize your widget or web page
according to the license.txt file included in the project.
*/


//
// Function: load()
// Called by HTML body element's onload event when the web application is ready
            to start
//
function load()
{
    dashcode.setupParts();
}
```

In addition to the invitation to modify the file, the file is also formatted in a way that is receptive to you looking at it with an eye to modifying it. In other words, the file has lots of comments and consistent indentation along with plenty of white space so that you can follow the flow of processing.

As the comment notes, you have to abide by the terms of `license.txt`. That file is located in the `Parts` folder at the top level of each Dashcode project (not the `Parts` folder within `mobile` or `safari`).

Identifying files you should not modify

A file that doesn't have an invitation to modify it probably should be off limits to your changes. Listing 17-2 shows part of ModeledXMLProxy.js, which is in the root-level Parts folder. Some comments are there, but nowhere do you find an invitation to modify the file. Note variable names, such as _xml-Root, that start with an underscore: It's a common convention that such variable names are used internally and are not for public use. Likewise, you see names that begin with DC (such as DC.ModeledXMLProxy). These files support internal Dashcode objects.

Listing 17-2:   Code You Should Stay Out Of

```
/** An object proxy for XML objects vended from an Ajax Controller
 *
 *  @declare DC.ModeledXMLProxy
 *  @extends DC.KVO
 */
DC.ModeledXMLProxy = Class.create(DC.KVO, {

    // The root of the xml tree
    _xmlRoot: null,      // Root
    _xmlNode: null,      // This node

    constructor: function(root,node,model)
    {
        this._xmlRoot = root;
        this._xmlNode = node;
        this._xmlModel = model;
        this._valueCache = {};

        if (model) {
            if (DC.typeOf(model) == "array") {
                this._xmlModel = model[0];
            }
        }
    },

    _typeOfChild: function(childName)
    {
        var type = "string";
        var toMany = false;
```

Identifying files you should be careful with

Listings 17-3 and 17-4 show examples of code you can modify carefully. The comment identifies the issue you should worry about: It's the code generator.

As you drag interface parts from the Library onto your canvas, the code generator updates files, such as `parts.js`, that contain references to the parts you're using. The code generator is on by default. To turn it off, you choose View⇨Stop Code Generator, and to turn it back on, you choose View⇨Start Code Generator.

The main reason for turning off the code generator is that Dashcode assumes that it can modify its own JavaScript files that have this warning in them. If you make changes to those files, Dashcode may overwrite your changes.

Unless you know what you're doing, you should not modify these files. If you do, the best thing to do is to copy your Dashcode project and make your changes in the copy. Test it, and if you're happy, you can either make the changes again in your main version, or you can rename the files so that the copy with the changes becomes your new main version.

Listing 17-3 shows you code from `mobile/Parts/setup.js`. You're invited to modify it, but also warned about turning off the code generator.

Listing 17-3:   Code You Can Be Careful With

```
/*
This file was generated by Dashcode and is covered by the
license.txt included in the project.  You may edit this file,
however it is recommended to first turn off the Dashcode
code generator otherwise the changes will be lost.
*/
var dashcodePartSpecs = {
    'footer': { view: 'DC.Text', text: 'Developed with Dashcode' }
};
```

Figure 17-2 shows the canvas and the source code involved here. In Listing 17-3, `dashcodePartSpecs` is declared and set to a JSON list called `footer` that contains two elements: `view` and `text`. This code winds its way through Dashcode to provide the Developer with Dashcode credit at the bottom of the mobile Safari app. `view` has the value DC.Text — remember that DC stands for Dashcode. And `text` has the text itself.

If you change the text on the canvas so that it reads *Developed with My Work* rather than *Developed with Dashcode,* as soon as you click out of the view on the canvas, the code is updated, as you see in Figure 17-3.

However, if you attempt to change the text in the code (not in the canvas), you'll find that you can't. Turn code generation off (choose View⇨Stop Code Generation), and you can change the text in the code and have it reflected in the canvas. After you make any code changes, turn code generation back on.

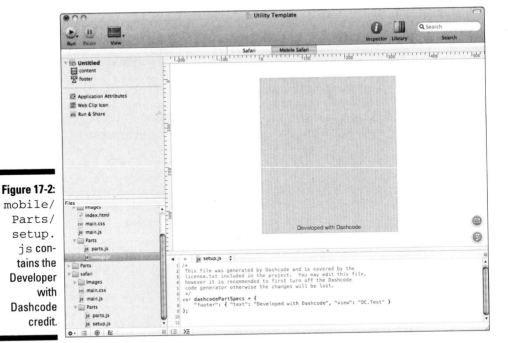

Figure 17-2:
`mobile/ Parts/ setup. js` contains the Developer with Dashcode credit.

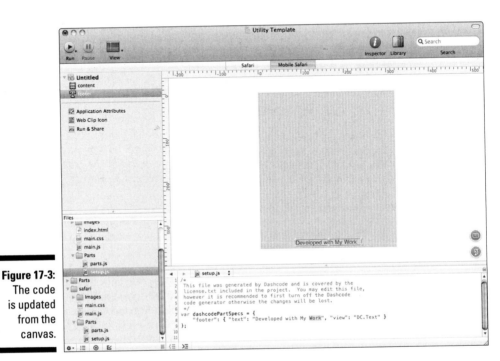

Figure 17-3:
The code is updated from the canvas.

You have to worry about turning code generation on and off only in files where you're warned to do so. These files form bridges between the user interface and the code, so they have to be kept in sync.

Listing 17-4 shows another file that you should be careful with. Here, in addition to the warning in the comment, the file formatting is a giveaway that you should not be working in the file unless you know what you're doing.

The file isn't formatted for easy modification or understanding. In fact, the spacing in Listing 17-4 has been slightly modified from the version that is installed as part of Dashcode. The reformatting just allows it to fit on the printed page; the spirit of the formatting remains intact. It is no more or less easy to read than it is in Dashcode.

Listing 17-4:   Code to Be More Careful With

```
/*
  This file was generated by Dashcode and is covered by the
  license.txt included in the project.  You may edit this file,
  however it is recommended to first turn off the Dashcode
  code generator otherwise the changes will be lost. This file
  is for files included by Dashcode directly. It will be replaced
  with an optimized version at deploy time.
*/
var dashcodePartSupport = {"core":
["../Parts/core/utilities.js","../Parts/core/core/base.js","../
Parts/core/core/array-additions.js","../Parts/core/core/
array-additions-ie.js","../Parts/core/core/set.js",
```

Using Transformers

Transformers are a remarkably powerful part of Dashcode. They build on a lot of components of Dashcode, so you may think they're complicated, but it's just a matter of taking advantage of the built-in structure. This section shows you how to use a simple transformer. Then you see how to create your own transformer.

Using a simple transformer

In fact, you've probably already seen a transformer at work in one of the Dashcode templates: The Browser Safari template lets you generate both a Safari and a mobile Safari product. This template uses data sources as well as the browser structure, shown in Figure 17-4, in the Safari version.

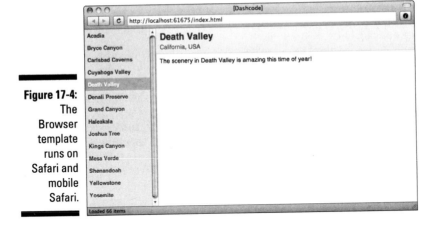

Figure 17-4:
The
Browser
template
runs on
Safari and
mobile
Safari.

Listing 17-5 shows the JSON data used in the data source for this template.

Listing 17-5: JSON data for the Browser template

```
{
    title: 'National Parks',
    items: [
        { name: "Acadia", location: "Maine, USA" },
        { name: "Bryce Canyon", location: "Utah, USA" },
        { name: "Carlsbad Caverns", location: "New Mexico, USA" },
        { name: "Cuyahoga Valley", location: "Ohio, USA" },
        { name: "Death Valley", location: "California, USA" },
        { name: "Denali Preserve", location: "Alaska, USA" },
        { name: "Grand Canyon", location: "Arizona, USA" },
        { name: "Haleakala", location: "Hawaii, USA" },
        { name: "Joshua Tree", location: "California, USA" },
        { name: "Kings Canyon", location: "California, USA" },
        { name: "Mesa Verde", location: "Colorado, USA" },
        { name: "Shenandoah", location: "Virginia, USA" },
        { name: "Yellowstone", location: "Wyoming, USA" },
        { name: "Yosemite", location: "California, USA" }
    ]
}
```

That data is presented in the interface, as shown in Figure 17-4. If you experiment with the data for a few seconds, you'll note that the information displayed for each park is the same. For Death Valley, the text, shown in Figure 17-5, is

```
The scenery in Death Valley is amazing this time of year!
```

Equally amazing, the comment for Grand Canyon is

```
The scenery in Grand Canyon is amazing this time of year!
```

Regardless of the time of year and which park you select, the scenery is always amazing.

Many people would agree that the national parks in the United States and in many other countries are amazing at any time of year, but at this point, you're interested in how that text is generated so identically.

In Listing 17-5, the only information available to the Dashcode project is the name of the park and its location. This means that the sentence is somehow constructed automatically from this data. It's done with a *transformer*.

The following steps show you how to trace down what happens and where it happens. It's a good case study in how to find your way around a Dashcode project — either a template, one that someone else has written, or even one that you wrote a while ago and that is no longer fresh in your mind.

1. **Run the project in the simulator to locate the data that is being transformed.**

   In this case, it's the text shown in Figure 17-4.

2. **In Dashcode, show that view on the canvas.**

   Expand the views and select the view that contains the data you're interested in, as shown in Figure 17-5. It's `detailDescription`.

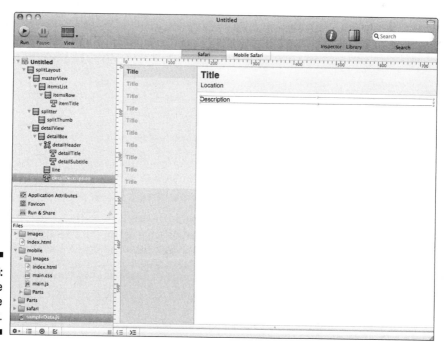

Figure 17-5:
Expand the views in the navigator.

3. **With the view selected, open the Bindings inspector.**

   In Figure 17-6, the `itemsList` data source is highlighted and shown in the data model view at the bottom of the canvas. You can see the binding for the `text` attribute of the `detailDescription` element in the interface, which is bound to the `name` attribute in the selection of `itemsList`. (If you want to go through the binding process, see Chapter 10.)

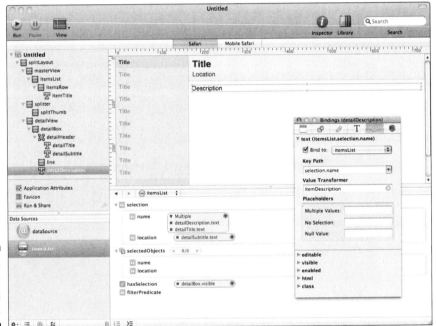

Figure 17-6:
Open the
Bindings
inspector.

4. **If necessary, open the Bindings inspector.**

   You see that Value Transformer is set to `itemDescription`, as shown in Figure 17-6. That code constructs the text.

5. **Use the arrow at the right of the field to open the code for `item Description`.**

   If you click in the Value Transformer field and not on the arrow, you get a list of the various possible transformers that you can use. If that happens, click in another field of the inspector to hide that list. The arrow reappears, and you can then click it. You've found the transformer! The code is shown in Listing 17-6.

Listing 17-6: itemDescription transformer

```
//
// Function: itemDescription()
// This method is a value transformer that returns the
// appropriate description of the selected item in the list
//
itemDescription = Class.create(DC.ValueTransformer,{
        transformedValue: function(value){
        return "The scenery in " + value +
          " is amazing this time of year!";
     }
   }
);
```

Listing 17-6 shows the standard format of a transformer. Listing 17-6 uses
some JavaScript that is a bit beyond the scope of this book, but have no fear:
The format is always the same, and you always manipulate the same section.
What you're looking for is the internal function into which the value of the
data source is passed. (In this case, it's the name of the park as identified
in the binding: `itemsList.selection.name`. (See Step 3 in the preceding
list.) That value is passed into the value transformer specified in the Bindings
inspector. You don't have to worry about all the steps in the process (the
JSON array to the data source to the data model to the Bindings inspector):
The untransformed value is delivered to the code in Listing 17-6.

What is returned from the transformer is that value subject to a
transformation:

```
return "The scenery in " + value +
   " is amazing this time of year!";
```

Follow the steps shown earlier in this section to get to that code and modify
it to return *is very amazing*, and you see how easy it is to modify the
structure.

The code shown in this transformer is very simple, but it's the prototype
of all transformers. You're running in JavaScript, so you have access to any
JavaScript functionality that you want. For example, if you're dealing with temperature data, here's the transformer that would convert Fahrenheit to Celsius
assuming that the Fahrenheit value is properly formatted. If you need to
format it, you can simply add that code (many tutorials offer this exact code
on the Web):

```
return (value - 32.0) * 5.0 / 9.0;
```

In practical terms, this transformer architecture means that you can use a
wide variety of data sources in your apps and widgets. In many cases, the
data in external data sources is the data you want to use, but it may not be in

the exact format you or your users want. Don't worry: Just construct a transformer to reformat it. JavaScript has a wide variety of tools for reformatting data and performing basic operations on it, so you can often do your transformation by using common code that already exists. Just plug it into the right place, and you're ready to go.

Creating your own transformer

Often, modifying an existing transformer (see preceding section) is sufficient. But if you need to build a transformer of your own, it's just as easy a process. Here's what you do:

1. **Select the view that displays the transformed value.**

   You may have to create that view.

2. **With that view selected, open the Bindings inspector.**

3. **In the value section, select a data source to bind to that view.**

   If you don't have a data source yet, you can select the generic `dataSource` from the pop-up menu, but you have to come back and fill in a data source before you run your app or widget.

4. **Type the name of the transformer you will create, as shown in Figure 17-7.**

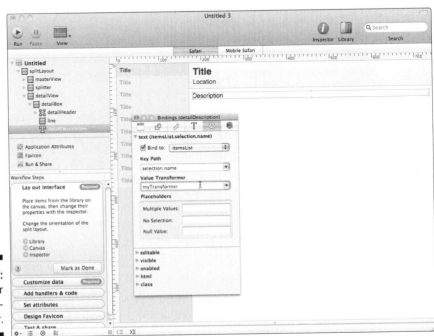

Figure 17-7: Name your new transformer.

When you click out of the transformer name field, the shell of your transformer is created for you.

Listing 17-7 shows the shell of your new transformer.

Listing 17-7:   Shell of the New Transformer

```
myTransformer = Class.create(DC.ValueTransformer,{
    transformedValue: function(value){
      // Insert Code Here
      return value;
    }
    // Uncomment to support a reverse transformation
    /*
       ,
    reverseTransformedValue: function(value){
      return value;
    }
    */
  }
);
```

All you have to do is to insert the code you want after the `Insert Code Here` comment. The value of the data model item is passed in as value, and you do something to it and then return the transformed value. Note that in these examples, the transformation has been a single line of code, but you're not limited to just one line. Of course, the more complex the transformation is, the more testing you'll have to do. Most transformations are pretty simple in part because you get the biggest return on your (minimal) programming investment.

A second set of comments lets you make your transformer more powerful. Removing them gives you the code shown in Listing 17-8.

Listing 17-8:   A Transformer and Reverse Transformer

```
myTransformer = Class.create(DC.ValueTransformer,{
    transformedValue: function(value){
      // Insert Code Here
      return value;
    },

    reverseTransformedValue: function(value){
      return value;
    }
  }
);
```

This code creates two functions: a transformer and a reverse transformer. The first one is executed if the value passes a test; otherwise, the reverse transformer is executed.

Using built-in transformers

When you select your text field and bind it to a data source, you can then select a transformer. You can type the name of a transformer, and Dashcode creates the shell for you (see preceding section). But a collection of transformers is also built into Dashcode. Click in the Value Transformer field to open the pop-up menu of built-in transformers, as shown in Figure 17-8.

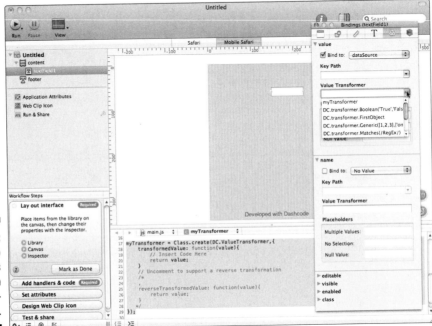

Figure 17-8: A pop-up menu lists built-in transformers.

You can use these transformers or modify them. You should change the name of a transformer that you modify, particularly if you'll be using it for different purposes with different data.

The built-in transformers are located in the top-level Parts folder. From there, go to core (an alias), then the true core folder, and then transformers.js. This is advanced JavaScript code, so I don't detail it in this book, but if you're experienced with JavaScript, you'll see that you can perform various transformations and tests on whatever values may be returned from the data model.

One thing that's useful is that this code has nothing to do with Dashcode. If you're not a JavaScript whiz, you can take this code to a friend who does know JavaScript and ask what it does or how to make it do what you want. All that your friend needs to know is that Dashcode is going to pass in `value` (it doesn't really matter how that happens), and the code that exists or that your friend will write has to return the transformed `value`.

As a starter, note that it's the `DC.transformer.Boolean` transformer that enables you to set values that are true or false and that then trigger the transformer or the reverse transformer.

Writing Your Own Handlers

You can combine handlers with the new tools and knowledge about Dashcode that have been presented in this chapter. Start by selecting a view in the canvas or in the navigator. It can be a button, a field, or any other view — including the background.

Open the Behaviors inspector, as shown in Figure 17-9. The template you started from is irrelevant; all that matters is that you select a view. Click around to select different views in the canvas or the navigator, and the list of events changes. Not every view responds to every type of event.

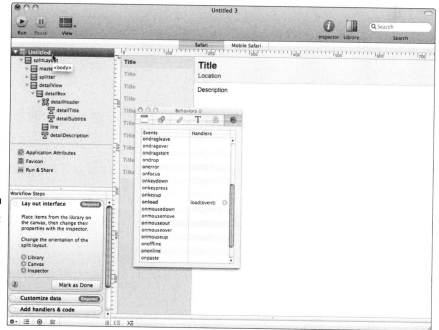

Figure 17-9: Use the Behaviors inspector for a selected view.

If you click the top-level view in the navigator (called Untitled if you just created a new project and haven't saved it yet), you find a long list of events that you can handle. Scroll down as you see in Figure 17-9, and you see that one of those events — onload — already has a handler attached to it.

This event is present and attached to the load handler for all Dashcode projects — Dashboard widgets as well as Safari and mobile Safari apps. As is the case with transformers, if a handler is shown, an arrow lets you open the relevant code, which is highlighted, as shown in Figure 17-10. (You may have to show the Source Code pane.)

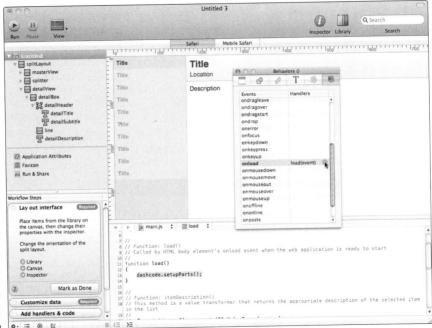

Figure 17-10: You can go to the code for any handler.

If no handler is present, you can click in the field and type the name of a handler you want to create. The shell of the code is created for you just as it was for a transformer. You can also click in the field to see a pop-up menu of existing handlers in exactly the same way you did for transformers. When you click in the handler field, it changes to an editable text field, as shown in Figure 17-11.

You can use the disclosure triangle at the right to then disclose the menu of existing handlers, as shown in Figure 17-12. These processes are repeated over and over in Dashcode. (It may take you a few moments to get used to the timing of the various interface changes.)

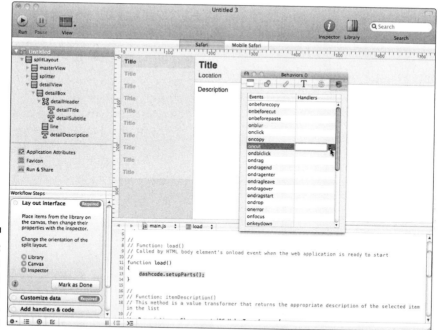

Figure 17-11:
Enter a name in the editable field.

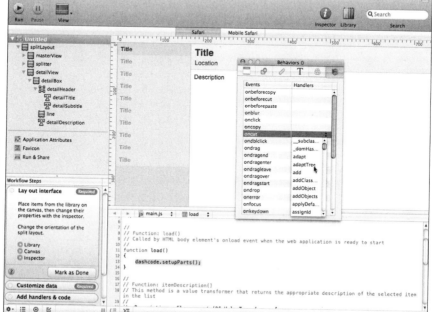

Figure 17-12:
With the editable field shown, the disclosure triangle lets you open the pop-up menu.

Chapter 18

Improving Your Interface

*I*nterfaces are always important, but in the world of apps and widgets (not to mention the mobile devices on which so many of them run), interfaces are more important than ever. These devices just don't have the room to accommodate some of the interface elements that exist in traditional software, and the intense focus of apps and widgets means that fewer options clutter up the screen.

This chapter addresses some of the interface extensions that you can work on with Dashcode.

Getting Deeper into Data Sources and the Data Model View

Bindings and data sources are incredibly powerful tools that let you integrate data from the Web and from files with list elements in Dashcode, not to mention the Stack Layout part that lets you swap views in and out. (Parts II and III focus on these issues.)

Because these tools work so well with files and data flows, you can easily lose sight of the fact that they also work very well with small amounts of data — even single data elements that users can type themselves.

The following sections explore a variety of techniques you can use to combine data sources and bindings with one another and with user-supplied input. If you've read earlier chapters in this book, you've seen exactly the same sort of thing before, but, when you're using single points of data, new opportunities open up. You can use several basic patterns and strategies to manage data that does not come from the Internet or from files.

Looking closer at the data model view

You can work with the data model view and its components without caring too much about the details: It's really very simple because each property in a data model view has a name, a binding control, and — possibly — one or more bindings that are displayed. Each one also has an icon indicating its data type. Furthermore, when you link a file or URL to a data source, you can see the data so that what it is and the type of data that it is becomes obvious.

Figure 18-1 shows the data model view from the Browser template that's available for both Safari and mobile Safari. It contains test data for you to use.

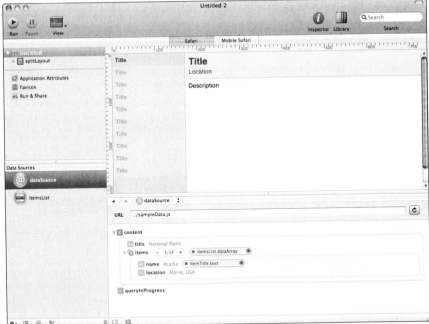

Figure 18-1:
The Browser template comes with a data source built into it.

The icons to the left of each item's name provide you with two pieces of information:

- ✔ Each icon identifies the type of data involved.
- ✔ Each one indicates whether it's a single data element or an array of elements.

The icons are distinctive in their design and color so that you can easily distinguish them from one another. Figure 18-1 gives you an idea of the icons, but you can't see the colors in print. Go into Dashcode, choose File⇨New Project, and choose Browse for Safari, using either the mobile Safari or Safari version. Show the Data Sources pane and look at the icons in all their colored glory.

Working with arrays of data

Arrays are indicated by a slight shadowing of the icon as if there were several of them stacked up. In Figure 18-1, compare the icons for content and items. content is a single data element, while items is an array with the multiple-icon image to the left.

In the case of a single data element, you see its value — for example, the value for title is "National Parks." In the case of an array of elements such as items, you see an oblong indicating which value is being shown (1/14 in Figure 18-1), while arrows let you move forward and back in the array.

You can use the disclosure triangle to collapse an array, such as items, which makes it clear that content consists of two elements: title and items (see Figure 18-2). The thin gray line around those two elements reinforces this fact.

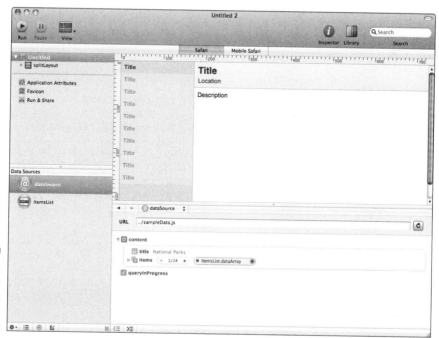

Figure 18-2:
You can
collapse
arrays.

You can also close everything up, as you see in Figure 18-3, to get a high-level view of the data source and its data.

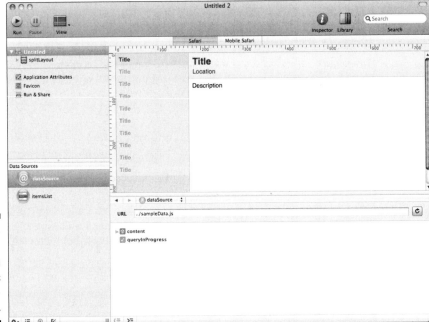

Figure 18-3:
You can collapse all elements of a data source.

Identifying property types

In Figure 18-1, earlier in this chapter, you see the icons for common data types:

- ✔ **String:** These include `title`, `name`, and `location`.

- ✔ **Boolean:** The check mark icon next to `queryInProgress` indicates a `true/false` Boolean. This property is interesting because it's not a basic data property; rather, it's a property of the data source and its operations. The property is filled in appropriately and, if necessary, by the data source.

- ✔ **Objects:** Dashcode can use these objects — bindable objects is the most important point here. `content` and `items` are a single object and an array of objects.

Figure 18-4 shows the data source for the RSS template for Safari. It's bigger than the Browser data source, but it has the same structure.

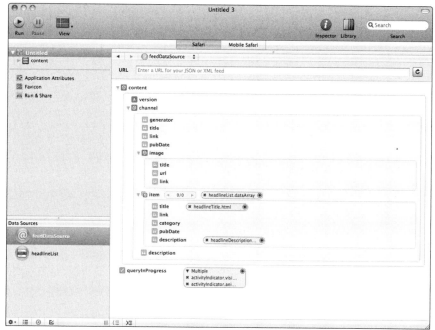

Figure 18-4:
The data
source for
the RSS
template for
Safari.

You need to know about two other property types:

- ✔ **Attributes:** As Figure 18-4 shows, you can have an attribute property (such as `version`). This attribute is used internally, according to the needs of the project and template.

- ✔ **Numbers:** A number sign indicates a numeral. Because it's a number, you can format it as you want. If the number needs to retain its formatting from the original data file through the data source and on into the project, specify it as a string — `"14.2"` rather than `14.2`.

The property type determines how the binding from data model view to interface element is established. Dashcode and JavaScript can do a lot of on-the-fly runtime conversions.

Moving data into and out of a data source

Forget for a moment the data sources you already know about: files or data flows with multiple records and multiple values in each one. A data source can manage a single data element (one field in one record to use database-speak).

Here's the recipe for using a single-value data source:

1. **Create a new Dashcode project for any platform using the Custom template.**

   Although the size of the canvas differs depending on whether you're working with mobile Safari, Safari, or a Dashboard widget, this example functions the same way in each environment.

2. **Reveal the list of data sources using the View menu, View in the toolbar, or the button in the lower left frame of the Dashcode window.**

   Because this project is new, you have a single data source.

3. **Change the data source's name to singleValueDS, as shown in Figure 18-5.**

4. **Add a Text Field part (editable) and a Text part (display only) from the Library, as shown in Figure 18-6.**

5. **Bind content to the textField, as shown in Figure 18-7.**

   When you release the mouse button, choose the value property of the text field as the other end of the binding from content, as shown in Figure 18-8.

6. **Similarly, bind content to the text field's text property, as shown in Figure 18-9.**

   value is normally a property of elements that you can edit, while text is usually an uneditable value.

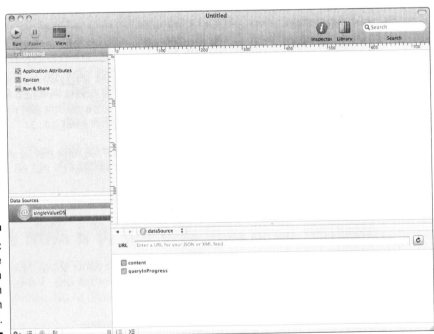

Figure 18-5:
Rename
the data
source in
the Custom
template.

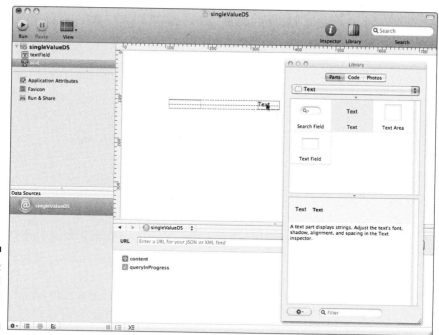

Figure 18-6:
Add text and
text field
parts.

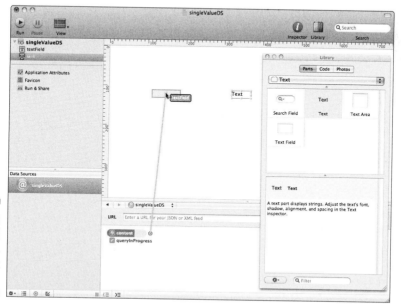

Figure 18-7:
Bind
`content`
to the text
field.

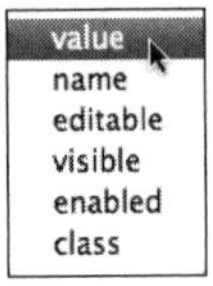

Figure 18-8:
Bind to the
`value`
property
of the text
field.

The canvas should look like Figure 18-10.

7. **Hover the mouse over `multiple` in the bindings list for content to show all the bindings.**

8. **Click Run to launch the project.**

9. **Enter data into the text field.**

The value appears in the other text field, as shown in Figure 18-11.

Experiment with typing slowly into the input field; the data transfers to the other field in (almost) real-time. The structure that is implemented here doesn't wait for the completion of the edit. In other environments, you may have to click out of the input field before the edit is completed and the data is transferred. That situation isn't the case here, but if you're used to clicking out of a field, it doesn't do any harm.

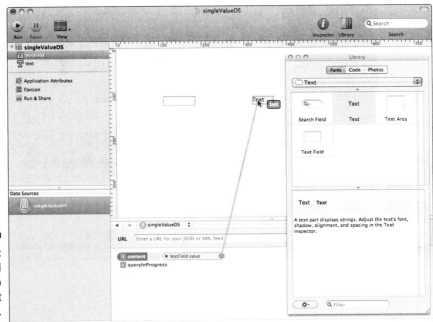

Figure 18-9:
Bind
content to
the text
element.

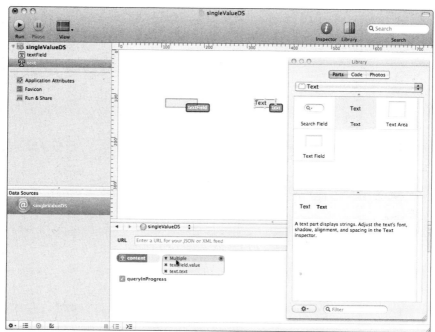

Figure 18-10:
Check
out the
bindings.

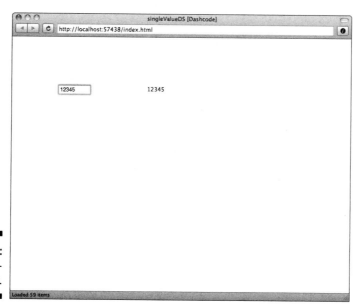

Figure 18-11:
The bind-
ings work.

Using a data source for a variety of bindings

You can use a data source with a single value (like the one shown in the previous section) in many ways. In the following example, a single text entry field drives several other objects as bindings pass data around. The example also reminds you that you can create bindings from the Bindings inspector as well as by connecting objects in the data model view to the interface.

Here's how you can use a data source as the intermediary between a data entry field and an interface object that receives the data:

1. **Add an indicator part from the Library, as shown in Figure 18-12.**

2. **Select the indicator and open the Bindings inspector.**

3. **Select the `singleValueDS` data source; set the property to `div`, which is the default name of the indicator (see Figure 18-13).**

   As soon as you make the change in the Bindings inspector, the bindings list in the data model view updates.

4. **With the indicator still selected, open the Attributes inspector and change its `id` from `div` to `myIndicator`.**

   Use accurate and specific names for views and variables so that you know exactly what elements you're working with.

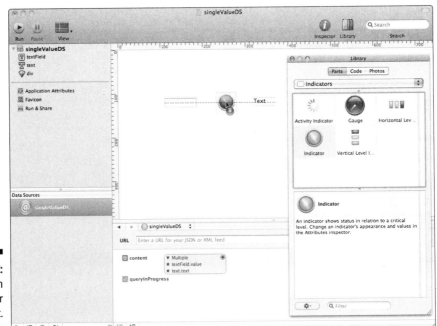

Figure 18-12:
Add an indicator part.

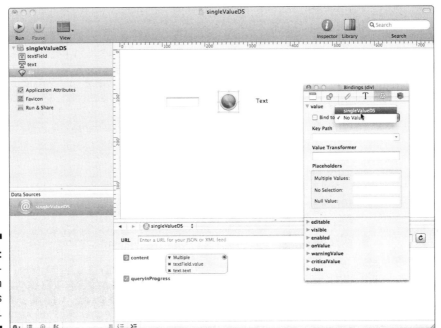

Figure 18-13:
Create bind-
ings with
the Bindings
inspector.

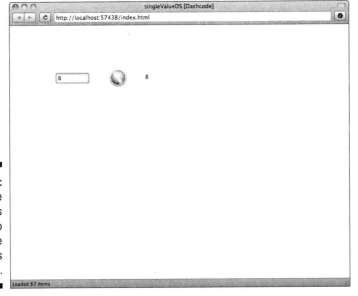

Figure 18-14:
Use the
Attributes
inspector to
change the
indicator's
ID.

5. **Click run to launch the project.**

   Enter data and watch as it is transferred through the data source to the text field and to the indicator, as shown in Figure 18-15.

   Experiment with the values set in the Attributes inspector to change the indicator's color to the caution or warning value.

6. **Add an activity indicator from the Library.**

7. **Bind the content property in the data model view to the activity indicator.**

   Its default name in the navigator is `activityIndicator`.

8. **Bind the content property again to the activity indicator — this time to the `activityIndicator.animating` property.**

   You can check this using the Bindings inspector for the activity indicator, as shown in Figure 18-16.

9. **Run and test.**

The activity indicator disappears when the text field doesn't have text in it. When text is entered, it controls the color of the activity indicator, as you see in Figure 18-17 (Try a sequence of 0, 5, 10, and 15 to see a good color show.)

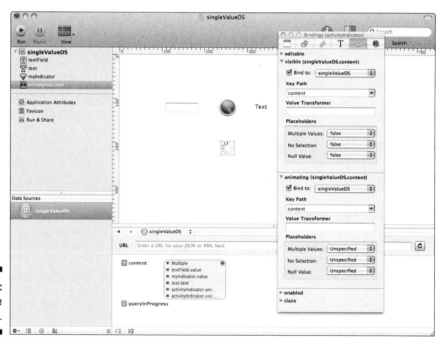

Figure 18-15:
Run the
project.

Figure 18-16:
Add an
activity
indicator.

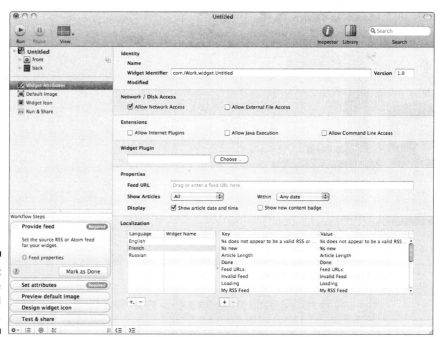

Figure 18-17:
Test the
completed
project.

Handling Localization

Localization is one of the most important features of Mac OS X. The localization architecture provides the ability to support multiple languages that the user can manage. Localization is supported by Dashcode, and while it's available for Safari Web apps, it reaches its greatest point with Dashboard widgets. This section offers an overview of the process (it's really not very complicated). For more information, log on to `http://developer.apple.com` and search for "localization dashboard widgets."

You provide all the basic localization settings for a widget in Widget Attributes, as shown in Figure 18-18. (Figure 18-18 is the RSS widget template with no modifications made to it except for the addition of French and Russian localizations for demonstration purposes.)

At the left, you add or delete languages; the box at the right provides key/value pairs for phrases and their translations in the selected languages. You add and delete from both boxes with the standard + and – buttons at the lower left.

If you choose to add a new language, you can choose from the pop-up menu, shown in Figure 18-19.

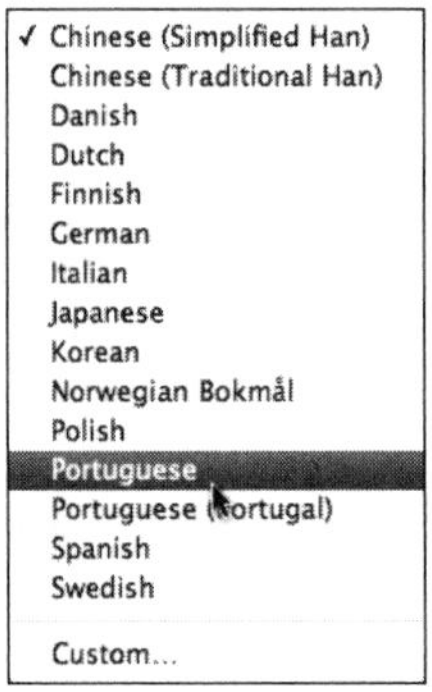

Figure 18-18:
Set up
localization
for widgets
in Widget
Attributes.

```
✓ Chinese (Simplified Han)
  Chinese (Traditional Han)
  Danish
  Dutch
  Finnish
  German
  Italian
  Japanese
  Korean
  Norwegian Bokmål
  Polish
  Portuguese
  Portuguese (Portugal)
  Spanish
  Swedish

  Custom...
```

The list of languages is standard in Mac OS X, but you can add your own, as shown in Figure 18-20.

The text in Figure 18-20 provides a clue as to how localization is handled. For each localized language, a folder called `lproj` is created. This folder usually has two files. Within the folders, the files always have the same names. (The language is part of the folder name, as in `en.lprog` for English.) The localized folders are in the Files list shown in Figure 18-21.

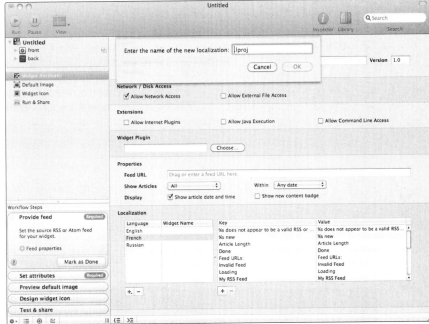

Figure 18-19: Choose a new language for localization.

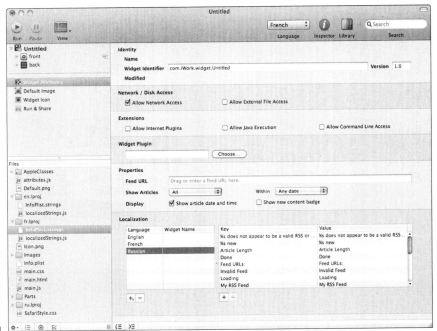

Figure 18-20: You can add a custom language for localization.

These files appear in each localized folder:

- ✔ **InfoPlist.strings:** This file contains information about the app that is localized. As you can see at the bottom left of Figure 18-21, you can provide a widget name for each language. This name is for the localized version of the widget, and it's part of the property list (`plist`) for the project. The property list can be accessed by the Finder, so it will be able to find the correct name even if the application isn't running.

- ✔ **localizedStrings.js:** This file contains the key/value pairs that you specify in the box at the right for each language. The program itself uses these localizations as it's running.

Dashcode creates and maintains these files; you don't modify the files inside the `lproj` folders. For example, if you modify a key with a new value (see Figure 18-22), Dashcode updates the appropriate file. (Keys are always displayed in alphabetical order by key, not value.)

Dashcode automatically stores the localizations you see in Figure 18-23.

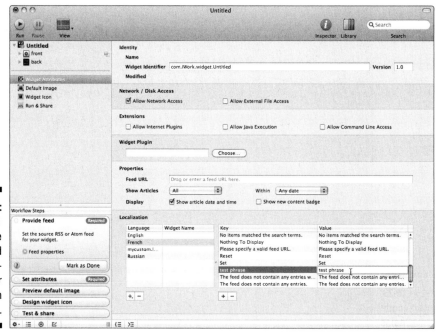

Figure 18-21:
`lproj`
folders are
created
automati-
cally for
each
language.

Figure 18-22:
Modify
localizations
in Widget
Attributes.

Figure 18-23:
Dashcode
maintains
the internal
localization
tables.

As you look at this structure, localization's purpose is basically to convert words or phrases from one language to another. In many cases, in addition to localization, you may want to add options for further customization. For example, you can certainly translate a phrase such as Sales Tax to another language, but if your widget provides a quick calculator of a product's final price, you may need an option to display the calculation as a sales tax rather than as a value-added tax. In this case (as in many others), it's not just the words that change but also the logic.

In short, you can usually do whatever you want to do with localization and customization with a combination of Widget Attributes and preferences.

If you're trying to localize a widget or app, see whether you can find a localization table from another widget in your target language as a starter. Do make certain that someone fluent in the language reviews your final localization.

Chapter 19

Testing and Monitoring Your Work

*W*hen your app or widget runs, your work is just beginning. Although some exceptions exist, in most cases, apps and widgets are designed to be run many times by many different people. After your Dashcode project runs for the first time, you move into another phase that includes distributing it, promoting it, responding to questions, and keeping a list of asked-for improvements.

You can certainly just wait for people to get in touch with you about problems and enhancements, but it makes sense to try to get ahead of the curve. Make sure that a variety of people test your work and that you set up channels of communication so that you aren't surprised when problems occur.

In keeping with the idea of getting ahead of problems, this chapter focuses not only on how to analyze and diagnose problems quickly, but also on how to prevent them.

The basic techniques for working with code are widely available in books and on the Web, so you don't find the standard advice about naming variables and using comments. You do find Dashcode-specific information about the built-in debugger and about some issues you may have not considered for a while.

Conserving Resources

Software requires a variety of resources in order to run. The most basic of resources are processor power to actually do the work, some kind of quickly accessible storage to store data as it's being worked on, and networking resources to communicate with other devices and software.

Enabling channels of communication for your Dashcode projects

Whether your Dashcode project is part of a large commercial enterprise, a cost-effective tool for a nonprofit organization, or part of a small business — possibly your own — a large part of its success often depends on you having effective channels of communication with your users and potential users. These channels of communication can mean actively promoting your app or widget on Web sites and in other media. They also can include having clear and easy-to-use ways for people to ask questions and get help. In these regards, Dashcode projects are no different from other projects.

This chapter shows you the technical tools to use in debugging and supporting your projects, but don't ignore the marketing side of things. A lot of information in books and on the Web can guide you in creating and supporting Web-based products, which is basically what apps and widgets are. (Even a widget that makes no calls to the Internet uses Web technologies extensively.)

Remember that apps and widgets almost never come with user documentation: If it's needed, you're probably thinking about a project that's too big or complex. Even so, some support is a good idea, even if it's a clear definition of what your project is all about.

If you're registered as an iOS developer at Apple's `http://developer.apple.com` site (a good idea, and it's free or inexpensive, depending on your status as a student, individual, or business), you can review the marketing materials for iPhone and iPad apps. Particularly important is the list of reasons why the App Store rejects apps. This list includes two reasons for rejection that can apply to Dashcode apps and widgets: The app doesn't do what it says it will do, or the app doesn't work.

Resist the temptation to try to make your app or widget into traditional software, but don't assume that the app or widget or your users can perform magic. The ability to get in touch with you or someone who can respond to issues is critical. For widgets, this information belongs on the back of the widget. For apps, you can construct a back side with the Info button, or you can construct another view to provide support.

And if you're tempted to provide separate e-mail addresses for different purposes, rethink matters. These tools are small and focused.

Some of these resources are interchangeable — for example, you can reduce your need for memory in many cases by storing and retrieving data over a network. The art of software design (and it is an art in many ways) is a matter of balancing those tradeoffs.

And just to make things more interesting, the costs of the basics (processing power, memory, and networking) vary over time. For a number of years, it's been a period of relatively cheap memory and pretty cheap processing power. Networking has been easily accessible, but that trend seems to be changing with the advent of smartphones that are rapidly eating up network capacity and with new ways of pricing network access. (The days of unlimited data transfers on smartphones are numbered.)

These trends affect all software development, but they particularly affect the development of apps and widgets. You may need to worry about resources that you've taken for granted for years. Old-timers can regale you with the tales of how they labored to conserve every byte of memory; they'll happily share some of the tricks with you, because after several decades of relative plenty, scarcity is coming. (To be honest, it's relative scarcity: No one is proposing the extraordinarily limited memory spaces of computers from a few decades ago.)

There's not much space

Developers haven't been counting bytes too much lately. Modern computers have so much more memory than they used to, and they also have very powerful virtual memory implementations that far exceed even mainframe capabilities from the past.

Here's a perfect example of tradeoffs: Virtual memory lets the developer work in a memory space that can appear infinite. This infinite memory is implemented by using more processor power. If memory becomes dramatically cheaper or processor power becomes dramatically more expensive, virtual memory may go into eclipse for a while.

The operating system does a great job of letting each app or widget have its own memory space that can seem unlimited, but good programmers know they must use that space wisely. That said, don't go overboard with packing data into every last bit of storage. (The need to fit a user ID into single words in the 1950s and 1960s arguably gave rise to some of today's security problems.) But develop a sense that everything you store in memory comes at a cost.

The best way to be a responsible user of memory is to release it when you no longer need it. Memory is automatically released in most cases when the process that used it terminates, but with the remarkably stable Mac OS X and iOS operating systems, processes can run for days or weeks without terminating. And it's amazing how much memory they can accumulate during that processing.

Apps and widgets run while other things occur

Just as you're working in an apparently infinite memory space, your app or widget is often running as if it were the only process on the computer: The operating system takes care of letting each app or widget appear to function as the only process on the computer.

But you're not the only process, and you can't do things that prevent other apps from getting their fair share of the processor. Telephony on iPhone is perhaps the most important other process: It needs to be able to preserve the connection so that calls aren't dropped. (Internet connections are a bit more forgiving. In part, this forgiveness is because these connections were designed for computers to use, and computers are a bit more patient than people are when it comes to timing.) As a result, you may have to pay attention to things such as memory use that you haven't worried about for years — if ever. The debugger lets you track these resources, but being careful about your use of resources as you use them is far easier than tracking them after you write the code and your problems.

Exploring the Debugging Tools

Dashcode has a variety of built-in debugging tools to help you track down problems and monitor how your app or widget is working. Because apps and widgets are built on JavaScript (which is interpreted rather than compiled), Dashcode can provide you with fairly precise information about where the app or widget is at any moment.

In compiled applications, the compiler often strips out the source code so that what is left are the instructions for the computer to execute. In interpreted scripts, such as JavaScript, the source code is interpreted at runtime and converted to machine instructions at that time rather than in a separate compilation process. (This overview is broad, and you should be aware that some preprocessors and optimizers can muddy the situation a bit.) Because the interpreter is looking at the source code as your code runs, it can show you what line it's currently looking at. The interpreter also can show you what actual machine instructions it's emitting for that line of source code.

The debugging tools let you get deep into the guts of what's happening inside your app or widget. Before your eyes glaze over, realize that you can do a great deal of productive debugging without looking at those hieroglyphics. When your Dashcode project doesn't run properly, the debugging tools can often pinpoint the line of code that has failed. If it's not the specific line of code, you can often find the general location in your code. So instead of having to look through all the files in your project as well as all the settings in the various inspectors, you can quickly get to the heart of the problem. The following sections demonstrate how you can use the debugger in this way.

The Debug menu lets you fine-tune options for debugging. The following sections use the default settings for the Debug menu, including Break on Exception, which stops execution when an error is encountered.

Creating a problem

The first step in demonstrating the debugging tools is to create a Dashcode project that contains a bug. As you can see throughout this book, Dashcode does its very best to prevent you from inserting bugs into the code, so creating a problem is easier said than done, but you can produce Dashcode projects with bugs in them.

Consider the *Developed with Dashcode* line, shown in Figure 19-1, which automatically appears at the bottom of templates. (It's the `footer` view inside `settings` inside `views` in the navigator.)

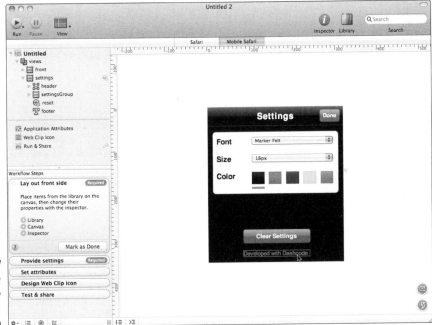

Figure 19-1: You can change the *Developed with Dashcode* credit line.

You can change the text just by selecting it in the canvas and typing new text. If you want to accidentally change *Developed with Dashcode* to *Developed with Dishcode,* you won't encounter any problems. That's the kind of mistake that Dashcode can't catch.

You can find the code that sets this text in Chapter 17. It's in `mobile/ Parts/setup.js,` and it's shown here:

```
"footer": { view: 'DC.Text', text: "Developed with Dashcode" },
```

Make certain that you choose View➪Source Code and that the pane below the canvas is open enough so that you can see the contents. This code is formatted a little differently than in the template in Chapter 17, but it's the same code. Chapter 17 presents the code as an example of code that you can modify but that you have to be careful with. In fact, in order to modify this code, you need to turn off code generation: Dashcode really is trying to make it hard for you to make a mistake that will cause the app or widget to fail. In this case, you want to keep going and create that problem (and then you can solve it).

Choose View➪Stop Code Generator to change the code and remove the quotation mark before the word *Developed.* The line of code should appear like this:

```
"footer": { view: 'DC.Text', text: "Developed with Dashcode" },
```

Figure 19-2 shows this code in the Source Code pane.

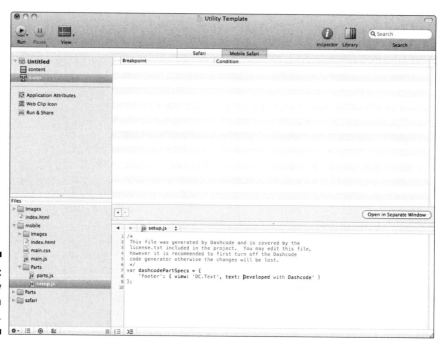

Figure 19-2:
Deliberately
introduce an
error.

As soon as you do so, the colored highlighting of text in the window readjusts itself: A missing or extra quotation mark throws everything else off, and it's a common typo. That's your first clue something is wrong.

Reviewing the run log

The Run button does more than run your projects in the simulator. You can also use it for debugging. When you click and hold the Run button, you can choose which particular tools you use to run it (see Figure 19-3).

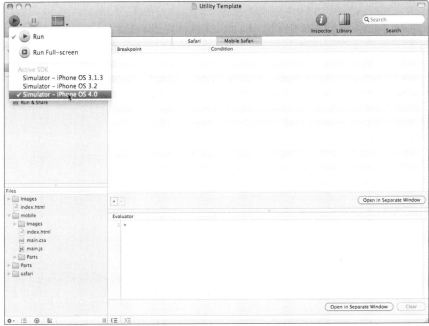

Figure 19-3:
You can choose your runtime configuration.

The ability to use these simulators requires that you install the iOS SDK through `http://developer.apple.com`. If not, Dashcode always uses its own code to run mobile Safari Web applications.

Choose View➪Run Log to show the run log, which replaces the Canvas pane at the top of the Dashcode window. The run log provides messages encountered as your app or widget runs. In most cases, as soon as you show the run log, you want to clear out the old messages: Do so by choosing Debug➪Clear Run Log.

Even though each message is stamped with its date and time, you can easily not notice the timestamps to think that error messages from a few minutes ago just occurred. Clearing the run log avoids this problem.

If you have the app that you modified with the missing quotation mark (see preceding section), you can run it now. The Dashcode window probably looks like Figure 19-4, and the simulator just hangs.

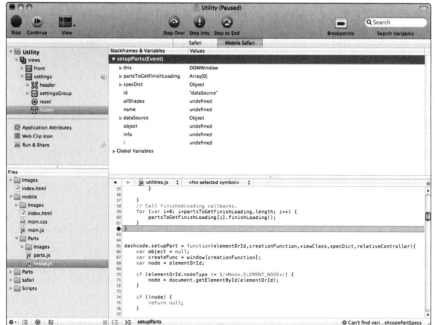

By default, the Stack Frame pane appears at the top; while you're looking at it, many people open the Source Code pane at the bottom so that they can compare the two. Whether you first look at the stack frame or the run log is up to you. Each one shows a different representation of what's going on. Many people like to go to the run log right away. Figure 19-5 shows what the run log looks like.

Because you created the problem (see preceding section), you know exactly where it is, but look at that code so that you can see how Dashcode reports the problem. As is a common situation with any debugging tool, Dashcode, gives you a general idea of what's wrong, but, particularly in cases of mismatched quotation marks, the actual problem is that the parser for JavaScript is thrown off.

Because the debugger is looking deep inside your app or widget, it may be reporting on code that you know nothing about, and it may be code that is correct. One way to approach such a problem is to look up the various references that Dashcode provides. Don't try to get to the bottom of each one. For your first pass, just check out each one quickly to see whether you see something you can work with. It's amazing how such a quick look at the debugger output can often help you find the problem.

Figure 19-5:
View the
run log.

In the run log, you see the message that the session started and then an error message: an X in a red circle. The run log shows you this message:

```
Can't find variable: dashcodePartSpecs
Parts/core/utilities.js  Line: 36
```

This message also appears at the lower right corner of the Dashcode window frame. You can click it to go to the line of code. If you go to that line of code, you see

```
for (var id in dashcodePartSpecs) {
```

This line of code is where the problem occurred, but nothing is wrong with it. What's wrong is that the variable dashcodePartSpecs, which is in a totally different file, was corrupted by the missing quotation mark. Because you don't immediately see something to deal with, move on.

Looking at stack frames

The stack frames display shows you the values of all variables at the moment when the project encountered troubles (refer to Figure 19-4). Disclosure triangles let you open up arrays and other multivalue items.

Some variables are declared but not initialized. Having uninitialized variables is perfectly normal, so don't panic yet.

If you don't see something immediately wrong, the next place to look is where the problem occurred — not the specific line of code, which often is obscure, but where in the code it was executed. As you go up one level and one more level, you gradually move from the world of complicated and obscure code to code that is documented with comments that let you know what is happening. (Being able to trace problems through the debugger is another reason why you should be generous with your own comments.)

The red arrow shown at line 62 in Figure 19-4 pinpoints the last line of the function that was executing when the problem occurred. If you can't immediately see what line 62 is doing check out what the function it's in is doing. Scroll up in the Source Code pane to the beginning of that function to see whether you can find any more clues. Here's the code you find:

```
//
// setupParts(string)
// Uses the dashcodePartsSpec dictionary, declared in the
//   automatically generated file setup.js to instantiate
//   all the parts in the project.
//
dashcode.setupParts = function () {
```

Things should start to click together now. `dashcodePartsSpec` appears in the error message and in the comment at the part of the function that failed. That's probably where the error is.

The comment tells you it's a dictionary in the file `setup.js`. And, in fact, that's the name of the array at the top of the file:

```
/*
  This file was generated by Dashcode and is covered by the
  license.txt included in the project.  You may edit this file,
  however it is recommended to first turn off the Dashcode
  code generator otherwise the changes will be lost.
*/
var dashcodePartSpecs = {
    "blackColorChip": { "view": 'DC.PushButton', "initialHeight":
    28, "initialWidth": 30, "leftImageWidth": 1, "onclick":
    "colorChanged", "rightImageWidth": 1 },
```

You're now in the place where the problem exists. Unfortunately, at this point, there's no substitute for some careful looking at the code. The messages you have tell you that the variable doesn't exist, and you can see that it does, so the problem is somewhere within all the data inside `dashcodePartSpecs`. Look at the code in the Source Code pane, and you can see from the colored highlighting that the delimiters have a problem. Before very long, you can home in on the missing quotation mark.

A little bit further down, you see the offending line. The quotation mark is missing at the beginning of the string, which causes Dashcode's syntax coloring to be off. Quoted strings in Dashcode source code by default are shown in purple. The string in the line that's wrong is shown in black and red. (In the following line of code, it appears in italics because colors aren't available in print).

```
"footer": { view: 'DC.Text', text: Developed with Dashcode" },
```

Using breakpoints

The strategy of using basic tools to track down errors works well in many cases, but sometimes you need to bring in another tool. Enter *breakpoints*. Instead of waiting for the project to encounter an error and stop, you can tell it to stop at a certain point. If the project stops at a breakpoint, it appears just as it does when it stops as a result of an error. A pointer indicates the line of code where it stopped, and the stack frames let you examine the contents of variables.

Many developers have used statements such as the PHP echo statement to print debugging data on the page that is being created. Such statements often work in conjunction with comments in the code so that the output may look like this:

```
OK to 1
After sorting
OK to 2
and so forth
```

Printing these trace statements was a standard way of working years ago. Because tracking down bugs isn't something that people do every day of the week (I hope), these old habits and simple tricks often persist.

But breakpoints are a much easier way of working. In particular, if you find yourself writing code to display the value of more than one variable, you need a breakpoint.

To create a breakpoint, show the code where you think the problem may occur. At the left side of the source code listing, line numbers are shown for each line. To create a breakpoint, click a line number, and an arrow appears, as shown in Figure 19-6.

When the line of code is about to be executed, the code stops, and a red arrow highlighted the location of the error replaces the breakpoint arrow (which is normally dark).

To remove a breakpoint, simply drag the arrow out of the left-hand column with the line numbers in it.

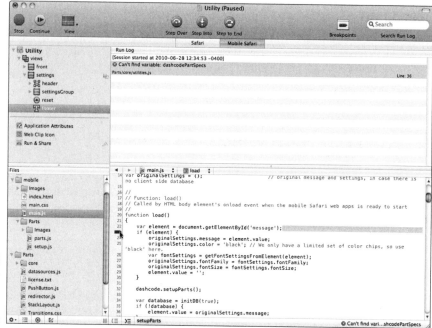

Figure 19-6:
Set a
breakpoint.

Control stops when the line with the breakpoint on it is about to be executed. A comment isn't executed, so control stops just before the next line after the comment that is about to be executed. If you have three lines of comments followed by a single line of executable code, setting a breakpoint on the first line of the comment causes Dashcode to halt just before the line of executable code that follows the comments.

When execution stops, you can check the stack frames for data values. If you don't see what you're looking for, you don't have to start over. After the project stops, you can step through it line by line and check out data in stack frames at each point. (Checking out the run log is of less use at this point because you're watching execution step by step, so you're seeing the run log being created.)

When you stop at a breakpoint, additional controls are visible in the toolbar (see Figure 19-7).

After you examine variables in the stack frame, you can use the three buttons in the center of the toolbar. Here's what they do:

✔ **Step Over** (⌘-O): This button steps over the line of code to which the arrow points. Because the breakpoint is activated before the line of code is executed, the effect is to execute that one line.

✔ **Step Into** (⌘-I): If the breakpoint is stopped at a call to a function, this button lets you step into the function and stop before executing the first line. You can then use Step Over to continue line by line. At the end of the function, control passes back to the calling function.

✔ **Step to end** (⌘-K): This button lets you continue to the last line of the function.

Note that the Continue button next to the Run button is also available when you're stopped at a breakpoint.

Breakpoints are useful for letting you inspect data, but by using the Step commands, you can trace the flow of execution. Misreading (or miscoding) a program is a very common problem. Only when you're confronted with the actual sequence of execution do you notice something like an unaligned `if` statement that causes you to branch out somewhere you never intended to go.

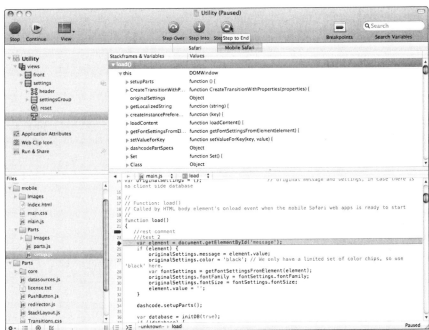

Figure 19-7: Step through breakpoints.

Monitoring Performance

You have another debugging tool at your disposal: a set of three dials that allows you to monitor your use of resources (memory, CPU, and network). As your project runs, the dials keep track of how you're using these resources.

A full discussion of these tools is beyond the scope of this book, but it's useful to display these dials (choose Debug⇨Show Performance Monitor) as you run the project.

What you're looking for is prolonged readings in the red zone. Occasional spikes as your app or widget runs is normal, but anything that causes a lot of resource use can cause a problem. For a very rough analysis, just watch the dials and keep track of what you're doing.

Part VI
The Part of Tens

The 5th Wave   By Rich Tennant

"Hold on Barbara. I'm pretty sure there's an app for this."

In this part . . .

This part provides tips and checklists to get you thinking about the big picture of Dashcode projects as well as tips that can save your users lots of time and aggravation. Remember, with Dashcode you're developing software for other people to use, so the software has to be easy for them — whoever they are — to use it.

Chapter 20

Ten Tips for Creating Better Apps and Widgets

*D*ashcode widget and apps can be simple to create and powerful for your users. Here are ten tips to keep in mind to make them even more useful.

Focus on One Thing

Many people criticize traditional application programs for being bloated — for being plagued by *feature creep.*

One reason for feature creep is that developers don't like to break things when they have a significant installed base of users. As a result, developers make certain that old features continue to work even as they add new features that do similar tasks. The idea is that old and new users alike appreciate the different tools they have available.

Apps and widgets are different from traditional application programs. They're relatively small, and they're designed to do specific tasks. In part because the economics of developing apps and widgets are so different from the cost of developing traditional programs (the costs can be much lower), you can be financially successful doing just one thing well. You don't have to be all things to all people.

The fact that you should clearly define and tightly focus your apps and widgets doesn't mean that you can't create a complex app. With Dashcode's development tools, you can bring a range of related functionality and specific expertise to a user's Dashboard widgets, as well as to Safari Web applications for iPhone or for Safari on a Mac.

The best way to get a sense of how focused you can be is to browse Apple's App Store for iPhone OS apps. The best-selling apps often have large numbers of users and are geared for a mass market. But browse through the other apps: You'll see a wide variety of apps that are so tightly focused to specific industries and types of users that you may not even be able to understand the descriptions. Read the comments, and you'll frequently find people complaining that the latest revision of app X is too complicated. (To be fair, sometimes users are set in their ways and don't want to learn something new — even then, the customer is always right.)

Instead of thinking about pouring everything you know about programming into an app or widget, think about pouring everything you know about a specific domain (baking, community organizing, selling gloves, and so on) into your app or widget.

Make certain that you can answer the question, "What does it do?" in half a dozen words. This type of focus is the hardest part of defining an app or widget. If you want to prove the point, think about one of the major desktop productivity programs that has been around for a decade or more — a word-processing program, for example. Try to answer "What does it do?" When you take a breath after five minutes or so, you'll realize why people are so excited about apps, Web apps, and widgets.

Make Your App or Widget Self-Contained in Every Possible Way

Do one thing, such as a game or productivity tool, that you can clearly define, but do it thoroughly without throwing in the kitchen sink. This tip is harder than you may think. Every time you think of something to add to your app or widget, make certain that it's essential and doesn't blur the focus. Remember that Dashcode apps and widgets are usually small, and you're in control. No Apple App Store reviews the process (which is both a plus and a minus). In this context, it can mean that if you want to take your brilliant idea for an app and widget and split it into several projects, that's fine. You can reuse your analysis and implementation with each version focused and self-contained.

In addition to making your app or widget self-contained, make certain that users know what it does contain and how they can get to it. The developer of one of the major desktop productivity applications from the last few decades addressed the problem of unintentionally hidden features of the program by constructing a game along the lines of, "Can you find the command to do X?" Unfortunately, this approach just emphasized how unwieldy the program had gotten, and the notion dropped from view.

Defining the boundaries of your project is essential. If you're writing a tool that lets people keep track of weather forecasts and the subsequent high and low temperatures and precipitation amounts, you may be tempted to include links to print and video weather reports from the past, as well as the sunrise and sunset times and wind speed — both predicted and actual. While that data surely enhances the app and makes it somewhat self-contained, before you know it, you'll be including the speed of ocean currents and sunspot activity.

If the app is designed to let people track the accuracy of weather forecasts (perhaps so that people can monitor the success rates of various local forecasters), you can make it complete and self-contained without adding all these features. To fulfill the mission, you can manage with just a few pieces of data:

- ✔ Date
- ✔ Name of forecaster/media outlet
- ✔ The difference between predicted and actual high temperature
- ✔ Difference between predicted and actual low temperature. Again, the values don't matter.

For the last two pieces of data, the actual values don't matter. You just include the difference between predicted and actual.

This data makes for a complete app or widget that includes everything necessary and nothing more. Over a period of time, people can gather the data easily and form conclusions or pursue other investigations. Maybe you'll find that you need additional data, but for a project of this type, you can then collect it. Starting out with everything doesn't guarantee that you'll have all the data you'll ever need, and it may make the app or widget and its interface too complicated for many people to use.

Add Internet Functionality for Necessary Additions

Many people equate the Internet with a Web browser — you stop what you're doing and go to a browser to continue what you're thinking of. Stopping what you're doing and switching to a browser was the pattern two decades ago, but it's not true now, and it's really not true with Dashcode projects.

Your users interact with a Safari Web app or with a Dashboard widget. From any Dashcode environment, you can let people get to the Internet — either by going to Web pages or by using XMLHttpRequest syntax to get a specific piece of information. Stop thinking in terms of browsers: You've got Web access in your Dashcode project, and you don't have to ask people to use a browser or type a URL.

Don't go too far, though. While you can theoretically create a browser inside your app or widget, you don't want to reinvent a Web browser. Bring the Web functionality to the app or widget.

Keep the User in Control

One reason for the popularity of apps and widgets is that the user is in control. (Some people would say for the first time in decades.)

Rarely does an app or widget come with an instruction manual. As a result, your user is in control and doesn't have access to pages and pages of documentation. But that scenario only works well if you've done your job.

The pieces all fit together: The user is in control in part by knowing what your app or widget can do and what information and commands it contains. You convey this information by the interface that you create, which is a tall order particularly when you're looking at the relatively small canvas you can use to draw on for a widget or Web app. (Even a Safari Web app designed for display in a desktop browser has a relatively small space because bookmarks, history, status areas, and other browser items take up significant chunks of the browser's window width.)

Keeping the user in control means that you have to trust your user. Some traditional application programs, such as bookkeeping software for small businesses, deliberately don't give the user too much control. The user is actually buying the expertise of the program and developer, and for that reason, the user expects to be led.

With the exception of educational software, most of the time, the user is going to be leading. You can guide and suggest, but control generally rests more squarely with the user than in many traditional applications.

Make Your App or Widget Interruptible

Dashboard widgets, along with Safari Web apps, all are interruptible. When you think about it, just about everything on a computer is interruptible: You can always pull the plug or turn off the computer. Although people talk about the need to make widgets and apps interruptible, what they mostly mean is that they are resumable.

Resumable means that any change to the app's state — including its data — is captured without the user having to take any extra action. Resumability is one of the biggest differences between apps and traditional application programs. It's taken quite a while, but developers and users agree that it's the software's responsibility to save the user's actions. When someone resumes using your app, the settings should be as they were the last time it was used; if you can display multiple views, in most cases, the last view displayed should be the same view that is shown even if six months have passed between the two uses of the app. Chapter 13 shows you how to make your widget or app resumable.

With the release of iPhone 4 and iOS 4 from Apple, this topic has received a great deal of attention. Multitasking is one of the important features of the new hardware and software.

Use Common Interface Tools

Safari Web apps and Dashboard widgets don't go through the App Store, which includes the review process. As a result, your users can decide for themselves whether your Dashcode project does what it claims to do (believe it or not, not doing what it promises is the No. 1 reason for App Store rejections) and whether it looks and behaves the way they expect a Safari Web app or a Dashboard widget to look and behave.

Within certain ranges, all Safari Web apps and all Dashboard widgets look the same. Many Dashcode projects use certain interface elements, and they all behave the same way. Users can simply look at your project's interface and quickly understand how to use it and what to do.

The following tips help you fit into design standards without making your app look as if it fell off an assembly line.

- ✔ **Use Library parts.** If you include customizable code, follow the comments in performing the customization. In many cases, you can go into the JavaScript code and make further customizations, but following the guidance from the comments in the Library parts is best.

- ✔ **Customize with the inspector**. Again, you can go into the code to override settings, but the settings that you should override are those that are in the various inspectors.

- ✔ **Never change a Library part's fundamental behavior.** The Behaviors inspector lets you attach a behavior to any selected view in your project. You can use one of the default behaviors, or you can write one of your own. You can easily convince yourself that your project's specific needs require you to redefine a Library part's behavior — for example, you can interpret a click on a button as meaning that the button's name should change from Option A to Option B. That behavior is most likely a pop-up menu's action, not a button's. (It may also be a check box.)

- ✔ **Avoid duplicate tools.** Dashcode projects are small, so you don't need to provide alternate ways of accomplishing a single task. If you have similar tasks, consider simplifying them into a common task with options selectable by pop-up menus, check boxes, or radio buttons.

Study every interface you can find. New devices coming to market use new ways to let people do everything from manipulate a calendar to edit video. Borrow what you can.

Beware of interfaces that make you think, "Look at that interface!" Look instead for interfaces that show you how to do something faster or more easily. An interface that draws attention to itself rather than the task it enables is generally not a good one.

Make Your App or Widget Predictable

Except for games, make your app or widget predictable, which helps keep the user in control. You can provide options and added features so long as you maintain focus on your primary objective, but make certain that you introduce them in a way that makes sense to the user and isn't a surprise.

This point can be interesting to consider in an app or widget that helps users make sense of data or even learn new concepts. How can it be predictable in this case?

Predictable can have a time dimension to it, which can make for interesting and pleasing apps and widgets. You may not be able to predict what an app will do next — yes, you can be surprised — but immediately after, if you say, "Oh, yes," or "Why didn't I see that?" the unpredictability is explained and, in many cases, welcome.

If you don't explain to the user why the app has done something, the user immediately feels left out of the loop and, more seriously, out of control of the app. In many cases today, an app or widget does know more than the user, but by revealing the process that it has gone through to make a recommendation or suggestion, the app keeps the user in control.

Talk the Talk and Walk the Walk

Apps and widgets are targeted and self-contained, and they rarely come with extensive documentation. It's rare to find a half-day seminar teaching people how to use one of them. (It's less rare to find a seminar teaching people how to build their own or expand on what others have done.)

One way to achieve these goals is to use the language of your users. Many large companies seek to parlay their existing software products into specific markets, and one of the pitfalls comes with terminology. For example, while it's quite true that a contact relationship software package designed for commercial use can also manage donors to nonprofits or the clients that those nonprofits serve, the terminology is different. Logically, the terms *patron* or *customer* are often the same thing, but to people in the field, they have very different meanings than *client*.

Dashcode makes it easy for someone with specific domain knowledge to share it with others using apps and widgets. A common mistake is to think about the large numbers of people who might use your Dashcode widget and then to generalize it so that the terminology isn't specific to one area — the area that you happen to know and that got you started in the process to begin with.

You can always reuse your analysis and design work, so think about keeping your target small and focused on what you know. Your users will respond to the familiar environment, and you can always come back and do another version for another group of people.

Focusing on specific domain knowledge is one of the key aspects of today's world of apps, widgets, and other lightweight software. The development costs are so low that you can successfully target areas that previously couldn't have justified the financial risk of customized development.

Don't Be Afraid to Start Over

Your investment in an app or widget isn't large compared to the investment you may have made years ago in traditional software, and it's not large in comparison to what you know about the subject area. Use your expertise and the advice of colleagues to fine-tune what you're doing, and if you have to start over, do so.

After you've built a few apps and widgets and familiarized yourself with the built-in templates, starting over is only a few minutes' work, either with the same template or a new one. Don't cling to the hours you spent developing your first Dashcode project; those hours were your learning curve. Get past it in your mind and remember that it's fine to rethink things and experiment with a totally different approach. Skip a lunch and come up with a new idea for people to consider. (Yes, the process can often be that fast.)

Provide Feedback Tools for Users

It's worth thinking about the difference between Dashcode projects and older applications. If you want feedback, an online survey that "only takes 5 minutes" is probably not a good idea for a widget that people use for half a minute a week.

Nevertheless, provide some kind of feedback and make it easy. For widgets, the back of the widget is the place for a URL. With Safari and mobile Safari Web apps, find a convenient place for such a link. When you're working on the limited space of an iPhone Web app, your eye may be drawn to the *Developed with Dashcode* credit line that appears on many of the templates. Do use a credit line to let people know how you've done things and to promote this exciting tool, but consider making that line a link to either a Web site or to another, larger view on a mobile Safari Web application. With additional space, you can provide the Dashcode credit, any other necessary credits, and links for comments and suggestions.

Depending what your app or widget does, you may want to let that link go to an interactive section. If you're building a Dashboard widget for use within an organization, such a section can let people provide comments and suggestions. Just be certain that you have the resources to think about, if not implement, suggestions that are made.

And, as has been stressed many times, remember that you're working in a very different scale from traditional applications. If a major software developer has a mailbox into which people can drop suggestions for the next version of the product, a count of two suggestions over a month would be considered a disaster. You're playing on a much smaller stage here, and you can be responsive to much smaller numbers of users.

Chapter 21

Ten Simplifications for Your Apps and Widgets

In This Chapter

▶ Giving your users the simplest interface possible

▶ Keeping your interface stable

▶ Accommodating differences in languages and handedness (left and right)

*W*hile simplifications to apps and widgets make them easier for users to use, they may make it a little more difficult for you to develop them. However, the increase in user satisfaction should pay off. Every time you're tempted to make it easier on yourself, remember to think about whether you're pushing your work off onto the user. Better yet, if you make it easier on yourself and on your users, you've hit pay dirt.

Use a Verb to Identify Every Interface Element You Can

You may think that using a verb to identify every interface element is about labels for buttons and other interface elements, but that's only a small part of it. When you talk about interface elements with colleagues, other developers, and friends or think about your app or widget, use a verb for every interface element.

Developers and managers frequently use other terms — sometimes humorous and sometimes historical — for the interface elements. Maybe you think of it as Carole's button or the blue slider, but in a strange way, that imprecision can find its way into your code. Even worse, when you write documentation or teach people how to use the app or widget, you can muddy the waters. Every interface element needs a set name that you use when you talk about it.

Some interface elements need a name only when you talk about them. For example, a sort button with an up-pointing arrow can let people know that it sorts the list next to or beneath it in reverse order. Place this sort button next to a similar button with a down-pointing arrow, and you've pretty clearly told the users what they do. However, when you're talking about these buttons, unless you're willing to go through a fairly elaborate pantomime, you need to make certain that you and your colleagues use the same terms to avoid confusion.

If you're working with code, there's one area where using a precise name becomes problematic. What do you do if you change the name of an interface element while you're working on the project? As a result of testing or user feedback, you may change the Process button to the Go button. What do you do with the code that's already been written? The testing team (even if that's only you) can come back to the development team (likewise, perhaps just you) with the news that users don't really like Process. But as a developer, you may have written code with variables that include the word *process*.

One solution that works for many developers is to use internal names that clearly show they're internal. For example, you may know from the beginning that you will include a Go button, so you may want to internally refer to it as UIGo (for user interface). While this solution isn't ideal, it helps preserve the distinction between code and other project internals and the user interface. You can even add a comment at the top of a file so that you can map the interface elements to the code: UIGo implements Process, for example. That way, you can change either name independently as long as you change the single comment that provides the mapping.

In particular, be careful about reversing names and meanings. One way to fit into the world of Dashcode apps and widgets is to user Apple's own internal rules for naming things. You can download the Apple Publications Style Guide, a several-hundred page PDF document, from `developer.apple.com`. It provides guidance on such issues as what verb to use to describe the process of choosing a menu command. (It's *choose*, not *select*; select is for objects such as graphics, sections of text, or icons.) Search for the title because its location changes from time to time. Apple updates this guide every year or so.

Sometimes you can identify interface elements simply with an icon or button. (After all, a button isn't called a graphical user interface for nothing.) You still need an accurate name to identify the interface element in your discussions, and you need an image that is absolutely clear to all your users. Some images are very culturally specific and can be quite mysterious to people who don't know the reference. On the other hand, some abstractions are far removed from what the objects they represent look like, but the abstractions have become so widely used that people understand them. (Take a look at the Home button in a Finder window: Do you live in a home that looks anything like that?)

Make Errors Impossible or Unlikely

Making errors impossible or unlikely is scarcely a new concept, but it still isn't adopted in much software. Decades ago, the cost of computing power and storage was so great that doing real-time checking was often problematic. (According to some reports, the first spell-checkers slowed down typing to such an extent that they were unusable!)

Now that computers have much more power and storage, you can do real-time checking so that errors are stopped before or as they happen. Your major tool in this endeavor is JavaScript itself, with an able assist from the various Dashcode inspectors. On many Web pages, JavaScript checks to see that an e-mail address field contains an @ symbol; other common JavaScript routines edit passwords in real time (for length, the presence or absence of special characters, and the like). Much of this code is available on the Web in various tutorials or examples.

Watch for interface tips and techniques to reuse. For example, if a field is to contain a telephone number, you can label it Telephone Number. In and of itself, that label takes up a bit too much valuable screen space. You can provide default data in the field that says Telephone Number, and that way, you'll save the space for the label. If you find the text in the field when you access it, you'll know that it's your default data, and you can ignore it. The user replaces the default data with real data, and you save the space for the label.

For example, many people in the United States and Canada recognize (xxx) xxx-xxxx as a telephone number format. Set the field to that value and ignore it when you're parsing input. But with this value in the field, people will often recognize it as a telephone number field, and the format will be clear. Keep your eyes open for the various ways in which engineers and designers encourage the correct data entry in the apps and Web pages.

Beyond suggestions, you can do some error-checking as close as possible to the actual error as possible. Here's where behaviors come in. As you see in Figure 21-1, you can attach a behavior to do your error-checking to any input field.

You can write JavaScript to do the actual error checking you see in Figure 21-2.

You have to decide what to do if you encounter an error. Remember, you're not in a standalone application program. If the text is too long, you can truncate it with JavaScript. You can reject it or replace it with a default value. What you really can't do successfully is to get into a back-and-forth exchange with the user in which various attempts are made to correct the error. See whether you can do an immediate fix and be done with it.

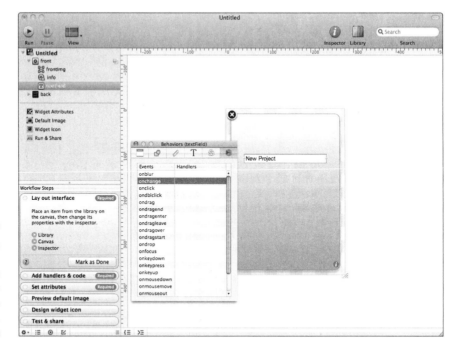

Figure 21-1:
Use the Behaviors inspector to catch errors immediately.

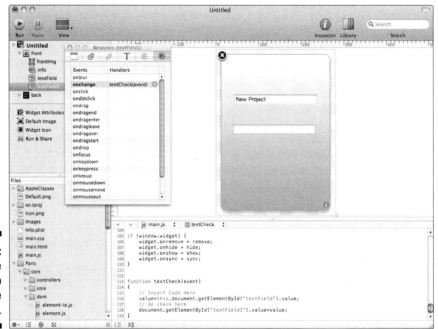

Figure 21-2:
Write the code to catch the error.

You may want to use the example of adding views to the Navigator in Dashcode. When you add a view or other part from the library, the view is assigned a unique default name that contains no spaces. You can then modify that name, but if your new name is illegal (perhaps because it contains spaces), the name automatically reverts to the legal and unique name that Dashcode created. This type of error-checking and correction is easy to implement in the context of a behavior that's implemented in JavaScript.

Use Localizations and Preferences for Set-and-Forget Customizations

Dashcode gives you two major tools for setting options, preferences, and localizations: preferences and the localization structure. Each tool is slightly more complicated than building specific values into your code, but that additional complication is worth it when it comes time to change these values or translate your app or widget.

You just have to organize your strategy for the data that can vary based on user preferences, localization choice, or even changes in your default settings that you hardcode (see Chapters 13 and 18). By opting into this controlled structure, you do a little more work up front in exchange for having an easier-to-maintain Dashcode project.

An added benefit to using these tools, which let users affect the appearance and behavior of the interface, is that you start to think about that interface somewhat independently of the text that it displays. Also, to the extent that preferences can govern what is displayed and in what sequence, you also think about your project somewhat differently.

Thinking about the difference between the interface and the functionality is good for you as you're developing your project. By creating a hard and fast distinction between the interface and the basic functionality, you often write clearer code that is easier to modify and maintain as time goes on.

Organize Lists and Groups from Complex to Simple Rather than Alphabetical

There's a lot to be said for alphabetical order. So much so, in fact, that alphabetical is the only order that many people think about for lists. Consider simplifying your Dashcode projects in several different ways.

Whenever you're thinking about a list of items and are considering alphabetical order, ask yourself whether you really need that entire list. In desktop applications, many designers consider lists of more than a dozen items to be too long for users to manage them effectively. (Notwithstanding the concerns of interface designers, you'll still find pop-up menus with lists of the nearly 200 nations of the world.)

The first way to make your lists simpler is to make them as short as possible. Also, use the Browser functionality that's built into Dashcode templates. Using this template, you can let users choose from a handful of items and then move into another handful for the selected item. With only three steps, you can easily turn a list of more than 200 hundred items into three hierarchical lists of no more than six each. This design choice is particularly important for the limited size of widgets and even Safari Web applications. When you have a much larger area to work with, you can display many more items at a time. However large the list is, what's important to the user is how much of it is visible at one time — that is, without scrolling it.

Recruit Right- and Left-Handed Testers

Using both right- and left-handed testers is a critical point for hand-held devices. Many people hold an iPhone in their nondominant hand (the left for right-handers) and then use the dominant hand to take notes and perform other on-phone tasks. You've got a host of issues to confront that you may never have thought about including the fact that many people hold a phone in such a way that their hand obscures part of the screen. The phone doesn't have a big screen, so any blocking may be problematic.

Along these lines, don't just worry about right- and left-handed testers. Testers are likely to be using your app or widget in a different way from other people. They won't be studying the interface and examining it thoroughly. Instead, they'll take a second or two to look at it, and then they'll act. If they don't get the response they expect, they'll move on.

Integrate with the User's Data So That It "Just Works" the First Time

Dashcode apps and widgets are focused and specific, which leads to some advantages over traditional applications. If you're writing an application for a traditional desktop, chances are you're writing something that many different people can use in many ways. You can use a word-processing program, for example, to write a research paper, a shopping list, or a yard sale sign. You can print the document on a single page, in landscape or portrait mode, or print only a subsection. Along with this power and flexibility comes the need for the developer of a traditional application to accept whatever the user provides by way of data.

Frequently (but not always) apps and widgets focus not on a generic task, such as word processing, but on a specific application for a task, such as creating a shopping list. Part of the focus includes the fact that apps and widgets generally bypass printing: You can print a Web page from a browser, but most of the printing features a word processing program needs to support don't exist in the land of apps and widgets.

Because the data you work with is generally a focused type of data, you can work with it in greater detail than the developer of a word processing application can work with generic text data. Take everything that you know about the user's data and incorporate it into your app. That includes the terminology but it also includes formatting and structuring for documents of all kinds.

In fact, when you're working with apps and widgets, you may want to forgo many of the word processing features. Remember: You've got access to a built-in database, so you can manage your data in the more structured world of a database designed for the specific data you're handling rather than the free-wheeling environment of word processing.

This functional focus makes it easy for the user to perform the specific task at hand so that the widget or app just works without the user having to set margins, arrange headings, or use any of the other word-processing tools so valuable in generalized desktop applications. The same principle applies to apps that are focused on other types of data: You can provide a widget or app that uses database or spreadsheet technology and that packages it up in a domain-specific way. This package is similar to providing a spreadsheet or database template so that the user can get down to the nitty-gritty of a specific task or project right away.

Everything that makes your app or widget familiar to users from the beginning will help them get involved with it. Familiarity is the key. If you use terminology and layouts that the user recognizes immediately, the user should be happy and productive.

Stay in Your Space Without Scrolling

On the relatively limitless expanse of a scrollable browser page, you can display a large amount of data, and users can navigate through it with the scrollbars. Although using scroll bars was a great way to navigate a few decades ago, this approach isn't terribly efficient today.

Templates such as the Browser template help you organize data so that navigation is simple for the user. Limit choices to half a dozen or so at a time; those choices will fit on even a small iPhone screen. By limiting choices, you can let users click through several layers of hierarchy without doing anything other than tap their finger. If the routine is tap-scroll-tap, the process becomes much slower than seeing your choices, tapping one, seeing the next choices, and tapping one of them.

Scroll bars, in some ways, are the enemies of the simplification that is at the heart of apps and widgets.

Make Certain Data Fields Are Big Enough for All Languages

Most of the simplifications in this chapter are for the user. This one is for you.

Even if you don't translate your app or widget into other languages, don't make it difficult for you or someone else to do so. That means, among other things, making fields big enough to be translated. Some people will argue that certain languages by their very nature take up more space to identify the same object than others do, but in fact it depends on the language and the specific words involved.

What is clear is that every time you leave only a pixel or two of leeway in a field that contains data, you're probably preparing for problems down the road. If the field needs to be enlarged, you can do so, but you may have to move other fields aside.

Test, Test, and Test Some More

No matter how small your app or widget is, test it repeatedly. At the beginning, you're probably the test subject, and you're not a very good one. You know how things are supposed to work, and you know what goes on in the background. The first time someone other than a developer runs new software, something often crashes immediately. After all, the software is designed to work to accommodate your view of the problem it addresses.

You can force yourself to try to think differently, but the best way to handle testing is to ask someone to test it and then leave the room. Give the tester exactly the information you expect a user to have (and in the case of an app or widget, that's usually very little data). Turn them loose and see what happens. Reassure them (and mean it!) that you want their honest impression of the software.

Testers get used up very quickly. As soon as someone has any experience with your software, they're not useful as a tester because whatever they learned the first time around colors their second experience. The good part is that with apps and widgets, the software is usually so specific and relatively small that testing it is easy.

Use Your Own Apps and Widgets

After testing comes production. Periodically use your own apps and widgets. If you're like many people, you may develop apps and widgets as an outgrowth of work you may already be doing. In other cases, you may develop them as an in-house developer for an organization. Don't let too much time elapse between your periodic reviews of the app or widget.

Keep an eye out for environmental changes. New versions of an operating system tend not to break apps and widgets — they're designed to be robust. However, always keep your apps and widgets in mind with any upgrades to hardware and software. In addition, if your app or widget accesses Internet resources, make certain that those resources haven't changed or moved.

Appendix

JavaScript Quickies

*J*avaScript is the language that powers Dashcode projects. You may never see it, but it's there, powering the parts from the Library that you use in your project as well as powering the entire infrastructure that lives in the files that are at the heart of every Dashcode project. (These files are added to each and every project that you create.)

Dashcode itself is not written in JavaScript. It's developed using Apple's Cocoa and Xcode development environment; the primary programming language is Objective-C. Some aspects of those tools have been re-implemented in Dashcode projects using JavaScript.

This appendix is designed to give you a high-level view of the most important things you need to know about JavaScript as well as examples of some types of JavaScript code that you'll encounter in your Dashcode projects.

For more information on JavaScript, check out *JavaScript and AJAX For Dummies* (Wiley) by Andy Harris.

Identifying your JavaScript Code

You deal with three types of JavaScript code in your Dashcode projects:

- ✔ **Code you write:** Occasionally, you need to write some JavaScript code for your project. You usually don't have to do too much of that, and what there is consists of code snippets — sections of code that you add to existing files that have been created for you. You rarely have to write a complete JavaScript code file.

- ✔ **Code you see:** Sometimes, you want to look into how the JavaScript from the Dashcode Library parts and the templates works. You may look into the Dashcode Library when you're debugging your project; it can also happen when you want to find out more about JavaScript — perhaps as you're modifying code as described in the next point.

✔ **Code you modify:** Most of the time, your experience with JavaScript consists of making modifications to code in the templates and Library parts. You have to be able to understand the basic structure of JavaScript files (so you can find the place where you need to do your work), and you need to understand the basic syntax (so that you know what to change and what not to change), and where to find more information.

Looking at JavaScript

JavaScript is one of the most widely used programming languages today. It's designed to run in Web browsers. Originally, Web pages were simply documents that were displayed by browsers, but before very long, designers of Web pages wanted to be able to have little snippets of code that would run as the page was being downloaded or as users interacted with it.

It's often JavaScript that runs quickly and quietly in the background of a Web page so that if you type an invalid e-mail address, you get a notification that it must have an @ in it. Likewise, JavaScript is often responsible for reminding you that a new password must have a certain number of letters and must have (or not have) certain special characters. Before the widespread use of JavaScript, you'd type in your data, click a Submit button, and the browser would transmit the data to the Web server where a new page would be downloaded saying either OK or displaying an error message. With JavaScript, that processing can happen in the Web browser on your computer and without the need for traffic over the Internet between the Web server and your computer.

JavaScript is now widely available, and, although a variety of dialects exist, the major syntax is available in most current Web browsers. Nevertheless, most browsers still retain an option that allows users to turn off JavaScript. This feature is a leftover from the days when people didn't trust JavaScript, in part because it was possible for it to generate malicious code. This problem has been largely bypassed today by curtailing some features that JavaScript can execute.

It's not worth discussing whether or not JavaScript is a good idea today. If you want to turn it off in your browser, you probably won't be able to view some important Web sites. And you certainly won't be able to view Dashcode project in Web apps.

For more information on JavaScript, the best online resource is Wikipedia — `http://wikipedia.org`. This appendix provides a few highlights of JavaScript that you need to know to work with Dashcode.

Putting the Script in JavaScript

Three basic types of programming languages are in use today. (Some hybrids are out there as well, but they're built on the following three types.) The differences among them affect how you work with them.

- **Compiled languages:** These are traditional programming languages, such as C, FORTRAN, COBOL, C++, C#, and Objective-C. You write your code, and a special program called a *compiler* translates it into instructions that a computer can execute, Typically, programming languages can be used on a variety of types of computers; it's the compilers that convert the language into specific code for a specific computer. The process of compiling a program consists of *parsing* the code into its logical chunks and then converting the code into executable instructions (*code-generation*).

  The compiler provides error messages if it encounters code that it can't process during the parsing operation or even later on in code generation. If you leave out a comma, misspell a variable name, or make any of a wide range of mistakes that a compiler can discover as it attempts to read your code, the compiler informs you of that fact and lets you know the code that causes the problem.

  Compilers don't catch logic errors. If you write syntactically correct code that computes interest on a bank account by multiplying the account balance by the number of quarts in a liter, a compiler won't catch that mistake.

- **Scripting languages:** There are no compilers here. You write your code, and it's parsed when it's needed. In the case of JavaScript, you write the code and store it in files that are referenced from Web pages. (You can also incorporate JavaScript code directly into the HTML of a Web page.) Because no parsing or code generation occurs when you write the code, any errors that occur during those processes happen at run-time — that is, when the page is displayed for a user who is viewing it in a browser.

- **Dynamic languages:** These languages are compiled in the traditional way, but certain chunks of code are linked into the executable instructions when the program runs. Objective-C is one such language.

If you are used to a traditional compiled language, you no longer have that compiler to check typos and incorrect syntax. Fortunately, Dashcode and many other development environments provide syntax-sensitive formatting to help you. (See "Turning on syntactical formatting in Dashcode," later in this appendix.)

Objecting to Everything

Many people first learned programming by developing some variation on the famous `Hello World` program: It prints the earth-shattering phrase, "Hello World!" or some variation of it on an output device — a printer or a display, in most cases. One of the earliest examples of this program appears in *The C Programming Guide* (Prentice Hall) by, Brian W. Kernighan and Dennis M. Ritchie. Here's the code that is shown there:

```
int main()
{
  printf("hello, world");
  return 0;
}
```

Already in the 1970s, the concept of object-oriented programming was beginning to become popular. One of the easiest ways to grasp the difference between object-oriented programming and the older form of programming is to look at Hello World in JavaScript:

```
<script type="text/javascript">
  document.write('<b>Hello World</b>');
</script>
```

This is an example of one use of JavaScript. You can write JavaScript in other ways, but in this section, the object-oriented features are what matters.

Understanding objects and their methods

In both code examples in the previous section ("Objecting to Everything"), some housekeeping code surrounds the single line of code that's important. In C, the line of code that matters is

```
printf("hello, world");
```

In JavaScript, the important line of code is

```
document.write('<b>Hello World</b>');
```

In C, the code you write uses statements and calls to functions and procedures that the program has created or that are built into C itself. In the JavaScript code, the program interacts with an *object* (the HTML document that is being created for download to a browser), and it is a routine that is built into the document object that is called. In C, `printf` is a function in the C language, in the JavaScript code, `write` is a method (pretty much the same as a function), but it belongs to the document object, not to the programming language.

In C and other languages of that type, you can create your own functions, and in JavaScript and similar languages you can create your own objects as well as their methods and properties.

Most JavaScript today is embedded in Web pages that are being prepared for download to a browser. (Sometimes, the JavaScript is located elsewhere, but it is usually called from the Web page that is being constructed.) `write` is the most common method of the document object.

Using object properties

JavaScript objects can have properties in addition to methods. Methods do things, but properties are data values. For example, the document object has properties such as

- ✔ **referrer:** The page that requested the page that is under construction
- ✔ **url:** The URL of the page being constructed
- ✔ **title:** The page title

Objects can contain other objects — that is, a technique that is used commonly in the Dashcode Library code. When an object contains another object, the term that is used is *containment*. Perhaps the most common example of containment is when Library parts use JavaScript code to find a specific part that is contained in a part. For example, containment is how Dashcode can find a specific view in your content. (See the JavaScript snippets in the second part of this appendix.)

For example, a document can contain one or more forms; each form can contain one or more buttons and other input objects. And each of those input objects can have its own properties, such as a name, a value, and a state such as `checked`.

Using objects with their methods and properties may seem to be a bit more complicated than the unstructured world of earlier programming languages where you can just create something like a button and refer to it by name, but object-oriented programming actually makes the code much more maintainable. Instead of naming items and being done with it, you need to refer to items such as buttons by locating them within a document and then within a form. As JavaScript code grows larger and more complex, this more structured approach really pays off. (And the JavaScript code that Dashcode creates behind the scenes is very complicated, indeed.)

Using object events

In addition to having properties (data) and methods (actions), objects can respond to events. Each object has a specific set of events it responds to. For example, document objects can often respond to events such as `onclick` or `onmouseover`. This style of programming replaces the older style in which a loop of code (an *event loop*) keeps running over and over. Each time the loop executes, it checks to see whether a click has happened, a mouse has moved, and so on. With event programming, you let the environment do the checking: All you do is specify what should happen when the event occurs for a specific object.

What to Look for in JavaScript Code

Although not all JavaScript code uses the object-oriented constructs described in this appendix, most of the Dashcode Library code does. You don't really have to know too much about how to write the code yourself. What you need to know is the basic structures described in this appendix so that you can make the customizations that are necessary for your app or widget.

As you work with JavaScript, the following sections cover a few tips to keep in mind.

Statements end with a semicolon

A JavaScript statement ends with a semicolon. That means that you can have several statements on one line, and that one statement can span several lines. The semicolon is what ends the statement.

Comments matter

JavaScript recognizes two types of comments. Two slashes cause anything following them on that line to be ignored. In Library parts, these comments often guide you to adjustments you should make.

For example, here's code from the Library Fade In part:

```
var itemToFadeIn = document.getElementById
  ("elementID");   // replace with name of element to fade
```

The statement ends with the semicolon. The double slashes introduce a comment telling you to replace `elementID` with the name of the element you want to fade.

You can also have comments that span several lines. You can bracket them with /* and */, or you can make each line into a comment. Here is the multi-line syntax:

```
/*
Purpose of this code: Center text.
Written by: Jesse Feiler
Updated: 4/25/2010
Comments: This is an example.
*/
```

Alternatively, you can write it like this:

```
// Purpose of this code: Center text.
// Written by: Jesse Feiler
// Updated: 4/25/2010
// Comments: This is an example.
```

 Document what you're doing so that when you or someone else comes back to it, you'll know what's going on. Even more important than documenting code, make certain that you update the documentation when you make changes.

Capitalization matters

JavaScript is case-sensitive. In this book, any code or snippet that is shown in code font uses the appropriate capitalization. For example, the url property of a document object isn't the same as a URL property (which is not defined). If you're used to a language that is forgiving about capitalization, case-sensitivity in any language may trip you up. You can stare at the apparently-correct syntax for days without noticing that it isn't capitalized properly.

Indenting doesn't matter but is a great idea

Except within quotation marks and between variable names and reserved words, spaces don't matter in JavaScript, and that includes the spaces you use to indent and line up code. Because the spaces don't matter, feel free to use them to organize your code visually. The Dashcode developers do this in the Dashcode JavaScript files that are part of your apps and widgets. Some of the code is meant for you to customize, but other sections are internal. You can tell from the spacing which is which. When the code has few spaces or comments and isn't indented, it usually isn't designed for you to mess with it.

Turning on syntactical formatting in Dashcode

Dashcode can format your code as you type it. You turn on syntactical formatting by choosing Dashcode⇨Preferences with the Formatting tab, as shown in Figure A-1. (Make sure that you turn on the syntax-based formatting checkbox at the upper left corner.)

Formatting your code as you type makes reading your code easier. It also helps make up for the lack of a compiler.

Dashcode parses your code as you type it; if you leave out a comma, a quotation mark, a parenthesis, or a bracket, the code won't parse properly. A compiler would give you an error, but with syntax-based formatting, you see color-coding that doesn't make sense. For example, a missing closing quotation mark may cause several lines of code to be colored as a quotation.

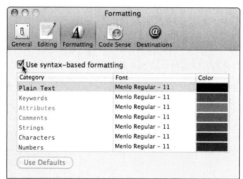

Figure A-1:
Turn on
syntax-
based
formatting.

JavaScript Snippets

The following sections provide some snippets from common code used in the Library. It doesn't hurt to print them and hang them from a bulletin board so that you can refer to the spelling and spacing as you need to. (Of course, using the code from the Library means you don't have to retype anything.)

A word to the wise: Remember that in `getElementById` and `setElementById`, it's `Id`, not `ID` or `id`.

Get an element value by ID

This code occurs in most Library code snippets that begin with Get. The following code is from the Get Slider Value code part in the Library:

```
// Values you provide
var sliderValue = document.getElementById("elementID"); // replace with ID of
             slider

// Slider code
sliderValue = sliderValue.object.value;
```

The first line of code gets an element from the document using its ID. This element is usually the name of a view you created in your widget or app (most often by dragging it from the Library). The second line gets the object property of the element with that ID and then gets the value of object.

Set an element value by ID

This code occurs in most Library code snippets that begin with Set. This code is from Set Indicator Value code part in the Library.

```
// Values you provide
var indicatorToChange = document.getElementById("elementID"); // replace with ID
             of indicator to change
var newIndicatorValue = 100;
  // new indicator value

// Indicator code
indicatorToChange.object.setValue(newIndicatorValue);
```

Index

• N •

...le & Macs

...d For Dummies
...3-0-470-58027-1

...one For Dummies,
...Edition
...3-0-470-87870-5

...cBook For Dummies, 3rd
...tion
...3-0-470-76918-8

...c OS X Snow Leopard For
...mmies
...3-0-470-43543-4

...siness

...okkeeping For Dummies
...3-0-7645-9848-7

...Interviews
...r Dummies,
...d Edition
...3-0-470-17748-8

...sumes For Dummies,
...Edition
...3-0-470-08037-5

...arting an
...line Business
...r Dummies,
...Edition
...3-0-470-60210-2

...ock Investing
...r Dummies,
...d Edition
...8-0-470-40114-9

...ccessful
...me Management
...r Dummies
...8-0-470-29034-7

Computer Hardware

BlackBerry
For Dummies,
4th Edition
978-0-470-60700-8

Computers For Seniors
For Dummies,
2nd Edition
978-0-470-53483-0

PCs For Dummies,
Windows
7 Edition
978-0-470-46542-4

Laptops For Dummies,
4th Edition
978-0-470-57829-2

Cooking & Entertaining

Cooking Basics
For Dummies,
3rd Edition
978-0-7645-7206-7

Wine For Dummies,
4th Edition
978-0-470-04579-4

Diet & Nutrition

Dieting For Dummies,
2nd Edition
978-0-7645-4149-0

Nutrition For Dummies,
4th Edition
978-0-471-79868-2

Weight Training
For Dummies,
3rd Edition
978-0-471-76845-6

Digital Photography

Digital SLR Cameras &
Photography For Dummies,
3rd Edition
978-0-470-46606-3

Photoshop Elements 8
For Dummies
978-0-470-52967-6

Gardening

Gardening Basics
For Dummies
978-0-470-03749-2

Organic Gardening
For Dummies,
2nd Edition
978-0-470-43067-5

Green/Sustainable

Raising Chickens
For Dummies
978-0-470-46544-8

Green Cleaning
For Dummies
978-0-470-39106-8

Health

Diabetes For Dummies,
3rd Edition
978-0-470-27086-8

Food Allergies
For Dummies
978-0-470-09584-3

Living Gluten-Free
For Dummies,
2nd Edition
978-0-470-58589-4

Hobbies/General

Chess For Dummies,
2nd Edition
978-0-7645-8404-6

Drawing
Cartoons & Comics
For Dummies
978-0-470-42683-8

Knitting For Dummies,
2nd Edition
978-0-470-28747-7

Organizing
For Dummies
978-0-7645-5300-4

Su Doku For Dummies
978-0-470-01892-7

Home Improvement

Home Maintenance
For Dummies,
2nd Edition
978-0-470-43063-7

Home Theater
For Dummies,
3rd Edition
978-0-470-41189-6

Living the
Country Lifestyle
All-in-One
For Dummies
978-0-470-43061-3

Solar Power Your Home
For Dummies,
2nd Edition
978-0-470-59678-4

...vailable wherever books are sold. For more information or to order direct: U.S. customers visit www.dummies.com or call 1-877-762-2974. ...K. customers visit www.wileyeurope.com or call (0) 1243 843291. Canadian customers visit www.wiley.ca or call 1-800-567-4797.

Internet

JUN 2 7 2012

Blogging For Dummies,
3rd Edition
978-0-470-61996-4

eBay For Dummies,
6th Edition
978-0-470-49741-8

Facebook For Dummies,
3rd Edition
978-0-470-87804-0

Web Marketing
For Dummies,
2nd Edition
978-0-470-37181-7

WordPress
For Dummies,
3rd Edition
978-0-470-59274-8

Language & Foreign Language

French For Dummies
978-0-7645-5193-2

Italian Phrases
For Dummies
978-0-7645-7203-6

Spanish For Dummies,
2nd Edition
978-0-470-87855-2

Spanish
For Dummies,
Audio Set
978-0-470-09585-0

Math & Science

Algebra I
For Dummies,
2nd Edition
978-0-470-55964-2

Biology For Dummies,
2nd Edition
978-0-470-59875-7

Calculus For Dummies
978-0-7645-2498-1

Chemistry For Dummies
978-0-7645-5430-8

Microsoft Office

Excel 2010 For Dummies
978-0-470-48953-6

Office 2010 All-in-One
For Dummies
978-0-470-49748-7

Office 2010 For Dummies,
Book + DVD Bundle
978-0-470-62698-6

Word 2010 For Dummies
978-0-470-48772-3

Music

Guitar For Dummies,
2nd Edition
978-0-7645-9904-0

iPod & iTunes For
Dummies, 8th Edition
978-0-470-87871-2

Piano Exercises
For Dummies
978-0-470-38765-8

Parenting & Education

Parenting For Dummies,
2nd Edition
978-0-7645-5418-6

Type 1 Diabetes
For Dummies
978-0-470-17811-9

Pets

Cats For Dummies,
2nd Edition
978-0-7645-5275-5

Dog Training For Dummies,
3rd Edition
978-0-470-60029-0

Puppies For Dummies,
2nd Edition
978-0-470-03717-1

Religion & Inspiration

The Bible For Dummies
978-0-7645-5296-0

Catholicism For Dummies
978-0-7645-5391-2

Women in the Bible
For Dummies
978-0-7645-8475-6

Self-Help & Relationship

Anger Management
For Dummies
978-0-470-03715-7

Overcoming Anxiety
For Dummies,
2nd Edition
978-0-470-57441-6

Sports

Baseball
For Dummies,
3rd Edition
978-0-7645-7537-2

Basketball
For Dummies,
2nd Edition
978-0-7645-5248-9

Golf For Dummies,
3rd Edition
978-0-471-76871-5

Web Development

Web Design
All-in-One
For Dummies
978-0-470-41796-6

Web Sites
Do-It-Yourself
For Dummies,
2nd Edition
978-0-470-56520-9

Windows 7

Windows 7
For Dummies
978-0-470-49743-2

Windows 7
For Dummies,
Book + DVD Bundle
978-0-470-52398-8

Windows 7 All-in-One
For Dummies
978-0-470-48763-1

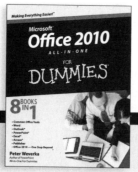